"If the only thing Fred Zaspel had accomp
Warfield's masterpiece sermons in his too-
the church yeoman service. But he has done much, much
tian Life* we are given the privilege of sitting at the feet of a Christ-centered, Bible-saturated,
gospel-loving theologian of the first rank and learning how to say, 'To me to live is Christ.'
A very welcome addition to what promises to be a valuable series."

Sinclair B. Ferguson, Retired Senior Pastor, First Presbyterian Church, Columbia,
South Carolina

"We are already indebted to Fred Zaspel for his work *The Theology of B. B. Warfield*—a book
that has introduced a new generation to the voluminous writings of a Princeton scholar
who was both New Testament interpreter and systematic theologian. Warfield's style feels
a tad impenetrable to many contemporary readers, but through Zaspel, Warfield, though
dead, still speaks. But can any devotional and practical guidance come out of old Princeton?
Zaspel's latest contribution, *Warfield on the Christian Life: Living in Light of the Gospel*, does
not simply answer with a resounding affirmative, but again faithfully unpacks Warfield and
shows him to be a theologian of head and heart. Above all, Warfield is an integrated thinker,
so he is ideally equipped to show how that which is central to the Bible, the gospel of God,
rightly shapes the Christian's entire life. And Zaspel makes this accessible."

D. A. Carson, Research Professor of New Testament, Trinity Evangelical
Divinity School

"B. B. Warfield was one of the great thinkers in the history of the church, and his writings
are a gold mine of biblical truth. Unfortunately, the sheer volume of his writings makes them
largely inaccessible to today's busy reader. But now, Fred Zaspel has done us a great service
by distilling—into one volume—the essence of Warfield's writings on the Christian life. This
book should prove to be a valuable asset to all Christians serious about growing in Christ."

Jerry Bridges, author, *The Pursuit of Holiness*

"B. B. Warfield looms large in the Protestant imagination as a theologian, one of the giants
in the land. What is less well known are the details and dynamics of his own approach to the
Christian life. Fred Zaspel has already written a substantial volume on Warfield as theologian;
now he opens up for us the world of Warfield's practical Christianity. Once again, fans of the
great Princetonian are in for a treat, and are deeply and delightfully in debt to Dr. Zaspel."

Carl R. Trueman, Paul Woolley Professor of Church History,
Westminster Theological Seminary, Philadelphia

"Following the publication of *Warfield on the Christian Life*, it will be impossible to continue
to claim that Princeton theology was 'all head but no heart,' or that Warfield himself was little
more than an Enlightenment rationalist."

Paul Helm, Teaching Fellow, Regent College; author, *The Secret Providence of God*

"B. B. Warfield is among the greatest theologians America has ever produced, and Fred
Zaspel is among his greatest living interpreters. Comprehensive, insightful, and remarkably
compelling, Zaspel's *Warfield on the Christian Life* is a masterful presentation of an understanding of the Christian life that values Christian experience and at the same time is 'deeply

and thoroughly theological.' While Zaspel's Warfield is a theological giant who enjoys the well-earned reputation as 'a theological army of one,' he is also 'a theologian of the heart' who recognizes that believers 'live unto Christ . . . not out of a vacuum but out of a mind and heart captivated and inflamed by an understanding of God's . . . saving activity in Christ.' This book is an important sequel to Zaspel's systematic summary of Warfield's theology, for it explains how Warfield could insist that truth 'fuels Christian living from beginning to end' without falling prey to a kind of Enlightenment rationalism. Enthusiastically recommended."

> **Paul K. Helseth,** Associate Professor of Christian Thought, Northwestern College; author, *Right Reason and the Princeton Mind: An Unorthodox Proposal*

"As Fred Zaspel shows, the Princetonians—and Warfield in particular—were very far from arid scholastics. The Princeton theology was wedded to a Princeton piety that was warm, spiritual, and gospel centered. Warfield's spirituality in particular grew from a profound encounter with Christ that was both personal and theological. Thank you, Dr. Zaspel, for showing us Warfield the christologian and man of God."

> **Kevin T. Bauder,** Research Professor, Central Baptist Seminary of Minneapolis

"'For Warfield the Christian life is but the outworking of the gospel.' Thank you, Fred Zaspel for bringing back to us the rich, contagious life and work of Benjamin Warfield. It satisfies the thirst this generation has for an authentic Christianity that flows from the deep well of a strong and informed theology."

> **Matthew R. Olson,** Former President, Northland International University

"Scripture and history show that spirituality rests wholly on a foundation of revealed truth, cordially received and loved. The best theologians have always been the most profound, trustworthy promoters of vital piety and transformation of life. We look to Augustine, Anselm, Calvin, Bunyan, Edwards, and a host of Puritan pastor-theologians as determinative of the truth of this observation. Now we must include B. B. Warfield in that imposing list of those who make clear the path, not only to live by the Spirit, but to walk by the Spirit. Fred Zaspel has condensed the marvelous insight contained in *The Theology of B. B. Warfield* and served it up as foundational to a robust practice of piety analyzed in this present work. Zaspel has laid out both the doctrinal and exegetical expertise of Warfield in showing how seriously he pursued true worship as the *summum bonum* of life. From divine revelation to the imitation of the Christ and the consummation of Christian hope, the Christian finds substantive truth on his side and is assured by that truth that God himself is near, to protect, direct, and finally perfect all the sheep for whom Christ died."

> **Tom J. Nettles,** Professor of Historical Theology, The Southern Baptist Theological Seminary

"I will reread, assign to my students, and give away Fred Zaspel's book *Warfield on the Christian Life,* not because it is an excellent commentary on Warfield—though it is—and not because it is highly readable—though it is—but primarily because I am a better Christian for having read it. I was mentally and spiritually invigorated, and you will be as well."

> **Joseph A. Pipa Jr.,** President, Greenville Presbyterian Theological Seminary

WARFIELD

on the Christian Life

THEOLOGIANS ON THE CHRISTIAN LIFE

EDITED BY STEPHEN J. NICHOLS AND JUSTIN TAYLOR

WARFIELD

on the Christian Life

LIVING IN LIGHT OF THE GOSPEL

FRED G. ZASPEL

FOREWORD BY MICHAEL A. G. HAYKIN

CROSSWAY

WHEATON, ILLINOIS

Warfield on the Christian Life: Living in Light of the Gospel
Copyright © 2012 by Fred G. Zaspel
Published by Crossway
   1300 Crescent Street
   Wheaton, Illinois 60187

Cover design: Josh Dennis
Cover illustration: Richard Solomon Artists, Mark Summers

First printing 2012
Reprinted with new cover 2014
Printed in the United States of America

Except for brief, scattered translations by Warfield, Scripture quotations not otherwise identified are from the ESV® Bible (*The Holy Bible, English Standard Version*®), copyright © 2001 by Crossway. Used by permission. All rights reserved.

Scripture quotations marked KJV are from the *King James Version* of the Bible.

Scripture quotations marked NIV are from the Holy Bible, New International Version®, NIV®. Copyright © 1973, 1978, 1984 by Biblica, Inc.™. Used by permission. All rights reserved worldwide.

All emphases in Scripture quotations have been added by the author.

Trade paperback ISBN: 978-1-4335-4319-7
ePub ISBN: 978-1-4335-2826-2
PDF ISBN: 978-1-4335-2824-8
Mobipocket ISBN: 978-1-4335-2825-5

Library of Congress Cataloging-in-Publication Data
Zaspel, Fred G.
 Warfield on the Christian life: living in light of the Gospel /
Fred G. Zaspel; foreword by Michael A. G. Haykin.
   pages cm. — (Theologians on the Christian life)
 Includes bibliographical references and indexes.
 ISBN 978-1-4335-2823-1 (tp)
 ISBN 978-1-4335-2826-2 (ePub)
 ISBN 978-1-4335-2824-8 (PDF)—
 ISBN 978-1-4335-2825-5 (mobipocket)
 1. Warfield, Benjamin Breckinridge, 1851–1921. 2. Christian
life. I. Title.
 BX9225.W236Z38   2012
 248.092—dc23   2011046600

Crossway is a publishing ministry of Good News Publishers.

VP		24	23	22	21	20	19	18	17	16	15	14
15	14	13	12	11	10	9	8	7	6	5	4	3	2	1

*For Kim
my best friend, soul mate,
and devoted wife*

CONTENTS

SERIES PREFACE

Some might call us spoiled. We live in an era of significant and substantial resources for Christians on living the Christian life. We have ready access to books, DVD series, online material, seminars—all in the interest of encouraging us in our daily walk with Christ. The laity, the people in the pew, have access to more information than scholars dreamed of having in previous centuries.

Yet for all our abundance of resources, we also lack something. We tend to lack the perspectives from the past, perspectives from a different time and place than our own. To put the matter differently, we have so many riches in our current horizon that we tend not to look to the horizons of the past.

That is unfortunate, especially when it comes to learning about and practicing discipleship. It's like owning a mansion and choosing to live in only one room. This series invites you to explore the other rooms.

As we go exploring, we will visit places and times different from our own. We will see different models, approaches, and emphases. This series does not intend for these models to be copied uncritically, and it certainly does not intend to put these figures from the past high upon a pedestal like some race of super-Christians. This series intends, however, to help us in the present listen to the past. We believe there is wisdom in the past twenty centuries of the church, wisdom for living the Christian life.

Stephen J. Nichols and Justin Taylor

FOREWORD

Theology, like clothing, has its fashions. And in the current climate of occidental evangelicalism, authors like B. B. Warfield seem increasingly out of place. Their interest in a rational defense and explication of the faith hardly appeals to various postmodern evangelical authors and their brave new world, which consists of mostly questions and few answers. In short, for far too many professing evangelicals, Warfield is simply passé. Why then take the time to remember him? What on earth can such an outmoded thinker have to say to a new generation that has moved far beyond both his interests and his way of expressing them?

Well, first of all, though theology has its fashions, we are not slavishly bound to wear the new duds any more than we are wed solely to the apparel of a bygone day. Wholesale rejection of past theological viewpoints simply because they are old is just as narrow-minded a perspective as the refusal to consider anything that is new.

Then, there are certain perennial issues in the history of the church, and Warfield, great theologian that he was, tackled them in a manner eminently worthy of serious consideration. The irrefragable power and infallibility of Scripture, for example, was just as much a concern of Augustine and John Calvin as it was of Warfield, and the latter's mode of affirming such was not as foreign to biblical categories as some think. In other words, because Warfield was widely read in the history of the church—witness his still-valuable treatises on Tertullian and Augustine—his defense of biblical inerrancy cannot simply be explained by tagging his thought an expression of modernity. And the same is true of other areas of Warfield's thinking.

Although his explication of inerrancy is a key reason for his being remembered, Warfield wrote about the entire range of theology, as this work by Fred Zaspel ably demonstrates. And because Warfield is indeed one of the great thinkers of the Christian church, his commentary on all matters Christian is great food for the soul of the contemporary believer seeking to live a life of faithfulness to Christ today.

Finally, a book like the one before you is necessary because reading Warfield, along with other Christian authors from the past, helps break the spell that the modern world casts over us. To paraphrase a recent comment that appeared in a *Washington Post* piece about classical school education: If you're not well versed in the history of Christian thought, you simply cannot be self-critical.[1]

So, take up and read this masterly overview of Warfield's perspectives on the Christian faith. There are riches here that will delight, enthrall, and edify.

Michael A. G. Haykin
The Southern Baptist Theological Seminary

---

[1]Julia Duin, "Embracing a Classical Education," *The Washington Post*, April 8, 2011, http://www
.washingtonpost.com/magazine/embracing-a-classical-education/2011/03/09/AFj6amwC_story
.html). The quote is from Jonathan Beeson, principal of St. Theresa Catholic School, Sugar Land,
Texas.

ACKNOWLEDGMENTS

On one level, of course, the subject matter of this book is already largely available in my previous volume, *The Theology of B. B. Warfield: A Systematic Summary*. There I surveyed the whole of Warfield's theological outlook and emphasized that, for Warfield, Christianity is a redemptive religion and that Scripture is given not simply to make us wise but to make us wise unto salvation. In all this I think it became clear that Warfield's view of the Christian life was deeply and thoroughly theological.

Even so, when Justin Taylor contacted me on behalf of Crossway to write this volume, I was eager to take it up. Certainly there is overlap, and if you have read the previous volume, you will notice that in places. But here not only is the material more condensed; the focus is more specific. And the nature of this volume also allows more extensive use of Warfield's published sermons. In the end, I trust our goal will have been reached: to provide a faithful representation of Warfield's understanding of the Christian life.

Many thanks to Justin Taylor and Steve Nichols for overseeing this project. This series, Theologians on the Christian Life, is a wonderful idea that I trust will prove of benefit to many. Many thanks also to Michael Haykin both for providing the foreword to this book and for his input and encouragement. He has been a wonderful and valued friend throughout my years of Warfield studies and writing.

ABBREVIATIONS

BSac	*Bibliotheca Sacra*
BT	*The Banner of Truth*
BTS	*Biblical and Theological Studies*. B. B. Warfield. Edited by Samuel Craig. Philadelphia: Presbyterian and Reformed, 1968
CT	*Christian Thought*
FL	*Faith and Life*. B. B. Warfield. 1916. Reprint, Carlisle, PA: Banner of Truth, 1974
JGM	*J. Gresham Machen: A Biographical Memoir*. Ned Stonehouse. Grand Rapids: Eerdmans, 1954
PGS	*The Power of God unto Salvation*. B. B. Warfield. 1903. Reprint, Grand Rapids: Eerdmans, 1930
PR	*The Presbyterian Review*
PRR	*The Presbyterian and Reformed Review*
PrS	*Princeton Sermons*. B. B. Warfield. Vestavia Hills, AL: Solid Ground Christian Books, 2009
PTR	*The Princeton Theological Review*
PWC	*The Person and Work of Christ*. B. B. Warfield. Edited by Samuel Craig. Philadelphia: Presbyterian and Reformed, 1950
SSW	*Selected Shorter Writings of Benjamin B. Warfield*. 2 vols. Edited by John Meeter. Nutley, NJ: Presbyterian and Reformed, 1970, 1973
SW	*The Saviour of the World*. B. B. Warfield. 1914. Reprint, Carlisle, PA: Banner of Truth, 1991
TBS	*The Bible Student*

W   *The Works of Benjamin Breckinridge Warfield.* 10 vols. 1927–1932. Reprint, Grand Rapids: Baker, 1981

        W, 1   *Revelation and Inspiration*, 1927

        W, 2   *Biblical Doctrines*, 1929

        W, 3   *Christology and Criticism*, 1929

        W, 5   *Calvin and Calvinism*, 1931

        W, 7   *Perfectionism, Part One*, 1931

        W, 8   *Perfectionism, Part Two*, 1932

        W, 9   *Studies in Theology*, 1932

        W, 10 *Critical Reviews*, 1932

INTRODUCTION

Christianity as a Supernatural Religion

In his classroom lectures at Princeton Theological Seminary, B. B. Warfield enjoyed saying to his students, "Gentlemen, I like the supernatural!" He reveled in the fact—and loved to emphasize in his teaching and writing—that Christianity is a thoroughly supernatural religion.

This may seem strange coming from the man who wrote the famous *Counterfeit Miracles*, a powerfully influential denial of the continued presence of the miraculous gifts of the Spirit in the church beyond the apostolic era. But for Warfield his discounting the continuation of the miraculous gifts reflected no embarrassment on his part concerning Christian supernaturalism. He was deeply convinced and passionately committed to the thoroughly supernatural character of Scripture, Christianity, and the Christian life itself. It is no exaggeration to say that his career was given to the defense of Christian supernaturalism. Throughout all his work he emphasized that the Christian faith and the Christian life are pervasively supernatural. Indeed, he insisted that the Christian himself is a walking miracle.

Nor in saying this did Warfield resort to "dumbing down" the definition of *miracle*. For him a miracle is nothing less than the immediate working of God above nature and apart from second causes. A miracle is that which cannot occur or be explained in terms of anything natural. And for him this is Christianity exactly—a supernatural religion, grounded in supernatural revelation, delivered and written for us by supernaturally inspired apostles and prophets, accomplished in a supernatural redemption by a supernatural Redeemer, and lived out in us by the supernatural influence and enablement of none other than the Spirit of God himself.

Historic Christian faith in Warfield's day had come under stringent attack. The modern "enlightened" mind could no longer tolerate such notions as incarnation, resurrection, and miracles. After Darwin it became increasingly difficult to speak of creation and divine involvement in the world and the affairs of men. Naturalism reigned, and many professing Christians began to feel embarrassed by their traditional doctrines, believing that in order to survive in this scientifically minded world Christianity would just have to make concessions or be left to the ghetto of outdated and discredited superstition. Centuries earlier Pelagius had taught a system of self-salvation, and Warfield frequently remarked that in the hands of Pelagius Christianity had become less a religion than a mere system of ethics. So also, he complained, in the anti-supernaturalistic atmosphere of his own day "the Christian life" became little more than an adherence to so many ethical notions. And so with genius of mind and great zeal of heart Warfield poured his energies into what was for him the delightful task of defending and expounding the Christian faith. And this he did at great length, always emphasizing that just as the Christian religion is in a class alone, apart from all other religions in that it is divinely given, so also the Christian life cannot be explained in terms other than divine activity for us and in us.

Warfield Lived in Light of the Gospel

Warfield not only taught that the Christian life was supernatural, but he also lived in this reality. He "liked the supernatural" because he had tasted of it himself. Having professed faith at age sixteen, and later having experienced a powerful revival that swept the campus of the College of New Jersey (now Princeton University), he told a friend that he gave himself to the Christian ministry simply out of a deep sense of love to Christ. He knew he was a sinner rescued by divine grace, and he knew the experience of one whose heart had been arrested by the Spirit of God and mysteriously drawn into loving communion with him. Frequently we read his joyful expressions of vibrant worship, of freedom from sin's enslaving grip, and of the continuously purifying work of God within his own heart and life. And those who knew him best report that more striking even than his towering intellect and academic powers were his deep love for Christ and his keen sense of dependence upon God for that supernatural aid promised and provided in the gospel.

In short, Warfield understood the Christian life in consistently gospel terms. "Living in light of the gospel" captures his thinking exactly. Christianity, he repeatedly insisted, is a redemptive religion, and the Christian life is but the outworking of that redemption. His firm grasp of the Christian faith, his fervent heart for Christ, his deep appreciation of grace, and his own Christian experience all served to make him one from whom we can learn not only what Christianity is but also what a *Christian* is and what the Christian life, by God's grace, can and ought to be.

PART I

PERSONAL BACKGROUND

CHAPTER I

BENJAMIN BRECKINRIDGE WARFIELD

The Man and His Work

At important moments in the history of the church, God has raised up men to give voice to his Word. There is Augustine, the theologian of sin and grace. He did not invent these doctrines, of course. But in his battle with Pelagius he gave them such clear and cogent articulation that ever since he has been recognized as the one who bestowed these doctrines to us. So also there is Anselm, the theologian of the doctrine of the atonement. And there is Luther, the theologian of justification. And there is Calvin, the theologian of the Holy Spirit.

Warfield: The Theologian of Inspiration—and More

In this same sense Benjamin Breckinridge Warfield (1851–1921) of "Old Princeton" is known as the theologian of the doctrine of inspiration. Those who hold to the historic doctrine today add very little to what Warfield said about it a hundred years ago. So also, any who reject that doctrine must contend with Warfield before their work is complete. He was the theologian of inspiration. This was his gift, in God's kind providence, to the modern church.

Impressive as all this is, it does not provide anything close to an adequate representation of this man, who was certainly one of the greatest—arguably the greatest of all—theologians America ever produced. Although the doctrine of inspiration was largely *the* issue of his day, and although he above all others provided exposition and defense of it, this was not what he would have considered his "center." And despite his many hundreds of published pages devoted to this cherished theme, it was not his leading area of theological attention. Staggering as his output on this theme was, Warfield was no mere single-issue specialist. His learning was massive, and he excelled in virtually every department of biblical studies. In terms of both the breadth and depth of his scholarship he was virtually without peer.

Warfield's Life

Warfield's life story, in one respect, is not particularly spectacular. He was not an activist, he rarely traveled, he founded no movement, and although immensely influential in his Presbyterian church (PCUSA) he was never one of its official leaders. He was a theologian in the Theological Seminary at Princeton, New Jersey, and he did scarcely little else. His story and his legacy are found, rather, in the many thousands of pages of theological writings that streamed from his pen for some four decades (from roughly 1880 to 1921). It is by his voluminous writings that he became one of the most outstanding and influential theologians of his day. And it is by means of these writings that his impact continues today.

Early Life and Education

Warfield's boyhood home was marked by the best of vital, Reformed piety and genuine godly concerns. Both his mother's and his father's families were rich with heritage: behind him were military officers, educators, influential ecclesiastical leaders, and governmental and political figures, even a United States vice president. Warfield's mother, Mary Cabell Breckinridge, was from the famous Scotch-Irish Presbyterian Breckinridge family of Maryland and Kentucky. Warfield's father, William Warfield, was descended from English Puritan forebears who had fled to America to avoid persecution. The Warfields were members of Lexington's Second Presbyterian Church, and it was here at age sixteen that young Benjamin made public profession of faith.

William Warfield was a successful cattle breeder, and Benjamin was reared in some degree of privilege. He received a private education and developed particular interest in mathematics and especially science, devouring with intense interest the newly published works of Charles Darwin. Because he was so intent on a career in science, he strongly objected to studying Greek. But with a touch of humor his brother Ethelbert (1861–1936) reports that

> youthful objections had little effect in a household where the shorter catechism was ordinarily completed in the sixth year, followed at once by the proofs from the Scriptures, and then by the larger catechism, with an appropriate amount of Scripture memorized in regular course each Sabbath afternoon.[1]

This early despising of Greek is ironic, given that Warfield was to become one of the great New Testament Greek scholars of his day!

Warfield was still just sixteen years old when he entered the sophomore class at the College of New Jersey in the fall of 1868. Mimicking his southern drawl, his college friends called him "Wo-field." School records indicate his involvement in a Sunday afternoon fistfight, of which it seems Warfield was the instigator! His maternal grandfather, Robert Jefferson Breckinridge (1800–1871), had been suspended from the school for a similar incident many years before. This incident earned Warfield the nickname "pugilist"— which some have found somewhat prophetic in light of the reputation he would earn as the great contender for the faith.

But Warfield evidently applied himself well as a student. He attained foremost rank in every department of instruction and perfect marks in mathematics and science, graduating with highest honors and first in his class in 1871 at age nineteen. He also won awards for essays and debate in the American Whig Society and was an editor for the *Nassau Literary Magazine*, for which he wrote several poems and other pieces.

Calling to Ministry

Following Warfield's graduation his father persuaded him to study in Europe, and in the spring of 1872 he began study in Edinburgh, Scotland, and then Heidelberg, Germany. His family was surprised to receive word from him midsummer that he would enter Christian ministry. It seems that a genuine revival swept the campus in his undergraduate days at the College of New Jersey and many young men went on to serve in Christian ministry. We have no record of Warfield's attributing his decision to this event, but a friend does recall his remark that he felt compelled out of love for Christ to serve him in this capacity. So in 1873, after a brief stint as editor of the *Farmer's Home Journal* in Lexington, he returned to Princeton, this time to the famous

[1] *W*, 1:vi.

theological seminary there, where he received instruction from men whom he came to admire deeply—especially the famous and by then elderly Charles Hodge (1797–1878) and his son Caspar Wistar Hodge (1830–1891). The younger Hodge was professor of New Testament, and he became something of a personal mentor of Warfield, their relationship forming an intimate and lasting friendship. It would be C. W. Hodge who, on behalf of the seminary, would write to Warfield in late 1886 inviting him to consider joining their faculty. For his entire life Warfield maintained deep affection for both the college and the seminary at Princeton, appreciating both the illustrious history of each institution and what he had learned from them.

In May of 1875 Warfield was licensed to preach by the Presbytery of Ebenezer, meeting at Lexington, Kentucky, and he served that summer as interim pastor at Concord Church in Nicholas County, Kentucky. After graduating in 1876 Warfield was the interim pastor of the First Presbyterian Church of Dayton, Ohio, from which he received a unanimous call to the pastorate. Warfield declined the call, determining instead to return to Europe for further studies.

Marriage

He was married on August 3 of that year to the brilliant, witty, and beautiful Annie Kinkead and then very soon took up studies in Leipzig. Warfield endured extended health problems that kept him from some studies while in Germany, but over the winter of 1876–1877 he took in various lectures.

His new wife was the daughter of a prominent Lexington attorney who in 1855 defended Abraham Lincoln. In the brief biographical sketches of Warfield that are commonly available, Annie is often reported to have been an invalid their entire married life, but it does not seem that this degree of debilitation came until perhaps 1893 (seventeen years into their marriage). A notice in the New York Times dated May 1, 1892, notes that Mrs. Warfield, Mrs. Woodrow Wilson, and other prominent ladies of Princeton served as "Patronesses" at a lecture event sponsored by the American Whig Society in Princeton on April 30. But about a year later, in July of 1893, Warfield sent a paper to be read at an event in Staten Island, New York, which he was unable himself to attend, the published version informs us, "owing to illness in his family."[2] It would seem that Annie's illness became severe during this period. There are reports of Annie's ill health from others at Princeton at the time, and by all accounts Warfield was a devoted husband in a very

---

[2]CT 11 (1893–1894): 163.

happy marriage. The Warfields had no children, and for many years he left his home only for the classroom. He was otherwise home nearly always in the company of his wife. And in the providence of God, without doubt, this contributed to his time in writing so extensively on so many subjects. It was reported by those who knew him that "he has had only two interests in life—his work, and Mrs. Warfield."[3]

Career and Stature

Following a stint as stated supply at the historic First Presbyterian Church in Baltimore, Warfield began his teaching career as professor of New Testament at Western (now Pittsburgh) Theological Seminary in Allegheny, Pennsylvania, in September 1878. Greek had now become his leading area of interest. And by the early 1880s Warfield had already begun to gain international recognition as a force of conservative Reformed theological scholarship. His landmark "Inspiration" (1881), coauthored with Archibald Alexander Hodge (1823–1886), and his "Canonicity of Second Peter" (1882) were especially noted, portending the brilliant career that quite obviously lay ahead for this young scholar. And in 1886 he became the first American to publish a textbook in New Testament textual criticism, a title that received accolades from all quarters and established him as a leading authority in the field.

His masterful work in New Testament studies, however, would prove to be the foundation of his famous life's work in theology. In 1887 Warfield returned to his beloved alma mater, Princeton Seminary, assuming the historic and prestigious chair of Didactic and Polemic Theology. We call it systematic theology today, and they did then also, but at Princeton, at least, the "polemic" dimension—establishing and maintaining the doctrines of Scripture at given points of controversy—was an especially important aspect of the theological task. And it was a work Warfield took up with great vigor.

The Theological Seminary at Princeton was now long and widely recognized as a land of biblical and theological giants. But both friends and foes of Old Princeton to this day acknowledge Warfield as the giant standing out above all the others. The breadth and depth of his voluminous works have impressed Christian students and scholars of all theological persuasions. Warfield was by all accounts one of the most outstanding and influential orthodox theologians of the era. Among Reformed orthodox theologians few have stood taller. This was the reputation he earned in his own lifetime, and the breadth and depth of his scholarship and exhaustive acquaintance

---

[3]*JGM*, 220.

with the theological, scientific, and philosophical literature and thought of his day constituted the high-water mark of Old Princeton. He was well equipped with all the tools of modern scholarship, thoroughly abreast of all the latest theories and methods of the critics, widely—indeed, seemingly exhaustively—read in all the various theological disciplines (whether of theological friend or foe), deeply informed by the historical development of Christian doctrines—Patristic (Greek and Latin), Reformed, and modern; German, French, Dutch, and English—and most of all demonstrating throughout his career an exhaustive exegetical grounding. Warfield was not only a well-informed theologian; he was a theologian perhaps without peer, certainly unsurpassed in all the English-speaking world.

The Naturalistic Worldview of Warfield's Day

"Enlightenment" thought in Warfield's day had come to its own, and naturalistic ideas dominated. The thoroughly supernatural character of the Christian faith was under assault at every point, the nature of inspiration most famously. Various "kenosis"[4] theories explained our Lord in purely human terms, and redemption had become much less than expiation through his substitutional sacrifice. Virtually the entire faith was being recast in thoroughly naturalistic terms, and Warfield vigorously gave himself to the exposition and defense of Christian supernaturalism—a supernatural God, a supernatural revelation, a supernatural Savior, and a supernatural salvation produced by nothing less than the supernatural workings of the Spirit of God. All this and nothing less, Warfield was deeply convinced, could enable us to sing not only *Deo gloria*, but *soli Deo gloria*. He understood that in this wide-ranging debate that raged, Christianity itself was at stake.

Warfield the Christologian

Warfield's own center of interest and concern was the person and work of Christ, and this constitutes his leading area of literary output. We might say that he was first and foremost a christologian. In his own heart of hearts he saw himself as a fallen sinner rescued by a divine Redeemer, and this—the person and work of Christ—is where we find the heartbeat of this great Princetonian. As he did with the doctrine of inspiration, so also Warfield provided for the church a massive exegetical grounding for the great truths of Christ's two natures, his redemptive work, and so on. Indeed, it was to

---

[4]From the Greek, *kenoō* in Phil. 2:7, meaning to "empty."

this end—God's redemptive revelation in Christ—that Warfield understood the doctrine of inspiration as so very vital.

Ultimately his was a fight for the gospel. Consistently at the center of Warfield's attention was the glorious message of divine rescue for sinners. If the attack was on the person of Christ, his concern was not academic only but soteriological—that we would be left without a Savior and without a gospel. If the attack was concerning the integrity of the Scriptures, his concern was not one of party spirit. It was that in the end we would be left without witness to Christ and, indeed, with a Christ who is himself mistaken as to the nature and authority of the book that was written about him. If the attack was an Arminian one, his concern was that the gospel would be so watered down as to devalue Christ and render him much less than the mighty Savior he is. Throughout even his most polemic writings Warfield's passion for Christ and utter dependence on a divine Savior are plainly evident. It is for this reason that Warfield was so passionate for historic Calvinism. For him, "dependence" on God was the very essence of true religion, and, thus, Calvinism is religion expressed in its purest form. That "God saves sinners" is the heart of both the Calvinistic system and the Christian faith itself.

Warfield the Man

Warfield was tall and erect, pleasant but dignified, rather heavy, something of an imposing figure, with ruddy cheeks, hair parted in the middle, sparkling eyes, and a full graying beard. Former student Charles Brokenshire (1885–1954) recalled, "He walked with head erect and well thrown back, and his face beamed with intelligence and amiability." He was "somewhat deaf," which made classroom recitation to him frustratingly difficult, but he was known for this method of teaching nonetheless. Brokenshire continues:

> His most interesting method of instruction appeared when he heard and answered some question in the classroom. Sometime he would use the Socratic method on a reciter and lead some student disposed to argue into a series of statements which drove the young liberal into the orthodox corner where "Benny" wanted him.[5]

"Benny" was the name used by his family—and by his students, but only behind his back, of course! He was always of good humor but also serious, somewhat reserved, and, as one former student reports, with a commanding

---

[5] Personal letter from Charles Brokenshire to John Meeter, June 25, 1942.

air of authority. Thoroughly informed as he was, on the one hand he could appear aloof and indifferent to the theological opinions of others, but on the other hand he displayed an obvious love for others and especially children. And he was always demonstrative in his support of gospel endeavors both at home and abroad.

Warfield was a scholar's scholar who enjoyed long hours daily with his books. He did not spend a great deal of time in social pleasantries such as after-dinner conversation. He was something of a recluse with his books and his pen, always diligent in his theological studies, and well read in all other fields of literature also, especially science.

In his writing Warfield would on occasion employ humor, even in his most involved theological works, sometimes a biting wit and even sarcasm. He was well spoken, with a pleasant southern accent. He preached in a conversational tone that was calm, deliberate, and unaffected but marked by deep spirituality and impassioned with the truth he expounded, yet without demonstrative oratory. Not his scholarship only but his Christlikeness also deeply impressed his students, and he was a man who was himself profoundly affected by the gospel he preached. It was written of him that he was a "devout and sweet-spirited Christian" and a "Christ-like man."[6] He was recognized as a Christian and a scholar in the best sense of both.

Overwhelmingly, Warfield is described by those who knew him as a "model Christian gentleman," a man of grace, great personal charm, generosity, kindness, good humor, and wit. One of Warfield's acquaintances summarizes his impressions of Warfield memorably.

> After a lapse of more than twenty years, Dr B. B. Warfield stands out as the most ideal Christian Character that I have ever known. . . . Dr Warfield possessed the most perfect combination of faculties of mind and heart that I have ever known in any person. His mind was keen and analytical in understanding facts and thoughts; and it was comprehensive in seeing all sides of a subject. He was so devoted to the truth as a man and teacher that his pupils could always trust his statements implicitly; and their confidence in him was never betrayed in any sense. He not only had the power of thought to comprehend a truth; but he also had a perfect command of language to give expression to his thoughts. His diction was precise and complete.
>
> But if Dr Warfield was great in intellectuality, he was just as great in goodness. Over a long period of years this man stands out in my mind as the most Christ-like man that I have ever known. In spite of his brilliance of mind, there

---

[6] *BSac* 78, no. 310 (1921): 124; "Letter from F. T. McGill to John Meeter," in *BT* 89 (Fall 1971): 18.

was no spirit of superciliousness, no purpose to offend the dullest pupil, no haughtiness of heart. With him there was never any sign of pretence [*sic*], or false front; for there was no spirit of hypocrisy in his inner heart. Rather there was always the spirit of humility and meekness and the spirit of kindness and gentleness toward others.[7]

Because of their massive learning and detailed, careful exposition, the theologians of Old Princeton are commonly referred to today as scholastic rationalists. But a broad reading of the Princetonians and of Warfield in particular will quickly demonstrate that this assessment is mistaken. The Princetonians are marked equally by the academic rigor and the fervent piety idealized in the seminary's official "Plan." Men such as Archibald Alexander, Samuel Miller, Charles Hodge, and J. W. Alexander in particular were known for their pastoral instincts. The sermons preached by Warfield and others at the Sabbath afternoon conferences in Miller Chapel, by themselves considered, demonstrate that while the Princetonians excelled in learning, they were at the same time men deeply affected by the gospel, with a keen sense of dependence on God, and consciously aware of the need of the supernatural influences of his Spirit in them. For Warfield himself, as we shall see, all theological learning has as its very practical goal the experiential knowledge of God.

As I have already alluded to, Warfield's heart beat hot for Christ. His passion for Christ and the gospel pulses prominently throughout the many thousands of pages of his works. He adored the Lord Jesus Christ, the incarnate Redeemer, and he loved to say so. And he loved to speak of our utter, helpless need of such a Savior from heaven. He was a "polemic" theologian, yes. And his polemics were powerful, supremely informed, insightful, and unrelenting, devouring the enemies of truth on all fronts. But they were polemics driven by a deep heart of love for and devotion to Christ. He was in fact the ideal of Old Princeton—the highest and best of informed scholarship matched by a humble piety and fervent love for Christ.

Samuel Craig, who was well acquainted with Warfield himself and his writings, affirms this in passing when he says,

What most impresses the student of Warfield's writings *apart from his deeply religious spirit, his sense of complete dependence on God for all things includ-*

---

[7]"Letter from F. T. McGill to John Meeter," in *BT* 89 (Fall 1971): 18.

ing especially his sense of indebtedness as a lost sinner to His free grace—is the breadth of his learning and the exactness of his scholarship.[8]

Craig's remark indicates that it was Warfield's personal sense of rescue that marked him first, although he is known more broadly for his great scholarship. Warfield said of Calvin, "It was not the head but the heart which made him a theologian, and it is not the head but the heart which he primarily addresses in his theology."[9] So also Warfield was a theologian of the heart, and tones of adoring worship of Christ mark his works everywhere.

Final Days

One of Warfield's closest friends was Geerhardus Vos (1862–1949), whom Warfield had helped bring to Princeton for the new chair of biblical theology. It was their regular practice for many years to walk together for refreshment and fellowship. On December 24, 1920, Warfield was walking along the sidewalk to the Vos home, just a few hundred yards across campus from his own home, when suddenly he grasped his chest and collapsed. Warfield spent the next few weeks recovering until, on Wednesday, February 16, 1921, he was finally ready to resume teaching. At the close of the class he returned home, where that evening a heart attack took him, this time fatally.

A former student remarked that Warfield had passed to his bright and happy reward where he can continue his studies to all eternity. J. Ross Stevenson, president of the seminary, wrote of Warfield's death almost a year later, "The Reformed Theology and the cause of evangelical religion have lost one of the ablest interpreters and defenders which America has ever produced."[10] Francis Patton remarked in his memorial address that it was a loss unquestionably felt throughout the greater part of the Christian world. "Nothing but ignorance of his exact scholarship, wide learning, varied writings, and the masterly way in which he did his work," he surmised, could prevent anyone "from uniting with us today in the statement that a prince and a great man has fallen in Israel."[11] J. Gresham Machen lamented in a letter to his mother after Warfield's funeral that as they carried him out, Old Princeton went with him, and that he was certain there was not a man in the entire church who could fill one quarter of his place.[12]

---

[8] *BTS*, xvii, emphasis added.
[9] *W*, 5:23.
[10] *The Expository Times* 33, no. 4 (1922): 153.
[11] Francis Patton, "Benjamin Breckinridge Warfield: A Memorial Address," *PTR* 19, no. 3 (1921): 369.
[12] *JGM*, 309–10.

There have been men of God in the past whose voice was needed and, it would seem, were sent of God for just the occasion and context in which they lived. Warfield was such a man. "The spoiler of liberals,"[13] he has been called, "the man who propelled orthodoxy into the twentieth century."[14] He was a theological army of one. Yet he commands a hearing still today. His vigorous theological endeavors, and his insightful understanding of the Christian life as one lived "in light of the gospel"—and his modeling of the same!—distinguish him as a teacher uniquely equipped to help us in our pursuit of Christ.

---

[13]Raymond Cannata, "History of Apologetics at Princeton Seminary," in William A. Dembski and Jay Wesley Richards, eds., *Unapologetic Apologetics* (Downers Grove, IL: InterVarsity, 2001), 71.
[14]Andrew Hoffecker, "Guardian of the Word," *Tabletalk*, April 2005, 12.

CHAPTER 2

TRUTH AND LIFE

The Role of Christian Doctrine in Warfield's Christian Life

Warfield was a Christian and a theologian, but for him these two categories are virtually one and the same. And we must recognize this if we are to understand him and profit from his instruction on the Christian life. For Warfield theology is not merely some added, optional dimension to the Christian life: it is the very stuff of Christian living. The Christian life is founded on and fostered by *truth*. Behavior, conduct, service, and personal expressions of godliness are of course essential also, and we will see that Warfield treats these subjects with a lively warmth that evidences their importance to him. But he understands these matters within a context that is distinctively Christian. For him, the practical expressions of our devotion and godliness are the outworking of redemptive truth divinely revealed to us in the pages of Scripture and rightly understood. We will see how this is so in later chapters, but we should note this understanding in Warfield up front. We live unto Christ, to the glory of God, not out of a vacuum but out of a mind and heart captivated and inflamed by an understanding of God's greatness and goodness and his saving activity in Christ. This is what fuels Christian living from beginning to end. Truth leads to life, and it is truth rightly understood that shapes Christian experience.

If life grows out of understanding, then it follows that *a firm grasp and robust appreciation of Christian truth is of primary importance to Christian living.* We must be very clear on this if we are to understand Warfield. For him, this is basic. Truth comes first. It is truth that God uses to produce and mold Christian living. Warfield's own piety was, at bottom, his response to Christian truth.

For Warfield, this follows from the very nature of the case. The fundamental truth that sets Christianity apart from all other religions is that it is a *revealed* religion. Christianity is not first about our reaching out to God. It is about his coming to us in grace, making himself known to us, his sinful creatures, in order to restore us to fellowship with himself. It is to this end that God has spoken. Thus, Christianity is a creedal, or doctrinal, religion. It is much more than that, of course, but it is a creedal religion at the very least and at its foundation. God comes first and foremost with a message to proclaim. It is a religion grounded in and advanced by the proclamation of divinely revealed truth. And a right understanding of that message is fundamental to all that it offers. The rescue it promises comes to us as this message is embraced, and our deepening acquaintance with this message advances the comforts and blessings it affords.

If the truth of God's sovereignty is intended for our comfort, then we should wholeheartedly search out an understanding of this truth. If we are designed to worship Christ for the enhancement of his praise and for our own joyful satisfaction, then we must increasingly grasp all that we possibly can of his glorious person and work. If faith consists in an utter dependence upon Christ, then we should seek to know all we can of his person and redemptive work. If in grace God has provided for our success and eventual victory over sin, then it is in the interest of our own encouragement to understand these gospel promises and to become fully acquainted with the abundant provision of the Holy Spirit and the prospect of our coming glory. In order for us to render due worship to God, our knowledge of him must be rightly informed, and so it behooves us to explore ever further the depths of his self-revelation in Scripture. The entirety of the Christian life and experience is our response to revealed truth.

So for Warfield, Christian doctrine is primary. God has revealed himself to us for our benefit. He has revealed himself in order to bring himself glory, to be sure. But he brings honor to himself in our redemption, and it is our increasing acquaintance with these truths that gives shape to Christian experience. We do not understand Warfield if we do not understand this.

One of the glories of the Christian life is that God has not only saved us according to his grand and gracious purpose, but he has also in grace revealed that purpose to us. He has not only set out to save us, so that in the end we will be part of his glorious kingdom, but he has let us in on it, so that we might marvel at the wisdom and mercy that lay behind it, so that we would have this to sing about, and so that we could rejoice in its present realization and in the prospect of its future consummation. It would of course have been enough if he had but saved us and let it go at that. But he has done more. He has not held back from us a realization of his redemptive work, but he has in love revealed to us "the mystery" of his eternal saving plan (Eph. 1:9–10) so that we would see his wisdom and grace and power at work on our behalf. And it has been the testimony of Christians for all the centuries that it is a deeper and increasing grasp of Christ's immeasurable love that grounds and sustains and advances our walk with God (Eph. 3:16–19).

That God has revealed himself in the written Word is a gift to be cherished, and with this blessing comes a corresponding privilege and obligation to learn and understand that Word. We will see how Warfield unpacks this in the next chapter. He complains that it is a symptom of a decaying faith indeed when the teaching of Scripture is neglected. And he judges that attitude of doctrinal indifference as contrary to the very nerve of Christian experience. It is Christian doctrine that gives shape to the distinctive Christian life and experience, and Warfield warns that to be indifferent to Christian doctrine is, simply, to be indifferent to Christianity itself.

Warfield argues that in this sense Christianity aims first at the mind. In terms of both evangelism and Christian growth Christianity offers first a message, a word from God—that is, doctrine. And thus Warfield will not allow a disjunction between doctrine and devotion. He insists, rather, that all Christian theology is itself "directly and richly and evangelically devotional."[1] Not every Christian is called to be a professional theologian, of course. But theology is nonetheless the business of every believer. It is the stuff of the Christian life.

This is not only Warfield's specific teaching on the matter; it is the character of his own Christian experience also. For him, the Christian experience is one that is shaped throughout by truth, truth that has deeply affected the mind and heart. And throughout his writings the doctrine he expounds is consistently an exercise of and an expression of devotion to Christ. Communion with God is not a mere feeling for him. It is the experience of God himself,

---

[1] *SSW*, 2:286; here Warfield cites the words of Alexander Whyte.

rightly—even if not fully—understood. And the Christian life, more broadly considered, is but the enjoyment of Christian truth rightly understood and gratefully experienced. For Warfield there is no substitute for this. Nothing else can so stimulate the Christian mind, enliven the Christian heart, and satisfyingly mold Christian experience.

We must understand this if we are to understand Warfield and appreciate his teaching on the Christian life. His understanding that Christian life grows in the soil of Christian truth is what shapes this book. We will expand further in the next chapter.

PART 2

FOUNDATIONS OF FAITH

CHAPTER 3

LEARNING AND LIVING

The Value and Authority of God's Word

We cannot do without the Scriptures; having them we need no other guide. We need this light to light our pathway; having it we may well dispense with any other.[1]

A Religion of the Book

Several times in his writings Warfield repeats the statement that Christianity is fundamentally different from all other religions in that it is a *revealed* religion. Christianity is not about our search for God or our means of finding him. Christianity is not a religion that works its way upward. It is all about God coming to us—God in grace making himself known to us and making a way for us to enjoy fellowship with him. God's self-revelation is therefore a redemptive act. He makes himself known in order to restore us to himself.

And so at the very heart of Christianity is, simply, a message—a revelation from God to us about what he has done to bring us to himself. Christianity is in its very essence a "word" and creedal religion. It is grounded in truth, propositions, a message from God that must be embraced.

---

[1] *SSW*, 2:570–71.

Warfield builds on this further. If Christianity is distinctively a revealed religion, then it is also uniquely *authoritative*. It does not offer itself as the best and highest of human thinking about God, or even the best or most successful of human efforts to know God. It professes to be nothing less than the unique and exclusive word from God, his very own self-disclosure and the record of the actions he has taken in Jesus Christ to bring us into fellowship with himself.

Warfield often quoted one of Rudyard Kipling's characters, who declares,

> The 'eathen in 'is blindness bows down to wood an' stone;
> 'E don't obey no orders unless they is 'is own.

That is to say, human religions lack authority. They form their own ideas and "discover" their own beliefs. By contrast the Christian is "under orders" because, unlike human religions, Christianity is a revealed religion—divinely revealed. We Christians are not our own touchstone of truth, and we do not confuse our ideas about God with his own self-revelation. We learn truth about God not from "inner lights" within ourselves but from God's own objective Word. Apart from this external authority there is no Christianity. This, at bottom, is Christianity's leading distinctive.

Warfield's Argument for Inerrancy

This was the starting point of Warfield's argument for inerrancy. Scripture is the word of God; it therefore cannot err in anything it affirms. Inspiration necessarily entails inerrancy. But his point at this stage is simply to affirm that Scripture is a word from God, his very own self-revelation.

In a crucial sense the nature of Scripture as God's own word is foundational to the entire system of Christian teaching. Apart from the doctrine of inspiration there is no sure reference point and therefore no well-grounded reason for the Christian hope or life. Without an inspired Bible the ground for any of Christianity's teachings is lost. Christians instinctively recognize the need for an external authority by which to measure their beliefs. And in that most important question of our standing before God we recognize that we need more than inner light or impressions: we need a sure word from God. We need from him a statement of his purpose of grace. To be assured of our safety beyond death, we need his own explicit assurance. And Scripture provides the answers. In God's Word we learn of Christ, of God's grace, of faith, and of salvation. Warfield asked, Where would we be without an inspired Bible? Where would the church be? How would we have learned rightly of Christ? What a confused faith Christianity would be without an inspired guide! Though it is theoretically possible to have a genuine Christianity without an inspired book, the fact is that this is how Christianity has been given to us, and without that inspired Bible we would have no reliable knowledge of Christ or of salvation, and no sure ground for hope. Instinctively, the church has always looked to Scripture as its source and measure of truth. As Warfield explains:

> Wherever Christ is known through whatever means, there is Christianity, and men may hear and believe and be saved. But God has caused his grace to abound to us in that he not only published redemption through Christ in the world, but gave this preachment authoritative expression through the apostles, and fixed it with infallible trustworthiness in his inspired word. Thus in every age God speaks directly to every Christian heart, and gives us abounding safety to our feet and divine security to our souls. And thus, instead of a mere record of a revelation given in the past, we have the ever-living word of God; instead of a mere tradition however guarded, we have what we have all learned to call in a unique sense "the Scriptures."[2]

In this sense, at least, the inspiration of Scripture is a foundational doctrine. And in this sense Warfield can assert, "Apart from the revelation of God deposited for us in the Scriptures, there is no Christianity. Obliterate this revelation—theology may remain, but it is no longer a Christian theology; religion may remain, but it is no longer the Christian religion." As the revelation of God in Scripture is ignored, a purely natural religion is left to make its advance.[3]

Truth and Life

Christianity, however, is more than a collection of various doctrines. Foundational and essential as Christian doctrine is, its goal is not merely to increase our understanding but also to redeem and radically transform our lives. Echoing 2 Timothy 3:15, Warfield emphasizes that Scripture is given not merely to make us wise, but to make us wise unto salvation. And for him "salvation" entails not only an initial faith and conversion, but a life adoringly and worshipfully given to Christ. "Christianity is neither a mere philosophy nor an empty illusion: it is objectively real and subjectively

---

[2] *SSW*, 2:541.
[3] *SSW*, 2:294–95.

operative, and finds its rooting both in its inspired record and in its spiritual efficacy."[4] Christianity, as we have seen, is distinctly a redemptive religion, and its happy goal, in brief, is to bring us to know God. It is to this end that God has revealed himself.

The Christian life is founded on and shaped by truth, truth revealed in Scripture. It is by means of God's self-revelation that we come to know him personally and experientially. And if that is the case, then here is established the duty and the privilege of increased acquaintance with God's Word. In this vein Warfield often speaks of Scripture not only as an infallible message, but therefore also as an infallible guide. Its commands and directives will never fail us. He loves to say that believing and obeying God's Word, we will always be *safe*. Here is a sure word from our Creator, a word that speaks always with supreme authority, and a word that will never lead us but in the way of truth.

Warfield is best known for his landmark defense of the doctrine of inspiration, and throughout his voluminous writings he often emphasized the note of biblical *authority*. This was, after all, the defining issue of the day, and he spoke to it more famously than any other. But the related theme of the *value* of Scripture to the Christian is a theme that recurs throughout with such obvious conviction as to show the prominent place it held in his thought.

Let us take his exposition of Colossians 1:9 as an example. Here the apostle prays, "asking that you may be filled with the knowledge of his will in all spiritual wisdom and understanding." The apostle's desire is that his readers be filled with knowledge, a knowledge of God's will, and this in order that they may walk worthy of their Lord, pleasing him in every possible way. Warfield comments:

> Obviously it seemed to the Apostle that the pathway to a right life lay through a right knowledge. It was only as they knew the will of God that they could hope to please Christ in action. Knowledge comes thus before life and is the constructive force of life. Thus the Apostle teaches us the supreme value of a right and profound and exact knowledge of Divine things. Not as if knowledge were the end—life, undoubtedly, is the end at which the saving processes are directed; but because the sole lever to raise the life to its proper height is just right knowledge. It is life—the right life—that the Apostle is praying for in behalf of the Colossians: but he represents knowledge—right knowledge—as possessing the necessity of means to that life.[5]

---

[4] *PTR* 8, no. 4 (1910): 688.
[5] *FL*, 542.

In Warfield's day Christian doctrine had come on bad times—much like our own day, in many respects. The very right of "doctrines" to exist and the duty of the church to expound them were questioned by many and even denied. One of the most popular slogans advancing this attempt to establish a Christianity that is free of theological baggage was that Christianity is not a doctrine but a life. Its ethic and its experience are essential, we are told, not its doctrines. The purpose of the Bible is to quicken life, not to satisfy our curiosity, and as we focus on doctrine we steer away from its proper and intended use. By the Bible God implants life and leads us to depend solely on God—and not facts or doctrines—for that life.

Warfield acknowledges the element of truth in this line of thinking that makes it deceptively attractive. Christianity is indeed a life, a blessed life in communion with the Son of God. But he insists that the whole body of Christian doctrine is designed to lead to this blessed life. He does not contend that doctrine creates this life—only the Spirit of God can do that, enabling us to hear the truth and respond to it. But it is truth—the gospel, doctrine—that the Spirit uses in regeneration. To make a sharp separation of life from doctrine is entirely foreign to Christianity and in fact turns it on its head. Ultimately it renounces Christianity altogether, reducing it to a feeling or an ethic. And so Warfield simply inquires what it is that produces the specific form of religious feeling and ethic that is distinctively Christian. Clearly, it is Christianity's doctrine, its teaching, that gives shape to its distinctive experience. Once again, knowledge of Christian doctrine is foundational to Christian living.

Not content to establish his argument from logic alone, Warfield argues the same from the inspired models of Scripture. The apostle Paul regularly organizes his letters in a way that reflects this understanding exactly. The transition marked in Romans 12:1 stands as a famous example. "I appeal to you *therefore*, brothers, by the mercies of God, to present your bodies as a living sacrifice, holy and acceptable to God, which is your spiritual worship." Warfield points out that the "therefore" or "because this is so" is significant. He has just finished a lengthy exposition of Christian doctrine (Romans 1–11), and turning to matters of ethics and behavior he explicitly grounds his exhortation in his previous doctrinal instruction. In this way the inspired apostle reveals his understanding that Christian life is grounded in and built upon Christian teaching.

All this follows the understanding of the Lord Jesus, who taught that sanctification is grounded in Christian doctrine: "Sanctify them in the truth; your word is truth" (John 17:17). The word our Lord brought from heaven and gave to his apostles was to be—for them and all believers after them—that which shapes Christian life and experience.

In short, Christianity is a religion that has a message to proclaim, and thus it is preeminently a doctrinal religion. It seeks by the propagation of truth to save the lost and rule their lives.

Moving one step further, Warfield argues that if Christian truth is essential to Christian life, then increased understanding of Christian truth is essential to advanced godliness and stability. The character of our theology will shape the character of our religion, and any defective view of God's character will be reflected in the soul and the peace of conscience we are meant to enjoy. If we have no doctrine, we have no Christianity. If we have scanty doctrine, we have scanty Christianity. If we have profoundly informed convictions, we will have a solid and substantial Christianity. If we do not think right thoughts about God, we will not worship him as he desires and deserves to be worshiped, and we will not experience the life intended for us. If we misunderstand Christian doctrine, it will result in a distortion or dwarfing of our religious life in some measure. The deeper and clearer our understanding of Christian truth, the greater will be its sanctifying effect on us. "The character of our religion is, in a word, determined by the character of our theology."[6] It is therefore in the interests of the religious life, genuine Christian living and experience, that we seek increasingly to understand God's self-revelation in Scripture more completely. Only so will it exert its intended influence.

Here, then, is the value of God's Word. It is given redemptively: God has set out by it, and not apart from it, to restore us to his fellowship and to his image. In other words, Scripture is foundational to life. "We cannot do without the Scriptures; having them we need no other guide. We need this light to light our pathway; having it we may well dispense with any other."[7]

Warfield highlights all this in the last paragraph of his lecture given at his inauguration to the chair of New Testament Exegesis and Literature at Western Theological Seminary in 1880. His lecture was a fervent defense of the church doctrine of inspiration against the advances of modern criticism. After an extensive counterattack and vindication of Scripture as the word of God, he closed with these words of Christian devotion:

How can I close without expression of thanks to Him who has so loved us as to give us so pure a record of his will,—God-given in all its parts, even though cast in the forms of human speech,—infallible in all its statements,—divine

---

[6] *W*, 9:80.
[7] *SSW*, 2:570–71.

even to its smallest particle! I am far from contending that without such an inspiration there could be no Christianity. Without any inspiration we could have had Christianity; yea, and men could still have heard the truth, and through it been awakened, and justified, and sanctified and glorified. The verities of our faith would remain historically proven true to us—so bountiful has God been in his fostering care—even had we no Bible; and through those verities, salvation. But to what uncertainties and doubts would we be the prey!—to what errors, constantly begetting worse errors, exposed!—to what refuges, all of them refuges of lies, driven! Look but at those who have lost the knowledge of this infallible guide: see them evincing man's most pressing need by inventing for themselves an infallible church, or even an infallible Pope. Revelation is but half revelation unless it be infallibly communicated; it is but half communicated unless it be infallibly recorded. The heathen in their blindness are our witnesses of what becomes of an unrecorded revelation. Let us bless God, then, for his inspired word! And may he grant that we may always cherish, love and venerate it, and conform all our life and thinking to it! So may we find safety for our feet, and peaceful security for our souls.[8]

---

[8] W, 1:424.

CHAPTER 4

REDEMPTION ACCOMPLISHED

God to the Rescue

Warfield often emphasized that because mankind is created in the image of God there is within each of us a sense of right and wrong, and with that a relentless sense of justice. Because of this innate sense of justice there is also within each of us an inexpungible sense of guilt. We know—even if we deny it—that we are dependent on and accountable to our Creator. And we know that we have violated his law at many points. Instinctively we are aware of a coming judgment, even if at all costs we suppress this knowledge, seeking to escape it (Rom. 1:32). Because of all this, there is in the heart of every man and woman an ineradicable longing for some means to appease the God whose law we have transgressed. It is this longing and need that Christianity, in its very essence, is designed to answer.

Warfield loved to speak of Christianity, therefore, as a distinctly *redemptive* religion. Christianity is "a sinner's religion," "a religion for sinners." Its central message is not one of human values or life but of divine rescue. "In the centre of its centre, in the heart of its heart, salvation is deliverance from sin."[1] For Warfield, Christianity *is* redemption. This—redemption—is what Christianity *means*.

---

[1] *SW*, 46.

This redemptive process begins, from our view of things, in God's self-revelation. Warfield speaks of revelation as one of God's redemptive acts because it is for our salvation that God makes himself known. His providence and history itself are likewise to be understood in a salvific context. God has set out to honor himself in human history by means of his gracious and powerful salvation of sinners. But this saving work, of course, centers on the person and work of God's Son, our Lord and Savior, Jesus Christ.

> And in proportion as the grace of the saving God in Christ Jesus is obscured or passes into the background, in that proportion does Christianity slip from our grasp. Christianity is summed up in the phrase: "God was in Christ, reconciling the world with himself" [2 Cor. 5:19]. Where this great confession is contradicted or neglected, there is no Christianity.[2]

Moreover, just as Christianity is itself a redemptive religion, so also the Christian life is grounded in and thrives on a right appreciation of the person and work of Jesus Christ. This is our point of reference throughout our Christian experience.

The Person of Christ

Fundamental to the Bible's doctrine of salvation is its doctrine of the person of Christ. The value and efficacy of Christ's work rest on the dignity of his person. As we saw in the previous chapter, the church's historic doctrine of the person of Christ in Warfield's day had come under sustained attack. For liberal theologians, Jesus of Nazareth simply could not have been God come as man. To give lip service to this traditional understanding they would often speak of God the Son as surrendering his deity in the incarnation and then, in his glorification, as returning to his former glory. But by one evasion or another they would not allow that the historic Jesus was, in fact, both God and man as the church had taught since the beginning and confessed in the early creeds. Jesus to them was a man—a good man, the best man, the ideal man, and the great teacher, but still just a man and not God.

Such a "shrunken deity," as Warfield would refer to the Jesus of liberalism,[3] is not worthy of our worshipful adoration. And as for any Christian, but especially in his context, it is important for Warfield to speak instead of Christ as the supernatural Savior who is both God and man. He speaks often and

---

[2] *SSW*, 1:50.
[3] *W*, 3:375.

at length of the deity of Christ, the Lord from heaven. And he expounds the humanity of Christ in unique and memorable ways. He takes as his starting point this historic doctrine of the person of Christ and insists that the Bible can make no sense without it.

The Deity of Christ

Warfield expounds the deity of Christ as something presupposed in the Old Testament presentation of the coming Messiah. Expectations and prophecies of David's greater son in the Psalms, for example, often employ language that goes well beyond what is appropriate to one who is merely human. If someone will reject the deity of Christ, Warfield contends, he must either set aside the Psalms altogether "or sing them with bated breath."[4]

Psalm 45:6 provides a clear example: "Your throne, O God, is forever and ever." It is impossible to miss the fact that the psalmist here provides plain testimony to the divine nature of the coming Messiah. What purely human king could be addressed as "God" and his sons be constituted as princes over the whole world (vv. 7, 17; cf. Heb. 1:8)?

Similarly, in Psalm 110:1 David speaks of his coming son as "my Lord."

> The LORD says to my Lord:
>   "Sit at my right hand,
> until I make your enemies your footstool." (cf. Heb. 1:13)

Jesus himself used this verse to silence his opponents (Matt. 22:41–46). How can David's son also be David's Lord? The psalm clearly anticipates, in the Messiah, one who is more than merely human.

The Old Testament prophets spoke of "the coming one" in transcendent terms—a coming King and a coming God. He is the "Mighty God, Everlasting Father, Prince of Peace" (Isa. 9:6). Though he belongs to the category of man, to be sure ("Son of Man"), he comes from heaven, rides on the clouds, and stands before God as one who belongs (Dan. 7:13–14).

Warfield surveys this Old Testament expectation at length (see also Jer. 23:6; Zech. 13:7; Mal. 3:1) and concludes that the anticipation of a divine Messiah is "the soul of the entire Old Testament." It was no merely human Redeemer that was to come. The hope of Israel lay in a perfect theophany—the coming of God himself.

---

[4] *W*, 3:10.

The Gospel writers, in turn, present Jesus as the fulfillment of just this expectation. Warfield stresses at length that the Gospel writers' emphasis on Jesus's miracles, his foreknowledge of all things, and his own claims all reflect their conviction that Jesus was not merely human but of divine origin and nature. They emphasize that Jesus was one who had come from heaven (John 1:14; 17:5; cf. the many "I came," "I have come," and "I was sent" passages, e.g., Mark 10:45), the fulfiller of the "coming of God" promises of the Old Testament Psalms and Prophets (e.g., Matt. 1:21, cf. Ps. 130:8; Matt. 1:23, cf. Isa. 7:14; Mark 2:19–20, cf. Hos. 2:19; Mark 14:62, cf. Dan.7:13–14). Consistently he is presented as the "Lord" (Luke 2:11) and this especially in connection with Old Testament passages referring to the "LORD" (Yahweh; e.g., Mark 2:28; 11:3). They present him as claiming himself to be the sovereign judge over all (Matt. 13:41; 16:27; 24:31), the one who will send "his" angels to gather God's elect (Mark 13:27). "Who is this Son of Man," Warfield asks pointedly, "surrounded by his angels, in whose hands are the issues of life? . . . Who is this Son of Man at whose behest his angels winnow men?"[5]

Beyond this, the Gospel writers present Jesus as the one whom God alone can know and the one who alone can know God (Matt. 11:27; Luke 10:22), who enjoys full equality with God (Matt. 28:19) and is himself God (John 1:1–3, 14, 18), who is one with God (John 10:30), and who therefore reveals God to us (John 1:1, 18; 14:8–9). The presupposition of every line of the Gospels—indeed, of the entire New Testament—is that Jesus is the Lord from heaven, the unique, transcendent God come to his people.

In the book of Acts and in the Epistles it is the lordship of Jesus that is proclaimed and expounded in depth and at such great length. To be sure, the recognition that "Jesus is Lord" (Rom. 10:9; 1 Cor. 12:3) expresses the very essence of Christianity, and "serving the Lord Christ" is the distinctive mark of the Christian. It is the Lord himself who is our Savior, and it is Jesus who is Lord—"the Lord of glory" in fact (1 Cor. 2:8), "God over all, blessed forever" (Rom. 9:5), "the great God and our Savior" (Titus 2:13). One no less than this has come to our rescue. Warfield goes to pains to demonstrate from every portion of the Bible that Jesus is a divine Savior.

The Two Natures

Yet he is not God only. Since the incarnation he is man also. And Warfield expounds the humanity of Christ in ways that are warm, memorable, and spiritually enriching. We will see much of this in due course, but it will be

---

[5] *SSW*, 1:153–54.

useful at this point to notice how the Bible presents a Savior who is both fully human and fully divine.

Luke notes for us that the young boy Jesus "grew and became strong, filled with wisdom," and that he "increased in wisdom and in stature and in favor with God and man" (Luke 2:40, 52). Warfield draws observations from this that inspire worshipful adoration of Christ, the ideal human, as we shall see. But he is careful also to stress something here that is essential to the gospel. These words from Luke display for us the *real humanity* of our Lord. He grew and advanced both in stature and in wisdom—and in corresponding favor with God and with men. Quite clearly he was a real boy and a real man. He advanced at every level—physically, intellectually, and spiritually. He learned. This accords well with those Gospel passages in which Jesus admits ignorance of the time of the coming day of judgment (Matt. 24:36; Mark 13:32). And often in the Gospels Jesus seeks information through questions. In short, there are no human traits lacking in the Gospel writers' portrait of Jesus. He was the object of temptation. He was conscious of dependence on God. He was a man of prayer. He exercised faith. And he learned obedience through the things he suffered.

All this and Luke's remarks remind us that our Lord was a man in mind and heart and spirit as well as in body. He was whatever it is to be a man—a man without error and without sin, but a man nonetheless. And he grew—not only during his youth but, we must assume, throughout his life—in knowledge and wisdom and piety and in moral strength and holiness.

Warfield stresses at this point that we need not be afraid of emphasizing too strongly our Lord's complete humanity. Luke does it himself! And Warfield reminds us that it is "gain and nothing but gain"[6] that we should recognize the full humanity of Christ as clearly as possible. Christ became—and thus is forever—all that man is. As the book of Hebrews tells us, "He was made like his brothers in every respect" (Heb. 2:17).

The danger arises only when we acknowledge his humanity without also recognizing his deity. Although the biblical writers present the Lord Jesus as all that man is, they do not represent him as *only* what man is. They also present him as all that God is. Right alongside the plain declarations and indications of his true and complete humanity there runs an equally clear series of declarations and indications of his deity.

For example, he is represented as ignorant of certain matters (Matt. 24:36 = Mark 13:32; cf. Luke 2:52). But he is equally represented as knowing all

---

[6]*SSW*, 1:162–63.

things (John 16:30; 21:17). He asks questions in order to acquire information, but he also knows the secret prayer of Nathaniel (John 1:47), the whole life of the Samaritan woman (John 4:29), the very thoughts of his enemies (Matt. 9:4), and "all that is in man" (John 2:25). All through his youth he grows and increases in wisdom and in his perception of God's will. Yet even at age twelve he confounds the rabbis with his penetrating questions from Scripture.

The Gospel writers make no attempt to keep these two lines separate: they are interlaced continually. Jesus is told of Lazarus's sickness, but he knows already that he is dead (John 11:3, 6, 11, 14). He asks, "Where have you laid him" and weeps for Mary and Martha, and yet he knows from the beginning that Lazarus will be raised. Everywhere we see these two strands of thought reflecting the two natures of our Lord. He is not presented as acting inconsistently. Nor is he inconsistently represented, now as acting in one order and now in another. Rather he is presented in that dual life that was his, with two natures constantly in complete possession. All that God is, is attributed to Jesus; yet all that man is, is attributed to him also. And neither line of presentation is more convincing than another. He is man, *and* he is God. He acquires information through his human nature but knows all things through his divine nature.

All of this is very clearly presented to us in the pages of Scripture. And Warfield counsels us that the only problem involved is that of our understanding it all. The facts are plain, even though a full comprehension of it all lies beyond us.

Because we have difficulty comprehending it, errors have crept into the church. Over the centuries some have pared down this or the other side of the equation, denying either Christ's deity or his full humanity. But the only way to do justice to the biblical representation of Jesus is to allow both lines of teaching to stand with full weight. Jesus as the God-man was in constant possession and use of *two natures*. He is perfect in deity and perfect in humanity—two distinct natures in one person. This is the doctrine of the person of Christ we have inherited from the very beginning of the Christian era and memorialized in the pronouncements of the Nicene and Chalcedonian councils. And if this "solution" is not the right one, that Christ possesses two natures in one person, then the puzzle remains insoluble.

Warfield acknowledges that it is difficult to conceive of two complete and perfect natures united in one person. But he reminds us that once it is conceived, all that the Bible says about Jesus follows and fits together with ease. He in whom dwells both an infinite and a finite mind both at every moment of time knows all things and as fully human is throughout all time advancing in knowledge. This is mystery, but it is simply and precisely the mystery of the incarnation. And without this mystery there could be no real incarnation at all. This is the glory of the incarnation. "It presents to our adoring gaze not a humanized God or a deified man, but a true God-man—one who is all that God is and at the same time all that man is: on whose mighty arm we can rest, and to whose human sympathy we can appeal."[7]

"We cannot afford to lose either the God in the man or the man in the God," Warfield admonishes. "Our hearts cry out for the complete God-man whom the Scriptures offer us." For if he is man, made like us, he is able to pour out his blood. And because he is God, his blood is of infinite value to save. And since he is both God and man in one person, then we can speak of God "purchasing his church with his own blood" (Acts 20:28). Warfield worshipfully adds, "And unless God has purchased his Church with his own blood, in what shall his Church find a ground for its hope?"[8]

This doctrine of the two natures of Christ is stated perhaps most clearly in Philippians 2:6–8, where the apostle Paul speaks of Christ,

> who, though he was in the form of God, did not count equality with God a thing to be grasped, but emptied himself, taking the form of a servant, being born in the likeness of men. And being found in human form, he humbled himself by becoming obedient to the point of death, even death on a cross.

This passage was the subject of much discussion in Warfield's day, and Warfield himself provided frequent and lengthy analysis of it. The substance of the apostle's statement is clear and to the point: God the Son became true man. In becoming man he did not cease to be God, but he did become truly human, and this he did in order to save us by dying for us. This is the glorious condescension of our Redeemer, and our faith rests in no one less.

That Christ is both God and man is essential to his saviorhood, and we worship him accordingly. This is the linchpin of the gospel—the glorious Son of God stooped to become all that we are in order to bring us rescue. Only in recognition of this great condescension of grace do we learn the love of God for us. And only here is our faith and love drawn out to its full

---

[7]*SSW*, 1:166.
[8]*SSW*, 1:166.

height. "For you know the grace of our Lord Jesus Christ, that though he was rich, yet for your sake he became poor, so that you by his poverty might become rich" (2 Cor. 8:9). The Lord of glory in human flesh—no Christian heart will be satisfied with anyone or anything less.

The Work of Christ

Warfield is careful to emphasize that the incarnation of the second person of the Trinity was not an end in itself. Marvelous as it is to behold, it had another end in view—human redemption. "Christ Jesus came into the world to save sinners" (1 Tim. 1:15; cf. Heb. 2:17). This is the rationale of the incarnation. It was a remedial scheme. It had human sin as its occasion and salvation as its goal. In the words of our Lord himself, he "came not to be served but to serve, and to give his life as a ransom for many" (Matt. 20:28). He came as the Redeemer, and so he went to the cross. He lived so that he might die and, by dying and rising, bring many to life.

Warfield comments that this title *Redeemer* is more endearing to us than all other titles our Lord bears, for "it is the name specifically of the Christ of the cross."[9] It brings before our eyes one who suffered in our place. And this—the Redeemer suffering in our place—is the very nerve of the New Testament presentation of Christ, the hinge on which the Christian gospel turns, and the center of our worship. Frequently in combating the trend in liberal theology to affirm the value of Jesus while deprecating the redeeming significance of his cross, Warfield insists that it is not Christ merely that we preach. It is Christ *crucified* that constitutes our message.

> A Christless cross no refuge for me;
> A Crossless Christ my Savior may not be;
> But, O Christ crucified! I rest in thee![10]

Whatever else is entailed in what the Bible calls salvation (and there is much more, as we shall see), rescue—deliverance from guilt—stands first. According to the biblical writers, this rescue is accomplished for us by the Lord Jesus in his death on the cross. When we say that "Christ died for us," we confess that we are sinners deserving of divine judgment and that our only rescue is found in the Lord from heaven who on the cross bore our curse in our place.

---

[9] *W*, 2:373.
[10] *SSW*, 2:667.

Satisfaction

To appreciate our salvation rightly, Warfield stresses, we must understand the death of Christ in terms of *satisfaction*. Other theories have been developed throughout the centuries of the church emphasizing that Christ's death constitutes a victory over Satan, or that it effects a change in the believer himself, and so on. While Warfield finds much that is true in these theories, he insists that we have not reached the heart of the issue until we see in Christ's death a satisfaction made to God for sin. The atonement of Christ was necessary, first, because of the justice of God, who is outraged by human sin. In its first aspect, the atoning work of Christ has reference to God, "terminating" on him. This understanding is necessary, Warfield argues, given the biblical estimate of sin. "If we are sinners, and in proportion as we know ourselves to be sinners, and appreciate what it means to be sinners, we will cry out for that Savior who only after He was perfected by suffering could become the Author of eternal salvation."[11] That is to say, sinners need an atonement that expiates (or removes) sin, that delivers them from sin, and that reconciles them to God.

Substitute

At the heart of this doctrine, Warfield insists, is the pervasive biblical presentation of Christ as a *substitute*. "One has died for all, therefore, all have died" (2 Cor. 5:14). He "who knew no sin" was made sin for us (2 Cor. 5:21). "He himself bore our sins in his body on the tree" (1 Pet. 2:24; cf. Rom. 8:3; 1 Cor. 5:7; Eph. 5:2; Heb. 2:17; 1 Pet. 3:18; 1 John 2:2). Christ took our "law-place," as Warfield well describes it, and satisfied—paid in full—the judicial debt incurred by our sin. He assumed our every obligation, every fault, every sin, and every debt, and standing in our place bore the divine curse (Gal. 3:13). This is the heart of the meaning of Christ's death—he was our substitute bearing our sin and answering to God on our behalf.

Sacrifice

Warfield reminds us further that if we speak of substitution in a biblical sense, we cannot avoid the concept of *sacrifice*. Israel's elaborate sacrificial system was designed in large part to illustrate the removal of God's wrath by means of substitutionary sacrifice. The sin of the worshiper was transferred to the animal, and the animal was offered in his place. Of course no

---

[11] *W*, 9:297.

animal could acceptably bear the curse of human sin (Heb. 10:1–4)—such offerings were merely temporary and symbolic. And the biblical writers regularly describe the death of Christ in these sacrificial terms, such as in their frequent reminder that salvation is "through his blood" (cf. Rom. 3:25; 5:9; 1 Cor. 10:16; Eph. 1:7; 2:13; Col. 1:20; Heb. 9:12, 14; 1 Pet. 1:2, 18–19; 1 John 1:7; 5:6, 8; Rev. 1:5). Christ himself describes his death in just these terms: "The Son of Man came not to be served but to serve, and to give his life as a ransom for many" (Matt. 20:28); "This is my blood of the covenant, which is poured out for many for the forgiveness of sins" (Matt. 26:28). And his apostles after him likewise describe his death in sacrificial terms (1 Cor. 5:7; Eph. 5:2; Heb. 7:27) and as having obtained the effects of sacrifice (Rom. 3:25; 1 Cor. 15:3; 2 Cor. 5:21; Eph. 1:7; Col. 1:14, 20; Titus 2:14; Heb. 1:3; 9:28; 10:12; 1 Pet. 2:24; 3:18; 1 John 2:2; 4:10; Rev. 1:5). In short, when the New Testament writers—as they so often do—connect forgiveness with the "death" or "blood" of Christ, they remind us again that our release from sin and guilt came only by the propitiatory and expiatory sacrifice of our Redeemer.

Here we have reached the very center of the gospel. "The blood of Jesus,— O, the blood of Jesus!" Warfield exclaims. "When we have reached it, we have attained not merely the heart, but the heart of the heart of the Gospel."[12] This doctrine of the sacrificial death of Christ is not only essential to Christianity,

> but in a very real sense it constitutes Christianity. It is this which differentiates Christianity from other religions. Christianity did not come into the world to proclaim a new morality and, sweeping away all the supernatural props by which men were wont to support their trembling, guilt-stricken souls, to throw them back on their own strong right arms to conquer a standing before God for themselves. It came to proclaim the real sacrifice for sin which God had provided in order to supersede all the poor fumbling efforts which men had made and were making to provide a sacrifice for sin for themselves; and, planting men's feet on this, to bid them go forward.[13]

Redemption

This broader context helps clarify the meaning of yet another biblical concept: *redemption*. Warfield demonstrates at great length that both in biblical and in extrabiblical usage the language of "redeem" or "redemption" did not refer to deliverance, merely, but to *deliverance upon payment of a ransom*

---

[12] *SW*, 88.
[13] *W*, 2:435.

price. He suggests that it might be better to translate the New Testament words as "a ransoming" or "to ransom," and to speak of Christ not only as a "Redeemer" but as a "Ransomer." The terminology emphasizes that a deliverance is obtained at the payment of a cost. Hence, Christ himself declares that he came "to give his life as a ransom for many" (Matt. 20:28; Mark 10:45), and that he "lays down his life" for his sheep (John 10:11) and for his friends (John 15:13). Similarly, the apostle Paul tells us that Christ "gave himself a ransom for all" (1 Tim. 2:6; cf. Gal. 1:4; 2:20; Eph. 5:2, 25). Still more fully, the apostle Peter reminds us, "You were ransomed from the futile ways inherited from your forefathers, not with perishable things such as silver or gold, but with the precious blood of Christ, like that of a lamb without blemish or spot" (1 Pet. 1:18–19). And in Hebrews 9:12 the notions of sacrifice and redemption are linked together explicitly: "Christ entered once for all into the holy places, not by means of the blood of goats and calves but by means of his own blood, thus securing an eternal redemption." By his one-time shedding of blood, Christ both "entered the holy place" and "obtained eternal ransoming." And so in brief the apostle Paul writes of Christ "in whom we have redemption through his blood, the forgiveness of sins" (Eph. 1:7; cf. Col. 1:14). This is the distinctive character of Christianity—Christ's dying in place of his people, securing our deliverance by the sacrifice of himself in payment for our sin.

Reconciliation

In turn, Warfield explains, the gospel "finds its key-note in a doctrine of *reconciliation*. The core of Paul's Gospel is indeed expressed in this one word, Reconciliation"—a reconciliation secured by expiation.[14] God's wrath has been turned aside from us, having been exhausted on our substitute, who offered himself in our place as a sacrifice for our sins, and as a result we are restored to fellowship with him. This is the great offer of the gospel. It is a "message of reconciliation" (2 Cor. 5:19)—a message of peace, fellowship with God through the work of our Redeemer. And the gospel ministry itself is, therefore, "the ministry of reconciliation" (2 Cor. 5:18).

Presupposed in this doctrine of reconciliation is a deep sense of sin and guilt and its Godward effects. Sin has outraged God's justice and has separated us from him. There is enmity. We are by nature children of wrath. We are settled in our opposition to God, and because of our rebellion God is wrathful toward us. But in Christ this enmity has been removed; indeed, the

---

[14]*SW*, 147, emphasis added.

sin causing it has been abolished, and peace with God has been established (2 Cor. 5:19, 21; Eph. 2:14, 16)—"external peace between an angry God and sinful men, and internal peace in the response of the human conscience to the restored smile of God."[15] This is the great distance Christ has brought us. And this is the joy of the Christian experience. We are God's beloved people, secured by him at great cost.

Christ the Object of Our Adoration

For Warfield, all of this is absolutely essential, even central, to Christian living as biblically understood. It is imperative for the Christian to understand these basic truths and think through them carefully in order to live worshipfully. These truths expand our minds and enlarge our hearts and instill a deep sense of adoration. We must never think that we can "get beyond" these truths. They must always be with us, front and center, informing and filling our hearts with loving praise.

This is perhaps the leading mark of Warfield's piety. His mind and heart were caught up with the person and work of Christ, and, stemming from this, he continually manifests a keen sense of helpless yet adoring dependence on his glorious Redeemer. He revels in the love of God displayed in the incarnation and the cross. His expositions of these themes are characterized not merely by precise theological definitions. He does provide marvelously exact definitions, of course, and he views this exercise as essential and basic to genuine, heartfelt worship. All throughout, his expositions are marked by the language of humble and grateful adoration. Here is the great Savior, eminently qualified, glorious in his condescension, and mighty in his saving virtues. This is the one in whom we rest, the great Redeemer from heaven who has lovingly come to our rescue and in whose blessed person and work we are forever safe. This is the one by whom and in whom we live. And this is the one *for* whom we live.

---

[15] W, 9:278.

CHAPTER 5

RIGHT WITH GOD

Our New Standing

When Warfield states that *deliverance from guilt* stands first in the New Testament conception of redemption, he is speaking in judicial terms. He is speaking of legal guilt, not felt guilt. More basic than what we feel is where we stand, and until the problem of *our standing before God* is addressed, nothing else matters. And so, again, deliverance from guilt is primary. This leads us, next, to consider the doctrine of justification, a doctrine apart from which, for Warfield, discussion of the Christian life would be impossible.

Justification by Grace

Warfield perceptively reminds us that the gospel "is not *good advice*, but *good news*."[1] By this he means to stress that salvation is a work done *for* us, which we receive freely by grace. The gospel, he goes on to say, does not declare what we must do to earn salvation for ourselves. It proclaims, rather, what Christ has done to save us. Our standing before God is a privilege secured for us by the Lord Jesus Christ; there is nothing we contribute. We are right with God only because of what we have in Christ.

Warfield is careful to clarify that in justification God acts as judge and not merely as a sovereign. A sovereign may pardon a criminal, but even

---

[1] *PGS*, 50, emphasis original.

though pardoned, the man remains guilty. But in justification God acts as a judge. He does not merely pardon; marvelously, he declares us to be *righteous*. Justification is his official pronouncement that we have met the law's requirement. It is his judicial declaration that we are just.

But how can a just God declare sinners righteous? The answer is at the heart of the "good news." Warfield explains that although this gift of righteousness comes to us freely, it does not come without cost. The "good news" is that the cost was paid for us by the Lord Jesus Christ. The apostle Paul explains that God justifies only on the ground of the ransoming work of Christ.

> We are justified by his grace as a gift, through the redemption that is in Christ Jesus, whom God put forward as a propitiation by his blood, to be received by faith. This was to show God's righteousness, because in his divine forbearance he had passed over former sins. It was to show his righteousness at the present time, so that he might be just and the justifier of the one who has faith in Jesus. (Rom. 3:24–26)

God does not—indeed, Warfield insists, God *cannot*—justify a sinner arbitrarily. That would be an unjust pronouncement of the judge (cf. Prov. 17:15). God can justify us only on the ground of a full satisfaction of his justice. And this we have in the sacrificial death of Christ. Acting as our substitute, Christ made payment for sin that fully satisfied the demands of divine justice. As Warfield explains:

> What Paul says is, that the ransoming that is in Christ Jesus is the means by which men, being sinners, are brought by God into a justification which they cannot secure for themselves. If the ransoming that is in Christ Jesus is the means by which alone they can be justified, that is only another way of saying that God, who gratuitously justifies them in His grace, proceeds in this act in view of nothing in them, but solely in view of the ransoming that is in Christ Jesus.[2]

Once again, what God requires of us—righteousness—he gives us in Christ. Here the term "imputation" is essential (Gen. 15:6; Ps. 32:2; Rom. 4:11, 22–24; 2 Cor. 5:19). Warfield defines imputation as "simply the act of setting to one's account." Just as Adam's sin was imputed to his posterity (Rom. 5:12), and just as our sin was imputed to Christ, so also Christ's

---

[2]"Redemption," in James Hastings, *Dictionary of the Apostolic Church*, 2 vols. (New York: Scribners, 1918), 2:305–6.

righteousness is imputed to us. The ground of justification is the imputed righteousness of Christ. "Therefore, as one trespass led to condemnation for all men, so one act of righteousness leads to justification and life for all men" (Rom. 5:18). "For our sake he made him to be sin who knew no sin, so that in him we might become the righteousness of God" (2 Cor. 5:21). God has not relaxed the standard and determined no longer to require righteousness of us. Nor is it a fictional righteousness that is imputed. God cannot merely pretend to be a righteous judge. No, but what he requires he provides. "The righteousness on the ground of which God accepts a sinner . . . is an absolutely real, and absolutely perfect righteousness. . . . It is the righteousness of Christ, provided by God in and through Christ." Christ performed the work required of us, and his merit is "imputed" to us—credited, "set to our account." This—righteousness provided for us by God in Christ—is "the sole ground" of our acceptance before God. And thus imputation is "the hinge" on which turn the doctrines of human sin, the satisfaction of Christ, and justification by faith.[3]

In brief, our sin was imputed to Christ, for which he stood accountable and rendered full payment. In exchange Christ's righteousness is imputed to us, and we now stand before God in the merits of his Son. This is a large part of what it means to be "in Christ." The righteousness in which we stand, the righteousness that renders us acceptable to God, is not a righteousness we have produced. It is the righteousness of Christ made ours by grace.

This was the apostle Paul's faith as he expressed it to the church at Philippi, that he would be found by God not having a righteousness that stems from his own doing, but having only that righteousness that comes as a gift from God (Phil. 3:4–10). Warfield points out that the apostle's teaching here is that "every item and degree" of our own righteousness is specifically excluded from the saving equation. Even faith, though demanded, is not allowed a place in the ground of our justification. "According to his express statements . . . we are saved entirely on the ground of an alien righteousness and not at all on the ground of anything we are or have done, or can do,—be it even so small a matter as believing." The apostle's whole point is to lay stress on the truth that "Christ Jesus is all." "The contrast is absolute," and the alternatives are mutually exclusive. Paul holds all personal efforts in contempt. All that we are and have, all that men can appeal to, the apostle counts not merely useless but loss—"all one mass of loss, to be cast away and buried in the sea"—so that we may instead gain Christ and be found in him. "On the

---

[3]"The Hibbert Journal," *TBS* 7, no. 3 (1903): 57; *W*, 9:302, 305; *FL*, 316.

one side stand all human works—they are all loss. On the other side stands Christ—he is all in all. That is the contrast." "The Gospel, to Paul, consists precisely in this: that we do nothing to earn our salvation or to secure it for ourselves. God in Christ does it all." There is never anything "in us or done by us, at any stage of our earthly development, because of which we are acceptable to God." We are accepted always and only "for Christ's sake, or we cannot ever be accepted at all."[4]

It is for this reason that Paul can declare that God "justifies the ungodly" (Rom. 4:5). This is certainly a surprising thing! In every other case we would consider it a miscarriage of justice for the judge to pronounce a guilty person righteous. But in Christ our record is clean, and divine justice is fully satisfied. God declares us righteous, not because we are righteous in ourselves, but because of our union with Jesus Christ, who has done for us all that God demands of us. And it is on this ground that the gospel invitation may be preached so freely. "There is no depth of degradation, return from which will not be welcomed by God. A sinner may be too vile for any and every thing else; but he cannot be too vile for salvation,"[5] for Christ is for us all that God requires of us.

This is the doctrine of justification—a pronouncement by God the judge that we are just (righteous), a pronouncement grounded not in anything about us but in Christ alone. Incredibly, righteousness—our right standing before God, grounded in the judgment of his law—is not something we give to God. It is something God gives us in Christ. "In Christ"—a more secure position we could never imagine. In what else could a sinner possibly hope?

Justification by Faith Alone

This, in turn, explains why it is so important for the apostle Paul to stress that justification is by faith alone, apart from any works. The righteousness by which we are brought into right standing with God is not our own but Christ's. This is the "good news"—what God requires of us he has given to us in Christ. Our reliance is therefore wholly on the Lord Jesus. The gospel fosters an attitude of entire dependence on Christ to the exclusion of everything else, and this defines Christianity as a religion of faith. The gospel is a gospel of trust. As Warfield writes, the whole of salvation, "in each of its steps and stages, runs back to God as its author and furtherer," and because of this, "a continual sense of humble dependence on God and of loving

---

[4]*FL*, 316–25; *W*, 7:113–16.
[5]*SW*, 24.

trust in Him is by it formed and fostered in every heart into which it makes entrance. Under the teachings of this gospel the eye is withdrawn from self and the face turned upward in loving gratitude to God, the great giver." "It must needs be by faith" that we receive all saving blessings, "for what is faith but a looking to God for blessings?"[6]

Warfield describes faith variously as "trust," "a confident entrusting of ourselves to Christ," "the instrument of reception," "looking to God for blessing," "casting" ourselves wholly upon Christ and on God, "utter dependence" or "resting" or "reposing" on God, a "self-abandoning trust," "an entire self-commitment of the soul to Jesus as the Son of God, the Saviour of the world." It is, in short, simply "the instrument of reception to which salvation comes."[7]

Faith is therefore of the very essence of Christianity, Warfield says. It is the "fundamental element of religion" on the human side, just as grace is the fundamental element of religion on God's side. Faith as "an attitude of dependence on God" is likewise "just the very essence" of true religion. "In proportion as any sense of self-sufficiency or any dependence on self enters the heart, in that proportion religion is driven from it." This is the only attitude becoming or even possible in weak and sinful man. If we are to be saved at all, it must be God who saves us. "Every sinner, when once aroused to the sense of his sin, knows this for himself—knows it in the times of his clearest vision and deepest comprehension with a poignancy that drives him to despair." And this despair is relieved only when he rests in God alone.[8]

In a word, given our sin and consequent unworthiness on the one hand and God's gracious promise of rescue on the other, faith—faith as trust, reliance, dependence—is our only possible approach to God. We are justified by faith alone, simply because we are saved by Christ alone. By our faith we acknowledge the sole sufficiency of Christ to save, that it is his righteousness and not our own that makes us right with God.

> Sometimes we are told that Justification by Faith is "out of date." That would be a pity, if it were true. What it would mean would be that the way of salvation was closed and "no thoroughfare" nailed up over the barriers. There is no justification for sinful men except by faith. The works of a sinful man will, of course, be as sinful as he is, and nothing but condemnation can be built on them. Where can he get works upon which he can found his hope of justifi-

---

[6]*PGS*, 213; *FL*, 170.
[7]*FL*, 155, 170, 397; *W*, 2:476, 481, 483, 502; 9:331, 467, 501.
[8]*FL*, 155, 320; *PGS*, 213.

cation, except from Another? His hope of Justification, remember—that is, of being pronounced righteous by God. Can God pronounce him righteous except on the ground of works that are righteous? Where can a sinful man get works that are righteous? Surely, not from himself; for, is he not a sinner, and all his works as sinful as he is? He must go out of himself, then, to find works which he can offer to God as righteous. And where will he find such works except in Christ? Or how will he make them his own except by faith in Christ?[9]

Justification in Christian Experience

Under the theme "Paul's argument from experience" Warfield expounds Romans 5:1–2: "Therefore, since we have been justified by faith, we have peace with God through our Lord Jesus Christ. Through him we have also obtained access by faith into this grace in which we stand, and we rejoice in hope of the glory of God."

Warfield takes his theme from the observation that the apostle Paul highlights an experience common to all believers, namely, that as a result of their justification by faith they have peace with God. The point, Warfield observes, is that as a result of seeking justification from God not by works but by faith in Jesus Christ, all believers experience the peace of a quieted conscience and acceptance with God. Paul does not exhort us here. He does not say that all believers *ought* to have this peace. His point is that all believers already have this peace, and it is to this consciousness of peace and joy that the apostle appeals: "Since we have been justified by faith, *we have peace with God.*" We have found in our own experience that peace with God has come by faith.[10]

Warfield then draws from this its primary implication: namely, that justification by faith is naturally adapted to produce peace and joy in the believing sinner. It is not without objective warrant that the believer enjoys this peace. Certainly, it is the Holy Spirit who produces this peace in us, but it is not an ungrounded emotion that he gives. It is, rather, a peace that rests on the nature of the transaction. Warfield explains at length that after we all have tried other means by which to find God's favor—self-efforts of various kinds, feverishly sincere though they may be—we still do not experience the peace we seek. We may give ourselves entirely to the service of God, but this alone does not clear the conscience. There yet remains that nagging sense of sin, a realization that we have not made the required grade. Briefly, in all our own attempts to please God, our conscience yet will not allow a sense of peace,

---

[9] *SSW*, 1:283.
[10] *PGS*, 57–90; *SSW*, 2:142–51.

for the recognition of demerit remains. "While walking the treadmill road of works no peace can possibly visit [our] hearts." But in being justified *by faith* the result is different—"peace and joy are the natural, or, indeed, the necessary fruits" of seeking salvation by faith alone.[11]

Warfield's point is that there is not only an objective, judicial peace established in our justification. But given that justification is by faith, a resting in the merits and work of Christ, it inevitably results in a subjective sense of peace with God also. This method of justification (faith) is perfectly suited to quiet our conscience. Indeed, it is calculated to satisfy the conscience and allay all feelings of guilt, for it fully answers the problem of sin. It rests on God's provision of a substitute—who supplies for us all the righteousness God requires of us and in whose blood perfect expiation of sin is made—and his gracious promise of full forgiveness in him. This method of justification does not leave us hoping that we have done well enough. It faces our unrighteousness squarely and makes full acknowledgment of it. But it offers full atonement and perfect obedience that may be made ours. It offers a substitute who does for us all that God requires of us. In Warfield's words, this method of justification "empties us of all righteousness which we may claim," and then it

> turns and points to a wonderful spectacle of the Son of God, become man, taking His place at the head of His people, presenting an infinite sacrifice for their sins in His own body on the tree, working out a perfect righteousness in their stead in the myriad deeds of love and right that filled His short but active life; and offering this righteousness, this righteousness of God, provided by God and acceptable to God, to the acceptance of the world.

And immediately Warfield says again, "Here is a mode of salvation which is indeed calculated to still the gnawing sense of guilt and quiet the fear of wrath." Here is an approach to God, a means of finding his favor, in which the conscience can safely rest. "We gaze on Christ and His sacrifice, and we know that God also sees it, and seeing it cannot condemn him who is in Christ."[12]

We will see more of this in due course, but we must note the shaping impact this doctrine is designed to have on the Christian heart and conscience. God has told us up front that, sinners though we are, he will have us as we come to him by way of Christ who has done for us all that God's law can require of us. And with this even the most lively and tender conscience can find

---

[11] *PGS*, 69; *SSW*, 2:147–49.
[12] *PGS*, 76, 89; cf. *SSW*, 2:142–51.

no objection. God is perfectly satisfied with Christ who acted in our place. God's law can demand no more. And in this our conscience finally finds rest. Peace with God has been justly established.

It is on this ground, Warfield notes, that the apostle exhorts the Philippians to "rejoice in the Lord" (Phil. 3:1; 4:4; cf. Rom. 5:2–3, 11). Spiritual worship can only be that worship which is marked by a "boasting in Christ Jesus alone and the withdrawal of all confidence from the flesh." The Philippians must rejoice *in the Lord*, and could rejoice *in the Lord* precisely because it was the Lord's own righteousness in which they stood. They were, after all, "saved—not self-saving souls." This "alien righteousness," the righteousness of Christ freely imputed to us, is the whole ground of our joy and confidence before God.[13]

It is vitally important for the Christian to be fully aware—to live in the awareness—that his justification before God is grounded entirely in the work of Christ. Our acceptance with God is completely and perfectly established. There is nothing lacking. Our standing with God is not grounded in anything about us. With Paul we have renounced all that hints of personal merit in order that we may contentedly glory in Christ alone. The sense of assurance and peace and joy this gospel affords is what animates us.

We close with Warfield's fervent application:

And having once entered into our peace, let us turn and look with new eyes upon this life which we are living in the flesh. These difficulties, these dangers, these trials, these sufferings, how hard they have been to bear! We have deserved no better, but—nay, therefore—how hard they have been to bear! But we have been justified by faith—actually and truly justified by faith—and now we have peace with God. What a new aspect is taken by the trials and sufferings of life! They are no longer our fate, hard and grinding; they are no longer our punishment, better than which is not to be expected—for ever. They come from the hand of a reconciled God, from the hand of our Father. What one of them has not its meaning, its purpose, its freightage of mercy and of good? Shall we not follow the apostle here, and, as we find that peace with God has stolen into our hearts and that we are exulting in the hope of future glory, let that glory gild also our present pathway? Shall we not turn with new courage, nay, even with joy, to the sufferings of this present life, crying with him: "And not only so, but we also rejoice in tribulations, knowing that tribulation worketh patience, and patience triedness, and triedness hope, and

---

[13]*FL*, 316–25; *W*, 7:113–16.

hope putteth not to shame, because the love of God hath been shed abroad in our hearts through the Holy Spirit which was given unto us!"

What new light this is to shine on the weary pathway of God's saints! . . .

And then the future! We used to look forward to it, perhaps, with nameless dread, with fearful expectation of judgment. What a glory has been thrown upon it by our new standpoint! We are no longer at enmity with God: we are at peace with God. Our conscience tells us that: we gaze on Christ and His sacrifice, and we know that God also sees it, and seeing it cannot condemn him who is in Christ. And when did Almighty God begin anything which He did not finish? And such a beginning! A beginning in indescribable, in inconceivable love. Our hearts are fairly dragged out of us in wondering love as we follow Paul's *a fortiori* argument. "For while we were yet weak, in due season Christ died for the ungodly. For scarcely for a righteous man will one die; yet perhaps for a good man some one would even dare to die. But God commendeth His love toward us, in that while we were yet sinners, Christ died for us. Much more then, being now justified by His blood, shall we be saved from wrath by Him. For if, while we were enemies, we were reconciled with God through the death of His Son, much more, being reconciled, shall we be saved by His life."

What means this peace in my heart? It means that the sense of guilt is allayed, that I am justified before God by the death of His dear Son. What means this justification with God? It means *much more*—that I shall be saved, by the life of His Son, from wrath. Much more! It is then much more than certain! Shall we not exult? Shall we not say with the apostle: "Much more being reconciled, shall we be saved by His life, and not only so, but also as those that rejoice in God through our Lord Jesus Christ, through whom we have now received this reconciliation"? Do we face the future now, then, with calmness? Ah, no! that would imply doubt. Do we face it, then, with courage? No; that would imply danger. Let us with the apostle face it with exultation, as becomes those who rejoice in God through our Lord Jesus Christ through whom we have *received* this reconciliation; as becomes those who, having been justified by faith, have peace with God, through Jesus Christ, and rejoice in the hope of the glory of God.[14]

---

[14]*PGS*, 86–87, 89–90.

CHAPTER 6

CONVERSION

The Great Change

Freed from Sin's Grip

We have seen that in Christ's redemptive work *deliverance from guilt* stands first. But Warfield emphasizes that while it is first, it is not alone. This "judicial" deliverance is basic, and it stands first in the sense that other benefits flow from it. Christ has rescued us from the guilt of sin, and by doing so he has, next, freed us from the *power of sin* also.

Original Sin

In Romans 5:12–21 the apostle Paul explains that the guilt, punishment, and defilement of Adam has passed to all his posterity. This is the "imputation" of Adam's sin to humanity. A consequence of this is *original sin*, the inherent depravity of every child of Adam. Simply put, we are born sinners, with a bent toward evil and a natural aversion to God. We are "sons of disobedience" (Eph. 2:2). It is "natural" for us to rebel against God and his law. And it is all this, Warfield explains, that leads us to a doctrine of *inability*. In our state of sin we are disinclined to good and inclined to evil. It is not "in us," so to speak, to pursue God and turn to Christ in faith. We are "free" to do so in the sense that we may if only we will. But we are not *able* to do so on our own. In our natural condition we are so caught up by sin that our inclinations lead us inevitably away from God. Our problem is not that we lack the right faculties of the soul or the necessary intellect to understand or the freedom to do what we want to do. Our problem, very simply, as Warfield summarizes it, is that "sin reigns" (cf. Rom. 6:14). Sin is so ingrained in our disposition, it has so distorted our judgment and affections—in short, it has so deformed our soul—that apart from supernatural intervention we are left to our sin forever. We are free to do as we will. But what we "will"—what we desire—is sin, not God. As theologians for centuries have stated it, mankind in its fallen condition is *unable not to sin*. And so, humanly considered, salvation is "impossible" (Mark 10:26–27).

Divine Rescue

Warfield stresses all this not as an end in itself but in order better to appreciate our salvation as a gift of divine grace. It is only against this backdrop that we can rightly apprehend the biblical teaching of the divine initiative in salvation (2 Cor. 4:13; Gal. 5:5) and of saving faith as a gift of God (Eph. 2:8–9; 6:23; Phil. 1:29; 1 Pet. 1:21; 2 Pet. 1:1). We will not rightly understand Christ or judge him as worthy of our surrender and faith apart from the transforming work of the Spirit of God. The work of the Spirit is that of regeneration, renewal, a "repristination of man," as Warfield calls it.[1] Bringing us to life the Spirit awakens us to spiritual realities to which, before, we were blind and indifferent. Enabled now to "see" both ourselves and Christ aright, we eagerly run to him for safety and hide ourselves in him. It is in this sense that our worship is marked by praise and thanks not only for salvation generally but also for the faith by which we are saved (Col. 1:3–4; 2 Thess. 1:3).

All this is to say, our salvation is *rescue* in every sense—not only rescue from the guilt and punishment of sin but rescue from its enslaving corruption also. And this, of course, is a work of God alone (Mark 10:27). Now that we are "under grace," sin no longer reigns over us (Rom. 6:14)—its power is broken, and we are free to serve God. The saving work of Christ rescues us from both sin's guilt and its power. Warfield observes that it is for this reason the apostle Paul can affirm that those for whom Christ died not only died with him, but just as surely, therefore, live for him (2 Cor. 5:14–15). Redemption accomplished and redemption applied.

---

[1] *SSW*, 1:274–75.

Renewal and the Great Change

All of this is necessary for a right appreciation of what Warfield calls the biblical doctrine of "renewal." In Christ is provided not only an objective but also a subjective salvation from sin. Throughout Scripture it is taught not merely that by our sin we have incurred condemnation, but also that by it our hearts are filled with corruption. Sin is not guilt only—it is also depravity. And for our recovery from sin we therefore need not only atonement but also renewal. That is to say, salvation consists not in pardon merely but also in purification. There is a cleansing both of our record and of our very being.

> Great as is the stress laid in the Scriptures on the forgiveness of sins as the root of salvation, no less stress is laid throughout the Scriptures on the cleansing of the heart as the fruit of salvation. Nowhere is the sinner permitted to rest satisfied with pardon as the end of salvation; everywhere he is made poignantly to feel that salvation is realized only in a clean heart and a right spirit.[2]

Salvation, then, involves "a radical and complete transformation" of the soul (Rom. 12:2; Eph. 4:23). This is the work of the Spirit of God (Eph. 4:24; Titus 3:5) in every believer, constituting the believer a "new man" (Eph. 4:24; Col. 3:10). We who are saved are "no longer conformed to this world" (Rom. 12:2; Eph. 4:22; Col. 3:9), but rather we are shaped in knowledge and holiness after the image of Christ (Rom. 12:2; Eph. 4:24; Col. 3:10).[3]

This "great change" of conversion that is experienced by every believer upon entering the Christian life has both a Godward and a manward side. As Warfield says, God "renews," "begets," "regenerates," and "creates." And man consequently "repents" and "turns."[4] God regenerates, "recreating the governing disposition" of the soul, and conversion instantly and inevitably follows. Warfield recognizes this personally transforming aspect of salvation as the fulfillment of God's new covenant promise (Jer. 31:33; 32:39; Ezek. 36:26; 37:14). Here God promises the powerful inner workings of his Spirit in giving new life (a "new heart"), which manifests itself in inward and outward holiness. Growing out of this provision of the regenerating and sanctifying Spirit are all the New Testament exhortations to and descriptions of renewal, conversion, progressive sanctification, and glorification.[5]

---

[2] *W*, 2:440.
[3] *W*, 2:439.
[4] *SSW*, 1:267; *FL*, 455.
[5] *SSW*, 2:323.

Repentance indicates primarily a change of mind, and this change of mind leads to a transformed life. In Matthew 21:29 Jesus speaks of the previously disobedient son who "repented and went" as his father commanded him. So also in Jesus's application of the parable to the Jewish leaders, he scolds them for not "repenting and believing" John the Baptist. Repentance is a change of mind that issues in amendment of life. But in its largest view repentance also entails godly sorrow over sin (Luke 17:3–4). Warfield finds all this stated succinctly in 2 Corinthians 7:8–11, particularly verse 10: "Godly sorrow brings repentance that leads to salvation." Warfield summarizes that repentance as a turning

> from all wrong to all good, in which the trend of our life is altered, in which, in a word, we turn our backs on Satan and all the works of the flesh, and our face to God and his service. The repentance of the New Testament is a total change of mind and heart, not only from some sins but from sin itself.

And he finds this illustrated in the prodigal son, who "came to himself" and returned humbly to the father (Luke 15:17).[6]

Warfield goes further and argues that true repentance does not view sin merely atomistically in terms of so many evil acts. If we are ourselves sinful and guilty, then true godly sorrow and change of mind will have in view not only what we do but also what we are, our sins as well as our sinfulness. There will be a recognition of personal demerit and guilt. "He only has really repented who has perceived and felt the filthiness and odiousness of his depraved nature and has turned from it to God with a full purpose of being hereafter more conformed to his image as revealed in the face of Jesus Christ."[7]

Warfield notes the proper order in all this. There is *godly sorrow*, on which repentance rests; and there is the *change of mind* in reference to sin, repentance; and there is the resulting *alteration of life*, "the fruits of repentance." "Godly grief produces a repentance that leads to salvation" (2 Cor. 7:10); "repent and believe" (Mark 1:15; cf. Matt. 21:32); "repent and turn" (Acts 3:19; 26:20); "believe and turn" (Acts 11:21). All this is man's responsibility and work. However, Warfield is quick to point out that repentance is declared to be the gift of God (Acts 5:31; 11:18; 2 Tim. 2:25). This suggests a divine side, a previous activity on God's part that leads to the change these words describe. That is to say, our repentance and faith are the direct consequences of a deep transforming work of the Spirit of God in us, changing our disposition in reference both to sin and to God, thus enabling us to repent and believe.

---

[6]*SSW*, 1:270–71.
[7]*SSW*, 1:280.

This "conversion" shows itself not only in faith and repentance but in all of life. Faith results in newness of life (Col. 2:12). Warfield finds all this illustrated crisply in the response of Saul of Tarsus to Jesus on the Damascus road. Confronted with the glory of the risen Christ, Saul has but two questions. First he asks, "Who are you, Lord?" (Acts 9:5). And then he asks, "What shall I do, Lord?" (Acts 22:10). In the first question he is not asking for Jesus's credentials—he is acknowledging his lordship. And in the second question he consecrates himself to his service. Divinely enabled to see the true glory of Christ, Saul surrenders himself to him without qualification. This, Warfield insists, is not exceptional but typical. This is the experience, the instinctive response, of everyone who comes to Christ. A great change indeed.

This "great change" or transformation of life is described figuratively in the New Testament as a change of clothing (Eph. 4:24; Col. 3:9, 10; cf. Rom. 13:14; Gal. 3:27). The old man is laid aside like dirty clothes, and the new man is put on like a clean garment. Sometimes conversion is described in terms of a metamorphosis (Rom. 12:2). It is also spoken of descriptively in terms of reanimation (John 5:21; Rom. 6:3–4; Eph. 2:4–6; Col. 2:12–13) or a re-creation (Eph. 2:10; 4:24; Col. 3:10). And sometimes it is referred to, more technically, as sanctification, a making holy (Rom. 6:19, 22; 15:16; 1 Thess. 4:3, 17; 5:23; etc.). Sometimes, in reference more directly to its source, this new life is described as the "living" or "forming" of Christ in us (Rom. 6:9–10; Gal. 2:20; 4:19; Eph. 3:17; cf. 1 Cor. 2:16; 2 Cor. 3:18) and as the indwelling of Christ or his Spirit in us or our being led by the Spirit (Rom. 8:14; Gal. 5:18). The subjects of this work are referred to as "spiritual men," men led of the Spirit (1 Cor. 2:15; 3:1; Gal. 6:1; cf. 1 Pet. 2:5) as contrasted with "carnal men," "men dominated by their own weak, vicious selves" (see 1 Cor. 2:14; 3:3; Jude 19). All through the New Testament the great emphasis on God's "power" working in us has in view this goal of our moral and spiritual transformation.[8]

Warfield explains this initial break with sin in terms of "sanctification" also. When Warfield spoke of the doctrine of sanctification, it was usually in terms of its progressive aspect, something we will see in due course. But he understood that there is an initial aspect to sanctification also—"definitive" sanctification, as John Murray (1898–1975) later stated and developed it.[9] This aspect of sanctification emphasizes a "cleansing" of the soul at the very

---

[8] *W*, 2:458–62.
[9] John Murray, "Definitive Sanctification," in *Collected Writings of John Murray*, vol. 2, *Select Lectures in Systematic Theology* (Carlisle, PA: Banner of Truth, 1977), 277–93.

outset of the Christian life, a distinctive "setting apart" of the believer to Christ that entails an emancipation from sin's power. That is, an essential part of the Christian experience is sanctification in its initial aspect, a definitive break with sin at the very start.

The Necessity of Change

It is important to Warfield to note that this change of life is not an optional extra to the Christian but part and parcel of the experience of every believer. Jesus taught Nicodemus that "the radical transformation of the Spirit of God" is "the precondition of entrance" to the kingdom of God. Heart and life transformation is part of the warp and woof of salvation itself. Justification by faith is the root of our salvation, but sanctification is "its substance." "Nowhere is the sinner permitted to rest satisfied with pardon as the end of salvation; everywhere he is made poignantly to feel that salvation is realized only in a clean heart and a right spirit." It was the ancient new covenant promise that God would write his law on his people's hearts (Jer. 31:33), that he would take out the stony hearts and replace them with hearts of flesh so that they would now walk in keeping with his commands (Ezek. 11:19). All this is the promised work of the Spirit of God in the lives of all of God's people. God works in his people to renew them, and the response inevitably is that of repentance and conversion. God's work of salvation is such that "he who really is a child of God will necessarily possess marks and signs of being so."[10]

To borrow the language of the apostle Paul, dying with Christ we also rise with him to new life (Romans 6). Christ has died for us to this end—so that we, having died with him, will no longer live to ourselves but unto him (2 Cor. 5:14–15). Those for whom Christ died live for him and find their lives shaped by the constraint of his love (2 Cor. 5:14), and all of life is adjusted and shaped accordingly. Warfield stresses this: we cannot die with Christ and not also rise to life with him.

Simply put, transformation of heart and life is the experience of every person in Christ. Salvation inevitably entails a change of heart and life. There is no justification without sanctification, and regeneration necessarily, by the nature of it, results in sanctification. The Christian is one who has been freed from sin in both its judicial and its moral aspects.

---

[10] W, 7:91; 2:440, 447, 461; PR 10 (April 1889): 335; FL, 191.

A Sign of Grace and Ground of Praise

Warfield does not see this teaching as designed to make Christians question or doubt their salvation, although he certainly could not miss the fact that it does indeed expose many a false profession. Rather, he sees this doctrine as designed to give encouragement to the believer. This is not merely theoretical—it reflects real experience. And as such it demonstrates the reality of God's grace at work in us. It constitutes real evidence of our sonship that God is well on the way to making us like Christ.

Warfield treats this theme in his exposition of 1 John 2:28–3:2, entitled, "Childship to God." John tells us that we *are already* God's children. And evidence of this fact is found in our very own life of holiness. This is how we know we are God's children: we come more and more to act like our Father. Sonship implies likeness. A wicked man is a son of Belial. So also, a righteous man is a son of God. Both Paul and John teach this. We do not receive this life by our righteousness; it is freely bestowed by divine grace. But we demonstrate by our righteousness that this life has been made ours, that we are God's children. Paul teaches us that there is no son who has not received the Spirit of adoption and that there is no son who is not led of God's Spirit in his struggle against sins (Rom. 8:5–14). All of God's sons give evidence, by their godliness, of their sonship. John, thinking in terms of regeneration rather than justification, teaches the same. We who are born of God have in a real sense the life of God in us, and the seed implanted in regeneration is the seed of holy living. This is how we know God's holy seed has been implanted in us: it shows itself in holy living.

Warfield carefully points out that regeneration and sanctification, while different, are obviously related. First there is birth, then growth. And so John says that we already are God's children. Throughout his first letter he insists that the mark of a child of God is a righteous life. Yet Warfield does not claim perfection or imply in any way that those who are born of God have reached sinlessness in this life. "We are children," he assures us. We are *already* his children. But the apostle continues, "It is not yet made manifest what we shall be" (1 John 3:2). Righteousness is present, but not yet a complete righteousness. This is to come only "when we see [Christ] as he is." Born of God, we grow up to be like Christ, and while we have not yet reached that goal, it will be ours one day nonetheless. In the degree of godliness present in our experience today we see evidence that we are indeed God's children.

Warfield's purpose in this is to encourage the reader. Holiness is necessary evidence of all who believe. But it is evidence nonetheless, an objective demonstration of God savingly at work in us.

And so, in the end, this doctrine calls us to new levels of joyful praise. We have lived on both sides. We remember the enslaving tyranny of sin, and we now enjoy freedom. We have experienced the grace of God powerfully at work in us. The biblical promise and teaching of the deep and effective workings of the Spirit of God in us correspond exactly to our experience. We know that we are God's children, and we know it, in part, because we have begun already to experience his saving work as he describes it. The redemption Christ accomplished for us in his death has been applied to us, and it is evident. His work in us is not yet complete, but our hearts and lives are now his.

CHAPTER 7

HELP FROM ABOVE

The Holy Spirit at Work

Warfield's writings and worship are marked by a robust Trinitarianism. Of course at the center of his worship is Christ the Redeemer, as we have seen. But Warfield also basks in the loving providence of God the Father, who is, in fact, God over all—something we will examine more fully in chapter 11. And for Warfield, unlike the thinking of so many in our day, the Holy Spirit is anything but the "forgotten" person of the Trinity. Warfield makes a point to emphasize that the study of the person and work of the Holy Spirit takes us into virtually every branch of theology and that his work in us is pervasive and foundational to Christian experience. From conversion and to final glorification, it is the Spirit of God who secures and directs our every step in the Christian life.

The Conviction of the Holy Spirit

As we saw in the previous chapter, our experience of the Spirit begins at conversion. The Spirit brings renewal, and we are transformed from the inside out. One aspect of this work that Warfield underscores is the work of conviction, which is highlighted in a passage like John 16:7–11.

> Nevertheless, I tell you the truth: it is to your advantage that I go away, for if
> I do not go away, the Helper will not come to you. But if I go, I will send him

to you. And when he comes, he will convict the world concerning sin and righteousness and judgment: concerning sin, because they do not believe in me; concerning righteousness, because I go to the Father, and you will see me no longer; concerning judgment, because the ruler of this world is judged.

The Spirit's work of conviction focuses on three specific issues: sin, righteousness, and judgment. In the powerful operations of grace he opens our eyes to see our *sin and guilt*, epitomized in our rejection of Christ. He also brings us to see that we lack the necessary *righteousness* that is found only in Christ. And he brings us to see the impending *judgment of God* that comes because of our sin and unrighteousness. To all this we were blind until the Spirit of God opened our eyes in grace and made us see. "'Twas grace that taught my heart to fear!" This is the Spirit's work of conviction, and here he brings Christ's work for us to its initial success as we respond in loving faith.

The Sealing of the Holy Spirit

In Ephesians 4:30 the apostle Paul writes, "And do not grieve the Holy Spirit of God, by whom you were sealed for the day of redemption." Warfield comments that "sealing" expresses the related ideas of *authentication* and *security*. The focus is on the security of the believer who is marked out, authenticated as one who is redeemed by Christ and secured in him unto the final completion of redemption. The same emphasis is evident in Ephesians 1:13–14, where the apostle writes that we were "sealed with the promised Holy Spirit," who is "the pledge" or "earnest" of our inheritance. That is, the Spirit of God given to us is himself the down payment and guarantee of our full realization of our redemption. Part of his ministry is to work out all the promises to us and bring them to fruition.

Warfield emphasizes that while we are God's purchased possession, bought with the precious blood of Christ, this redemption is not yet complete. The "day of redemption" awaits us in the future, to which we who are purchased are to be safely brought. And for this great realization we have been sealed, "the Holy Spirit of promise" being both the foretaste and the pledge of it. The down payment has been made. The Holy Spirit is the "first fruits" of the glory to come, a glory we have already begun to taste by virtue of his presence in us. This is itself the guarantee that we who are bought by Christ will be kept to experience the fullness of salvation promised us. The Spirit of God having convicted us of sin and having drawn us to Christ in faith and having come to us himself as a pledge of final salvation—all of this will happily conspire to bring us safely to our appointed end.

A due recognition of our safety and the certainty of our final glory, in turn, serves as an incentive to holiness. Paul exhorts us, "do not grieve the Holy Spirit of God, by whom you were sealed for the day of redemption." Warfield carefully notes the connection: the appeal is not to fear but to gratitude. The Spirit of God has come to us as our pledge and foretaste of glory, and his presence in us is itself the guarantee that we shall reach final glory. And our recognition of all this ought to drive us, with a heart of thankfulness, to continue in faithfulness and godliness.

> If the Holy Spirit has done this for me; if He in all His holiness is dwelling in me, to seal me unto the day of redemption, shall I have no care not to grieve Him? Fear is paralyzing. Despair is destruction of effort. Hope is living and active in every limb, and when that hope becomes assurance, and that assurance is recognized as based on the act of a Person, lovingly dealing with us and winning us to holiness, can we conceive of a motive to holiness of equal power?[1]

The Spirit's Testimony to Our Sonship

The Holy Spirit has also come to us in order to assure us of our sonship and to bring us to a joyful experience of that sonship. Warfield cites Romans 8:16 as the verse on which the great Protestant doctrine of assurance is grounded and which most clearly expresses the ministry of the Holy Spirit in that assurance: "The Spirit himself bears witness with our spirit that we are children of God."

This doctrine of assurance holds that every Christian "may and should be assured that he is a child of God—that it is possible for him to attain this assurance and that to seek and find it is accordingly his duty." This is the affirmation of Romans 8:16. This text further affirms that it is the ministry of the Holy Spirit actively to instill in us an assurance that God is our Father, a conscious awareness that we belong to him. The verse is clearly designed to encourage the believer and engender confidence in the heart of the believer, and it points us to a testimony to our sonship by none less than the Spirit of God himself. We are not left to doubt and gloom; nor are we left to our own uncertain conjectures or imaginations. "The Spirit himself"

---

[1] *FL*, 297.

bears testimony that we belong to God as his children. This is the plain and emphatic affirmation of the verse.[2]

It is equally clear that this verse would caution us not to confound the testimony of the Spirit with the testimony of our own consciousness. Whether we should understand the verse as saying that the Holy Spirit bears witness "with our spirit" or "to our spirit," either way the Holy Spirit is clearly distinguished from our own spirit, and his testimony from ours. Indeed, this is the very nerve of the statement, Warfield comments—that the Christian is encouraged to realize the divine witness to his sonship.[3]

However, Warfield emphasizes the apostle Paul's apparent suggestion that the witness of the Spirit to our sonship is given in conjunction with the testimony of our own spirit, and thus it would be most natural to translate the phrase as "bears witness *with* our spirit." In this case the idea is that the Holy Spirit bears witness in conjunction with the testimony of our own consciousness. Both ideas are present—the witness of the Spirit and the witness of our own consciousness, a conjoined witness of both spirits in which the one gives confirmation to the other. Warfield supports this understanding with an appeal to verse 15, where Paul affirms that *we* cry "Abba." These two verses, then, affirm that the testimony to our sonship comes distinctly from the Spirit of God but confluently with the testimony of our own consciousness. It is not the one without the other.

This distinction is important, Warfield argues, for it will keep us from the abuse of the verse that too many have given it. Too many have latched onto the teaching of this verse regarding the Spirit's witness when in fact they have no other credible ground for assurance, subjective or objective. But the fact is there are signs that accompany genuine conversion, such as hatred of sin, love for the brethren, and so on. And the Spirit of God does not work in a vacuum. The assurance of sonship he gives is not a blind assurance grounded in nothing. He ministers assurance concurrently with our spirit, which would imply the presence of a reasonably well-grounded assurance—evidence of grace. The testimony of the Spirit is intended to serve not as a substitute for the testimony of our own spirit but "as an enhancement of it." Warfield explains:

> Its object is not to assure a man who has "no signs" that he is a child of God, but to assure him who has "signs," but is too timid to draw so great an inference from so small a premise, that he is a child of God and to give him thus

---

[2]*FL*, 179–82.
[3]*FL*, 182–83.

not merely a human but a Divine basis for his assurance. It is, in a word, not a substitute for the proper evidence of our childship; but a Divine enhancement of that evidence.[4]

Some want to ground assurance *syllogistically*—the promise is sure to those who believe the gospel; I believe the gospel; therefore, I am a child of God. Others disagree, grounding assurance *mystically* in the witness of the Spirit. But we do not have to choose between the two, and to debate the question in this way is fruitless. Both considerations play into the proper grounding of Christian assurance. The Spirit is the "efficient cause" of our assurance, but he is not the "formal ground" of it.[5]

In all this discussion about the mode in which the Spirit delivers assurance, Warfield cautions that we should not lose sight of the reality of the divine witness itself. The affirmation is that the Holy Spirit assures believers of their sonship. He does not give this sense of assurance in our hearts without reason but by giving "true weight and validity to the reasons that exist and so leading to the true conclusion, with Divine assurance."

> The function of the witness of the Spirit of God is, therefore, to give to our halting conclusions the weight of His Divine certitude. It may be our reasoning by which the conclusion is reached. It is the testimony of the Spirit which gives to a conclusion thus reached indefectible certainty. We have grounds, good grounds, for believing that we are in Christ, apart from [i.e., in addition to] His witness. Through His witness these good grounds produce their full effect in our minds and hearts.[6]

Thus the Holy Spirit both brings us to faith and gives us a sense of assurance that our faith is well placed and that we are God's children. We are assured in the gospel that if we believe in Christ, we will be saved, and we are then given assurance by the Spirit of God within us that this is so in our own particular case. He bears witness with our spirit that we are God's children (Rom. 8:16). As we might say it, God has not only told us that we are his children by faith, but God the Spirit has come to make us *feel* and *sense* that we are God's children as he ministers to us an awareness of his fatherly love.

---

[4] *FL*, 187.
[5] *FL*, 187–89; *PRR* 5, no. 19 (1894): 549.
[6] *FL*, 191–92.

The Love of the Holy Spirit

In his sermon on James 4:5 entitled, "The Love of the Holy Ghost," Warfield expounds at length this often-overlooked ministry of the Holy Spirit. The translation he prefers for this verse is the one that is suggested in the margin of the Revised Version: "Or think ye that the Scripture saith in vain, That Spirit which He made to dwell in us yearneth for us even unto jealous envy?" In the context James is addressing the problem of quarrels that had marred the fellowship of that infant church, and he traces the problem back to such unseemly and worldly vices as hedonism and greed and selfishness. Verse 5 constitutes James's rebuke against all this, a rebuke grounded in a reminder of God's love. Warfield summarizes the teaching of the verse as "a declaration, on the basis of Old Testament Teaching, of the deep yearning which the Holy Spirit, which God has caused to dwell in us, feels for our undivided and unwavering devotion."[7]

The imagery involved is not new to James: it is the figure of marriage describing the relation of the Christian to God. Because the Christian is "married" to God, any love for the world is an unfaithful breach of our vows—hence, in verse 4, the condemnation for adultery. Dallying with the rival lover is unfaithfulness to God our husband. For his part, God loves his bride deeply. And because he loves her, he pursues her and longs for her faithful affection.

Nor is there anything new in this teaching of God's love for his people. Indeed, James, writing the very first of the New Testament books, Warfield says, grounds his rebuke in the teaching of the Old Testament Scriptures as something of which his readers are already aware. James does not cite a particular passage from the Old Testament but seems to summarize its teaching on the subject. The prophets in particular are replete with passages that depict God as the loving husband chasing after the affection and loyalty of his unfaithful people (Jer. 3:20; Ezek. 16:38, 60–63; Hos. 2:18–20). This much is familiar biblical teaching for both James and his readers.

What James seeks to stress is the intensity of this divine love for us: God "yearns for us, even unto jealous envy." This again is not entirely new and reflects many Old Testament passages that speak of God as jealous for the love and faithfulness of his people (Ex. 34:14; Nah. 1:2; Zech. 8:2). But James does advance the notion not only with the use of the verb *yearns*, which appears also in Psalm 42:1, but also the adverb *jealous*, which expresses "the

---

[7] *PGS*, 121.

86

feeling which one is apt to cherish toward a rival." It is with "sickening envy," Warfield summarizes, that

> God contemplates our dallying with the world and the world's pleasures. He envies the world our love—the love due Him, pledged to Him, but basely withdrawn from Him and squandered upon the world. The combined expression is, you will see, astonishingly intense. God is represented as panting, yearning, after us, even unto not merely jealousy, but jealous envy. Such vehemence of feeling in God is almost incredible.[8]

Warfield insists this is no mere anthropomorphism but a blessed revelation of the heart of God toward us who belong to him. However difficult it may be to believe that God loves us with such passion, we must believe it, for he tells us that he does.

> What can we do but admiringly cry, Oh, the breadth and the length and height and depth of the love of God which passes knowledge. . . . Strain the capacity of words to the utmost and still they fall short of expressing the jealous envy with which He contemplates the love of His people for the world, the yearning desire which possesses Him to turn them back to their duty to Him. It is this inexpressibly precious assurance which the text gives us; let us, without doubting, embrace it with hearty faith.[9]

Warfield points out further that this love of God for his people is to be considered not in corporate terms only but in individual terms. Commonly in Scripture it is the larger body of God's people that is under consideration as the objects of his love—the house of Israel in the Old Testament and the church, his bride, the Lamb's wife, in the New Testament. And in such passages individuals, of course, share in God's love but only as they are part of the larger body: with some noted exceptions (Ps. 73:27; Rom. 7:4), the notion of love for the individual is generally not as prominent. But here the reference is explicitly the individual—it is the individual believer who is warned of the stirrings of God's loving jealousy in view of the believer's unfaithfulness to him.

The primary contribution of this text, however, is that it directly attributes this love of God for his people to the Holy Spirit. In this respect, the text is almost unique. In the Old Testament it is the Lord, the covenant God, who stands in covenant marriage union with his people, Israel, and who is

---

[8] *PGS*, 128–29.
[9] *PGS*, 129–30.

jealous over their loyalty. In the New Testament it is Christ the Lamb who loves and cherishes the church and has taken her to be his bride. But in this passage it is God the Holy Spirit who is said to love with yearning affection. God has given his Spirit to dwell within, and he does so in passionate love for us and with jealousy for our loyal affection.

On the one hand, this should not surprise us, for the persons of the triune God cannot be divided but always act in concert with one another. To say "God is love" is necessarily to confess the same each of Father, Son, and Spirit. But this particular emphasis is immensely useful in that it forces to our attention the love of the Holy Spirit for us—a notion that is not commonly given due consideration. We commonly give thanks to the Father for sending his Son in love to save us (John 3:16–17; Rom. 5:10; 1 John 4:10), for loving us such that we are given the privilege of being his children (1 John 3:1). And we commonly rejoice in the great love of Christ in giving himself for us (John 15:3; Eph. 5:2; 1 John 3:16). These glorious truths we never let escape us. But to draw comfort from this clearly revealed truth—that the Holy Spirit, who dwells within us, loves us also—this is too seldom the experience of the believer. But here it is for us, Warfield admonishes, intended for our use in just this way (cf. Rom. 15:30). And what a glorious thought it is,

> that the Spirit of all holiness is willing to visit such polluted hearts as ours, and even to dwell in them, to make them His home, to work ceaselessly and patiently with them, gradually wooing them—through many groanings and many trials—to slow and tentative efforts toward good; and never leaving them until, through His constant grace, they have been won entirely to put off the old man and put on the new man and to stand new creatures before the face of their Father God and their Redeemer Christ. Surely herein is love! . . . [and] what immense riches of comfort and joy this great truth has in it for our souls![10]

What but his love for us could explain his constant pursuit of us even in our most determined unfaithfulness? What love this is that outlives our shameful disregard and backslidings. "It is only because the Spirit which He hath caused to dwell in us yearneth for us even unto jealous envy, that He is able to continue His gracious work of drawing our souls to God amid the incredible oppositions we give to His holy work." And, in turn, what a great incentive to holiness this is. How could we "dally with sin" and "forget

---

[10]*PGS*, 138.

our covenanted duties to God" when we know that God the Spirit, dwelling within, lovingly pursues us with jealous envy?[11]

From here Warfield proceeds to explore this love more fully in light of the fact that the Spirit is given to "indwell" us. "See how close the love of God is brought to us. It is made to throb in our very hearts; to be shed abroad within us; and to work subtly upon us, drawing us to itself, from within." In light of this we may understand more clearly Paul's declaration that the flesh wars against the Spirit and the Spirit against the flesh (Gal. 5:17), the Spirit here seen as part of our own very being, striving from within to keep us to himself and from sin. Again, this enables us better to understand Paul's declaration in Romans 8:26 that the Spirit of God makes intercession for us with groanings of love when we do not know what to pray for.[12] The Spirit of God has not come to us as a temporary sojourner. He has not come to visit but to abide with us, to make his home within us, to settle in and make us his permanent dwelling. God has not covenanted with us halfheartedly. He takes us as his wife in permanent and not merely temporary union. He has come to abide in us forever, and his love for us is so great that from within he continuously pursues us, even through our sin. Though we run from him at times, he does not abandon us to ourselves, but remaining with us he strives within to woo us back to himself. His jealous love is undying and relentless. Indeed, it is precisely because we have fallen into such loving hands as these that we have hope for life and for eternity. He will not let us go but will always strive longingly and persistently from within us to keep us for himself.

Warfield summarizes this worshipfully.

See us steeped in the sin of the world; loving evil for evil's sake, hating God and all that God stands for, ever seeking to drain deeper and deeper the cup of our sinful indulgence. The Spirit follows us unwaveringly through all. He is not driven away because we are sinners. He comes to us because, being sinners, we need Him. He is not cast off because we reject His loving offices. He abides with us because our rejection of Him would leave us helpless. He does not condition His further help upon our recognizing and returning His love. His continuance with us is conditioned only on His own love for us. And that love for us is so strong, so mighty, and so constant that it can never fail. When He sees us immersed in sin and rushing headlong to destruction, He does not turn from us, He yearns for us with jealous envy.

---

[11] *PGS*, 139–40; *SSW*, 2:723.
[12] *PGS*, 140–41.

It is in the hands of such love that we have fallen. And it is because we have fallen into the hands of such love that we have before us a future of eternal hope. When we lose hope in ourselves, when the present becomes dark and the future black before us, when effort after effort has issued only in disheartening failure, and our sin looms big before our despairing eyes; when our hearts hate and despise themselves, and we remember that God is greater than our hearts and cannot abide the least iniquity; the Spirit whom He has sent to bring us to Him still labors with us, not in indifference or hatred, but in pitying love. Yea, His love burns all the stronger because we so deeply need His help: He is yearning after us with jealous envy.[13]

Such is the love of God the Spirit for us. Concluding his exposition of this theme Warfield simply directs our attention to the glory of it.

Could there be presented to us a more complete manifestation of the infinite love of God than is contained in this revelation of the love of the Spirit for us? God is love. Does not this greatest of all revelations take on a new brightness and a new force to move our souls when we come to realize that not only is the Father love, and the Son love, but the Spirit also is love; and so wholly love that, despite the foulness of our sin, He yearneth for us even unto jealous envy?

Could there be given us a higher incentive to faithfulness to God than is contained in this revelation of the love of the Spirit for us? Are our hearts so hard that they are incapable of responding to the appeal of such a love as this? Can we dally with the world, seek our own pleasures, forget our duty of love to God, when the Spirit which He hath made to dwell in us is yearning after us even unto jealous envy?

Could there be afforded us a deeper ground of encouragement in our Christian life than is contained in this revelation of the love of the Spirit for us? Is hope so dead within us that it is no longer possible for us to rest with confidence upon such love? Can we doubt what the end shall be—despite all that the world can do to destroy us, and the flesh and the devil—when we know that the Spirit which He hath made to dwell in us is yearning after us even unto jealous envy?

Could there, then, be granted us a firmer foundation for the holy joy of Christian assurance than is contained in this revelation of the love of the Spirit for us? Is faith grown so weak that it cannot stay itself on the almighty arm of God? Surely, surely, though our hearts faint within us, and the way seems dark, and there are lions roaring in the path, we shall be able to look past them all to the open gates of pearl beyond, whensoever we remember

---

[13]*PGS*, 143–45.

that the Spirit which He hath made to dwell within us is yearning after us even unto jealous envy![14]

That is to say, the love of the Holy Spirit for us is an exhilarating love, a sanctifying love, an enduring love, and therefore an assuring love.

The Leading of the Spirit

Warfield complains that while the doctrine of the leading of the Spirit has been much spoken of, it seems to be little understood. Too often it is understood to refer to a supposed mystical guiding of the Spirit in matters of, say, business, decision making, or the like. But none of this comes close to the biblical description of this ministry of the Holy Spirit. Romans 8:14 is the sole passage that speaks directly to the issue: "For all who are led by the Spirit of God are sons of God." The verse is almost without parallel in the New Testament, the only other being Galatians 5:18, where in a similar context Paul again employs the same phrase: "But if you are led by the Spirit, you are not under the law." These two passages, almost entirely alone, provide definition of this doctrine.

First of all, Warfield points out, Romans 8:14 makes it pointedly clear that this "leading of the Spirit" is not a ministry reserved for eminent saints only. It is a ministry of the Spirit that is common to all God's children: "As many as are led by the Spirit of God, these are the sons of God." This, indeed, is what differentiates the children of God from all others, which is the apostle's point in the immediately preceding verse: "But if any one has not the Spirit of Christ, that one is not His." It is entirely mistaken to refer this ministry to special sanctity or such. This ministry "is not the reward of special spiritual attainment; it is the condition of all spiritual attainment." Without it we would remain hopelessly the children of the Devil, and only by this are we enabled to cry "Abba, Father."[15]

Next, Warfield points out that the specific purpose of this leading is to enable us to overcome sin. In the previous passage Paul describes our inherent sin and its effects in us, and he answers this problem by pointing us to the Spirit of God dwelling within, giving new life, freeing us from bondage to sin, and bringing us to live no longer as debtors to the flesh. The Spirit implants a new principle of life, which becomes a new ruling power over us—leading us to holiness. This "leading of the Spirit," then, is simply a synonym for

---

[14]*PGS*, 147–48.
[15]*PGS*, 153–55; *W*, 8:122–24.

the process of sanctification. Far from a leading of eminent saints in business and other such decisions, this ministry is given to all God's children in order to transform them and lead them in the paths of holiness and truth.

Finally, Paul says, this leading of the Spirit is not sporadic, given on special occasions of special need or direction, but continuously affecting the Christian throughout the whole of his life. Its only object is the eradication of sin, leading to holiness, and therefore it has bearing on every activity of every kind—physical, intellectual, and spiritual. It is simply the power of God unto salvation at work in the believer, constantly leading to the goal of sanctification.

Warfield explains further with the following observations. First, he stresses the "extraneousness" of this influence. Something can be "led" only by an influence distinct from itself, and Paul's language here emphasizes this distinction. It is the Spirit of God, he says, who "leads" God's children. It is not merely the success of our higher regenerate powers over the remains of the old man yet lingering in us. It is nothing other than the Spirit of God bringing the heart into subjection. This is the significance of the corresponding terms "natural" or "self-led" man and "spiritual" or "Spirit-led" man. Our progress in godliness, the apostle affirms, is due specifically to the supernatural influence of the Holy Spirit.[16]

Second, Romans 8:14 emphasizes the "controlling power" of the Spirit's influence on the children of God. The Spirit is not a mere guide, pointing the way in which we should go. Nor is he a mere leader, going before us in the way or even commanding the way. Nor does he merely uphold us as we ourselves determine the way in which we should go. The language speaks of controlling influence. The word "led" that the apostle uses here is used of leading animals (Matt. 21:2), of leading the helplessly sick (Luke 10:34; 18:40), and of leading prisoners (John 18:28; Acts 6:12; 9:2). The term may at times be used in such a way that the idea of force retires somewhat into the background (John 1:42; Acts 9:2). "Yet the proper meaning of the word includes the idea of control, and the implication of prevailing determination of action never wholly leaves it." That is to say, the "leading" influence of the Spirit in the lives of God's children is a controlling influence. An outside power has come to their hearts to bring them to the attainment of holiness. He does not merely suggest this way to go. Nor does he merely point the way we ought to go. Nor does he merely rouse in our minds certain inducements toward righteousness. Rather he has taken the helm to

---

[16]*PGS*, 160–62.

bring us to holiness. We were formerly slaves to sin, but a new power has come upon us and broken that bondage—not that we should now be left to make the way ourselves, but that we should be "powerfully directed" on the course set for us. Accordingly the apostle tells us that although we have been emancipated from bondage, we are still bound—not to the flesh but to the Spirit, to live after the Spirit. In brief, the believer is under a new power, a new and beneficent control. There is One dwelling within us who has come to rule—to lead us in the way God would have us go.[17]

Apparently out of concern to avoid certain "higher life" teachings, Warfield cautions that this new power is not a substitute for our power; it is merely a new ruling, dominating power. To be "led" is not to be carried. The Holy Spirit "carried along" the prophets in their writing of Scripture (2 Pet. 1:21), but in "leading" his children he controls their action, "yet it is by their effort they advance to the determined end." The believer is not purely passive. Rather, under the controlling influence of the Spirit the believer strives to attain the goal while the controlling and sanctifying Spirit "supplies the entire directing impulse." The prophets could not be exhorted to "work out their own messages with fear and trembling." The Spirit of God "carried" them along for exactly this purpose. But the child of God is commanded to work out his own salvation with fear and trembling precisely because the Spirit of God within is influencing him to that end (Phil. 2:12–13). Under his control we walk the path he has set for us. "It is His part to keep us in the path and to bring us at length to the goal. But it is we who tread every step of the way." Weary and faint as we may become along the way, we continue under the Spirit's enabling control.[18]

Warfield concludes with a note of joy and praise for the "strong consolation" that is found for us in this "gracious assurance." It is designed to minister comfort and encouragement. Poor and weak as we are, we may fear that sin is too powerful for us. But the Holy Spirit is more powerful, and we need not despair, for he leads us. "If God be for us, who can be against us." "Sin has a dreadful grasp upon us; we have no power to withstand it. But there enters our hearts a power not ourselves making for righteousness. This power is the Spirit of the most high God." We must then move forward not in despair but in hope and in expectation of triumph, for the victory is assured. "The Holy Spirit within us cannot fail us," however rough may be the way we must tread. Under his influence the holiness God demands of us will be realized.[19]

---

[17]*PGS*, 162–67.
[18]*PGS*, 167–72.
[19]*PGS*, 172–79.

Spiritual Strengthening

Closely related to this is the notion of "spiritual strengthening." In Ephesians 3:16 the apostle Paul prays that "according to the riches of his glory he may grant you to be strengthened with power through his Spirit in your inner being." This ministry of the Spirit includes both the idea of "spiritual" as distinguished from physical strengthening and the idea of strengthening by the Holy Spirit as distinguished from any earthly agency. Paul's prayer here is for divine inner strengthening ministered by the Spirit of God.

This spiritual strengthening, Warfield explains, is identical with the abiding of Christ in our hearts by faith (v. 17). What is to be emphasized here is not the coming or arrival of Christ in the heart but his abiding. Christ has already arrived in their hearts, and Paul is praying that he will abide. Paul is not praying that these people will be converted, but assuming their conversion, he prays for their spiritual strengthening, and this he describes in terms of Christ abiding in their hearts. More precisely, their spiritual strengthening is dependent on the abiding of Christ in their hearts by faith—this is its source. Anyone who has read his New Testament, however, understands immediately that Paul is here speaking of the Holy Spirit—it is by the Spirit, the executive of the Godhead, that Christ indwells the heart, and the two, in this sense, are "one and the same great fact." But Paul's point is that Christ is the ultimate source and ground of the believer's spiritual strength. Still, it is the Spirit himself who strengthens us (v. 16).

This strengthening, in turn, is accomplished by his increasing our apprehension of spiritual things (vv. 17–19). By enlarging our grasp of the immeasurable love of Christ for us—a knowledge we need more than any other—the Spirit brings us to greater levels of spiritual attainment. Having grounded us firmly in a widening grasp of the love of Christ, he gives us strength to grasp spiritual truth, to which is added increased spiritual strength until finally we are made like him—"filled with all the fullness of God" (v. 19).[20]

God has determined graciously to bring about in us all that he demands of us, and he has given us his Spirit to strengthen us to this end.

The Spirit's Help in Our Praying

In the eighth chapter of Romans the apostle Paul is addressing the difficulty that attends the Christian life in a world of sin and curse, a difficulty made still more difficult on account of our own weaknesses. Yet the exhortation

---

[20]*FL*, 270–78.

is to perseverance, and the apostle's object in large part is to encourage the saints in this by reminding them of the ever-continuing help of the Spirit of God within them. One example of this work is his help in our praying.

> Likewise the Spirit helps us in our weakness. For we do not know what to pray for as we ought, but the Spirit himself intercedes for us with groanings too deep for words. And he who searches hearts knows what is the mind of the Spirit, because the Spirit intercedes for the saints according to the will of God. (Rom. 8:26–27)

In such fallen conditions, Warfield says worshipfully, prayer is the "vital breath" of the Christian. Indeed, in these days of distress the Christian must "live by prayer." The encouragement offered here is the affirmation that the Holy Spirit puts words to our prayers that are fitting—and, thus, effective. He works within us to ensure that we ask God for what we really need so that we will obtain what we ask. In our weakness we do not know what we should rightly pray for, nor do we pray with due fervency. Even in our sincerity we fail and do not know rightly what to pray for or how to pray. And besides our mere "weakness," we have also our remaining sin with its stubborn persistence. But by the Spirit of God working in our hearts, we are led to pray aright "in matter and manner" so that our petitions "are rendered acceptable to God, as being according to His will."[21]

The Spirit helps us in praying by making this intercession for us "with groanings too deep for words." This intercession, Warfield argues, is not an objective intercession made in heaven for us, as Christ intercedes. The intercession of which Paul speaks "is known to God not as God in heaven, but as 'searcher of hearts.'" Or again, it is "not an intercession through us as conduits" who are themselves unengaged. "It is an intercession made by the Spirit as our helper and not as our substitute." This groaning intercession is made by the Spirit "over and above" our own praying. That is, he works within so as to bring us to see rightly what we need and to pray accordingly. "They are our desires, and our groans. But not apart from the Spirit. They are His; wrought in us by Him." And thus by his hidden inner working in us, framing our thoughts, we are brought to pray according to the will of God.[22]

> Thus, then, the Spirit helps our weakness. By His hidden, inner influences He quickens us to the perception of our real need; He frames in us an infinite

---

[21] *FL*, 193, 197–99; *SSW*, 2:706.
[22] *FL*, 199–201.

desire for this needed thing; He leads us to bring this desire in all its unutterable strength before God; who, seeing it within our hearts, cannot but grant it, as accordant with His will. Is not this a very present help in time of trouble? As prevalent a help as if we were miraculously rescued from any danger? And yet a help wrought through the means of God's own appointment, that is, our attitude of constant dependence on Him and our prayer to Him for His aid? And could Paul here have devised a better encouragement to the saints to go on in their holy course and fight the battle bravely to the end?[23]

Summary

In all these ministries of the Spirit we are reminded that although the Christian life is one of struggle, even continuous struggle, it is not a struggle we must somehow perfect on our own. Nor is it a struggle in which the outcome is uncertain. By the Holy Spirit of God at work in us we are given every provision for success. He has come not only to bring us to Christ, but to secure us for glory with him and to effect in us the holiness required of us.

Let us go onward, in hope and triumph, in our holy efforts. Let our slack knees be strengthened and new vigor enter our every nerve. The victory is assured. The Holy Spirit within us cannot fail us. The way may be rough; the path may climb the dizzy ascent with a rapidity too great for our faltering feet; dangers, pitfalls are on every side. But the Holy Spirit is leading us. Surely, in that assurance, despite dangers and weakness, and panting chest and swimming head, we can find strength to go ever forward.

In these days, when the gloom of doubt if not even the blackness of despair, has settled down on so many souls, there is surely profit and strength in the certainty that there is a portal of such glory before us, and in the assurance that our feet shall press its threshold at the last. In this assurance we shall no longer beat our disheartened way through life in dumb despondency, and find expression for our passionate but hopeless longings only in the wail of the dreary poet of pessimism:—

> "But if from boundless spaces no answering voice shall start,
> Except the barren echo of our ever yearning heart—
> Farewell, then, empty deserts, where beat our aimless wings,
> Farewell, then, dream sublime of uncompassable things."

We are not, indeed, relieved from the necessity for healthful effort, but we can no longer speak of "vain hopes." The way may be hard, but we can no longer talk

---

[23] *FL*, 200.

of "the unfruitful road which bruises our naked feet." Strenuous endeavor may be required of us, but we can no longer feel that we are "beating aimless wings," and can expect no further response from the infinite expanse than "a sterile echo of our own eternal longings." No, no—the language of despair falls at once from off our souls. Henceforth our accents will be borrowed rather from a nobler "poet of faith," and the blessing of Asher will seem to be spoken to us also:—

> "Thy shoes shall be iron and brass,
> And as thy days, so shall thy strength be.
> There is none like unto God, O Jeshurun,
> Who rideth upon the heavens for thy help,
> And in His excellency on the skies.
> The eternal God is thy dwelling-place,
> And underneath are the everlasting arms."[24]

---

[24]*PGS*, 177–79.

CHAPTER 8

FROM GLORY TO GLORY

The Doctrine of Sanctification

For Warfield the Christian life is but the outworking of the gospel. Holiness is not an optional extra attained only by "super saints." It is but an entailment of salvation. We have been saved from sin and unto Christ, and this is not theoretical truth only. It is the Christian life. Godliness is the outworking of the gospel.

Warfield emphasizes this from many angles of Christian doctrine, as we have already begun to see. Another prominent example is his treatment of this theme in connection with our *union with Christ*.

The apostle Paul tells us that we have died with Christ and that we have been raised with Christ (e.g., Rom. 6:1–11; 2 Cor. 5:14–15; Col. 3:1). Behind this terminology lies the great fundamental fact of the Christian faith, that Christ died and rose again. These are not bare facts only. What is significant about these facts is their purpose and accomplishment: Christ died *for our sins*, and he rose again *for our justification* (Rom. 4:25). Yet there is further significance still. Since Christ died in our place, there is a sense in which we can say that we died with him. And if we died with him, we rose again with him also.

But again, this is no merely theoretical truth. It is experiential also. If we speak in any meaningful sense of dying and living with Christ, surely that has some ramifications for Christian living. And in fact, the apostle Paul speaks in these terms explicitly. "He died for all, that those who live might no longer live for themselves but for him who for their sake died and was raised" (2 Cor. 5:15). He died to take away our sins, not judicially only but experientially also—having died with him we have found that sin's grip has been broken. Having been raised with him we have begun to experience the newness of life to which he was raised. Our participation in the death and resurrection of Christ marks the end of our old life and our entrance "into acceptance with God and into all that is involved in that great word, life."[1]

In Colossians 3:1 the apostle Paul writes that we have been "raised with Christ." This presupposes that we died with Christ, something the apostle affirms also (v. 3; cf. 2:20). Warfield comments at length on the practical significance of all this.

> If we be Christians at all, we are such only in virtue of the fact that when He died, He died for us, and we, therefore, died as sinners with His death; and that when He rose again for our justification, we rose again into newness of life with Him,—the life that we now live is a new life, from a new spring, even the Spirit of Christ which He as the risen Lord has sent down to us. This is the great fact of participation in the saving work of Christ, with all that it involves. And what we have here is an assertion that such a participation involves seizing of us bodily and lifting us to another and higher plane. We were sinners, and lived as sinners; we lived an earthly life, in the lowest sense of that word. But now we have died with Christ as sinners and can live no more as sinners; we have been raised together with Him and can live only on the plane of this new life, which is not in sin, not "in the earth," but in heaven. In a high and true sense, because we have died to sin and been raised to holiness, we have already passed out of earth to heaven. Heaven is already the sphere of our life; our "citizenship is in heaven"—we are citizens of the Kingdom of Heaven, and have the life appropriate thereto to live.[2]

It is on this ground, Warfield notes, that the inspired apostle exhorts us to holy living: "If then you have been raised with Christ, seek the things that are above" (Col. 3:1). The command is simply that we live in keeping with our change of state in Christ. We have died with Christ and have been raised with him to holiness, and so we must live accordingly. We have passed out of the realm of sin and death, the apostle reminds us. We have been made citizens of the heavenly kingdom (Phil. 3:20; Col. 1:13). Therefore we must live and behave accordingly.

---

[1] *FL*, 351.
[2] *FL*, 351–52.

Once again, the Christian life is but the outworking of the gospel. We live in light of what Christ has done for us and in light of what we have become in him.

Warfield versus the Higher Life Teachings

One of Warfield's famous studies is an extended analysis of the various forms of Christian perfectionism and higher life teachings. This is not the place for a full review of this large section of Warfield writings. But the influence of the perfectionist–higher life teachings lives on today, and we can benefit from Warfield's critique at least in survey fashion as we seek to understand his doctrine of sanctification—a doctrine that he defined primarily in terms of the Christian's progress in holiness.

The relation of perfectionism to higher life teachings is genetic. The higher life teachers claim perfection neither for themselves nor for their followers. Like their perfectionist forebears, however, they do teach that the Christian can enter a stage of victory over sin and that this "higher life" is attained through a distinct act of faith. There were slight differences in emphasis among the various Keswick, higher life, and victorious life teachers, of course, but they all inherited these general traits.

The higher life teachings, both in Warfield's day and in our own, have several distinctives that dominate. First is the teaching that the higher life of victory over sin is entered by *a distinct act of faith*. We are justified by faith, they agree, but we are sanctified by a distinct and separate act of faith. Warfield rightly reminds us here that we are saved not by faiths but by faith and that justification and sanctification cannot be neatly separated. They are distinct, of course, but they cannot be separated. We are justified by faith, and justification, in turn, is the ground of all saving blessings—blessings that are unfailingly given to all who are justified. We are not called to trust Christ for justification and then at another time trust him for sanctification. This separation of sanctification from justification "forces from us the astonished cry, Is Christ divided?," Warfield exclaims. "And it compels us to point afresh to the primary truth that we do not obtain the benefits of Christ apart from, but only in and with His Person; and that when we have Him we have all."[3]

Second, the higher life teachings are also marked by what we might call *a doctrine of passivity or the suspended will*. That is, Christians are encouraged to "let go, and let God!" Let God accomplish our holiness for us! Indeed, we

---

[3] W, 8:569.

are even admonished and warned against "trying too hard." We are assured that this is God's work to do in us and for us. It is Christ who is to live in us and through us, and the reason we fail is that we have not yet handed the reins of our life over to him! The Christian's responsibility, so this teaching holds, is to turn over his life to Christ and then to continue resting in him to do the work that we cannot do ourselves. Just abandon to him—we are told that this is all we need to do. But all this, Warfield reminds us, misses entirely that large emphasis in the New Testament on Christian responsibility, Christian effort and striving, even warfare against sin. "Since we have these promises, beloved, *let us cleanse ourselves* from every defilement of body and spirit, bringing holiness to completion in the fear of God" (2 Cor. 7:1).

Moreover, the teaching is self-contradictory, for as passive as this all may seem, at the end of the day the responsibility still rests on the believer to "let go" and rest in Christ for his sanctification, and any sin is due to the believer's failure to yield. In this case the "higher" life can be lost as quickly as it is attained. And so Warfield criticizes the theory as resting not on Christ at all but on the human will. This reduces Christ merely to the instrument through whom we work. Indeed, he is helpless and unable to accomplish anything in us until we successfully abandon ourselves and yield to him. Ironically, (according to this teaching) on the one hand God is helpless to work in us unless and until we sincerely place ourselves at his disposal for this purpose. Yet on the other hand, Warfield points out, God is equally helpless to keep us in his hands once he has undertaken this work. We must surrender to him to do the work, yet we must continue to surrender or he can do nothing. And so he will keep us but only so long as we yield to him to keep us. We surrender control to him, but he is not in control after all. This makes for a very strange clay indeed, Warfield says, which must lie passive in the potter's hands, and yet the potter can do nothing with it unless it lets him! And so Warfield sees this teaching as sheer confusion: Christ will sanctify us so long as we allow him to do so, and he will keep us from falling so long as we do not fall.

Third, the higher life teachings promote a confusing *doctrine of "the two natures."* According to this teaching, when we are saved, we are given a new, holy nature, disposed to godliness. Yet, they say, the old nature remains. And while these two natures are in continual conflict, we must yield ourselves to the new nature and allow it the victory. This teaching in some ways resembles the New Testament teaching regarding "the flesh" versus "the spirit." But its terminology of "two natures" is confusing at best, and Warfield mocks it at many points. If it is my old nature and not me that sins, who, after all, has sinned? And which nature should repent? The old nature surely will not repent. But then the new nature has nothing to repent of! And where does this leave "me"? Who is the Christian in all this? Is he the old nature or the new? He surely cannot be the new nature, for the new nature would not have sinned. And neither can he be the old nature, for that would not try otherwise! And so if the Christian is neither the old nature nor the new, Warfield concludes, he must be some kind of nonentity. Warfield insists that whatever resemblance this teaching has to the New Testament is superficial, and he argues at some length that it is unhelpful, confusing, and should be discarded.

Fourth, Warfield points out that the higher life scheme views the Christian as gaining *victory over sinning*, but it does *not* view him as gaining *victory over sin*. Sins are avoided, but the sinful disposition is not progressively eradicated. "The old nature" remains unaffected, and we ourselves remain virtually unchanged. If we continue to trust and yield and surrender at every successive moment, then we cease to sin, at least consciously. But this is not the same as being made holy in any meaningful sense; it is merely being made more successful in overcoming sins.

Finally, closely related to the preceding and perhaps most serious of all, this teaching fosters the notion that *a person may be justified and remain under the dominion of sin.* Until we surrender our lives over to Christ and yield to his control, we are saved but still living under the reign of sin. This, Warfield says, is a fundamental misunderstanding of salvation itself. And in it two very different classes of Christians emerge, so this teaching would have us believe. There is the "ordinary" Christian—the rank and file believer who, although justified, is "carnal" and still not experiencing the higher life for which he was intended. And there is the victorious or "spiritual" Christian—the believer who in abandonment to Christ realizes success over sin. Warfield is appalled at this. It is the crass and unbiblical separation of justification and sanctification that we highlighted above. He sees this as fostering of pride on the one hand and hindering of genuine sanctification on the other. And he insists that there are not two classes of Christians but that Christians are to be found at every step of the spectrum, making their way to glory.

Warfield summarizes succinctly his own assessment of the higher life doctrine of the holiness movements.

A certain levity lies at the heart of "the Keswick Movement"; its zeal is to assure ourselves that we are actually and fully saved, rather than to give ourselves to the repentance which is due to our sins, to the working out of salvation with fear and trembling, to heavenly mindedness, and a life of prayer and a walk in love. It imagines that there can be faith without repentance and conquest of sin without moral struggle. The law, sin itself as evil desire in the regenerate, the determined fulfillment of the will of God in vital endeavor, are pushed into the background. It seeks, in a word, peace instead of righteousness, and the trail of a spiritual euthymia lies over it.[4]

The Doctrine of Sanctification

Against all this Warfield expounds the doctrine of sanctification in terms of every believer's progressive struggle against sin, a struggle marked, on the one hand, by a radical freedom from sin experienced in conversion and, on the other, by a final perfection in glory. For Warfield sanctification is a progressive experience growing out of an initial transformation of heart and life in regeneration by the Holy Spirit and culminating in the glory of the eschaton, when we will reach our goal, having been made like Christ. Warfield relishes the truth that the believer's sinfulness is more than matched by the grace of God in Christ and by the creative work of the Holy Spirit, and he insists that this is not abstract theory merely but the experience of every believer.

Just as in the parable of the sower (Matt. 13:3–9, 18–23) it is the condition of the soil that allows one seed to grow, so also in regeneration God renews our hearts and transforms our affections, giving a new character to our will and a fundamentally new direction to our lives. The Christian, in other words, is one who is both pronounced righteous (justified) and made holy (sanctified). Warfield then speaks of sanctification in three dimensions. First, he speaks of sanctification in *an initial and definitive sense*, the radical break with sin we experience in regeneration and conversion. Second, he speaks of sanctification in a *progressive sense*, and in keeping with the Reformed tradition generally this receives the bulk of his attention. Third, and finally, Warfield speaks of sanctification in *a final and perfected sense*. We will survey these in turn.

Initial Sanctification

Warfield describes sanctification as secured in our justification, on the one hand, and as rooted in regeneration and conversion, on the other. In regeneration and conversion there is, respectively, the imparting of new life and a radical break with sin. The Christian is not one who has been

---

[4]*W*, 7:339–40.

made objectively safe only. The Christian is one whose heart and direction of life have been transformed. We saw this above in Warfield's exposition of "renewal" and "the great change" (chap. 6). Warfield emphasizes that in salvation the believer is not left unchanged and merely rescued from hell. He speaks often of our rescue from sin's power and the cleansing and purifying effects of Christ's work in us. He labors the point that Christ's blood not only provides satisfaction to divine justice, but also cleanses us from sin's corruption. It effects a "renovation" of the whole man. "Nowhere is the sinner permitted to rest satisfied with pardon as the end of salvation; everywhere he is made poignantly to feel that salvation is realized only in a clean heart and a right spirit." This notion is essential to Warfield's argument that justification and sanctification cannot be separated and that there are not "two kinds" of Christians. All who are justified are also made holy in Christ.[5]

To be sure, in justification and sanctification, respectively, we are saved from the penalty and the power of sin, but Warfield cautions that we must be careful not to overstate this distinction. For what is the penalty of sin, he asks, and what is salvation from sin? "Is not our sinfulness the penalty above all other penalties of sin, and is not holiness just salvation from sin?" A realized and experienced holiness is itself "the very reward which is granted us in justification." Being declared righteous (justified) demands that we also are made righteous (sanctified).[6]

All this is to say, in contrast to the higher life teachers, that sanctification has to do not with actions only but with our very person and being. It involves a deliverance from natural corruption and a purifying of the believer himself. In sanctification there is more than a mere counteracting of sins: there is a liberation from sin itself and an eventual eradication of it altogether. The believer is one whose heart has been made holy, and the progress of sanctification is but the "working out" of this salvation already experienced (Phil. 2:12–13). We have been sanctified, and in this assurance we may press on to a further experience of it.

Warfield nowhere mentions this in connection with the Westminster Confession of Faith, but both his knowledge of and love for the confession were profound, and he might well have had it in mind.

They, who are once effectually called, and regenerated, having a new heart, and a new spirit created in them, are further sanctified, really and personally,

---

[5] *W*, 2:440, 446.
[6] *W*, 8:100, 570.

through the virtue of Christ's death and resurrection, by His Word and Spirit dwelling in them: the dominion of the whole body of sin is destroyed, and the several lusts thereof are more and more weakened and mortified; and they more and more quickened and strengthened in all saving graces, to the practice of true holiness, without which no man shall see the Lord.[7]

The emphasis here is clearly on sanctification in its progressive aspect. But notice the word "further" in the first sentence. "They, who are once effectually called, and regenerated, having a new heart, and a new spirit created in them, are *further* sanctified." This is the point here, and this is Warfield's emphasis. The Christian may rejoice that sin is no longer in charge. Its grip has been broken, and we have been set free from it in Christ. There is much progress to be made, to be sure. But the definitive break has been made: we no longer *have* to sin.

Accordingly, Warfield simply points out that wherever the gospel has been proclaimed and believed, its effects have always been evident in the transformation of lives. He speaks of "the regeneration of society" that has been effected "by the forces brought into the world by Christianity." In 1895 Warfield reviewed a new title that examined the character of early Christianity and demonstrated that Christians were people noted to be of superior life and character. Warfield remarks with appreciation that this is always the case: "It was in this sign that Christianity conquered, and in it that it must ever conquer, when conquer it will and does." And in virtually every soteriological context, Warfield insists that "the great change" is not a matter of theory only but of experience, that in salvation the sinner is radically and thoroughly transformed, and that this transformation is inevitably reflected in every believer.[8]

Progressive Sanctification

Warfield also speaks of sanctification in a progressive sense, and in keeping with the Reformed tradition this receives the bulk of his attention. He describes this aspect of sanctification, as we have already noted, in terms of a continual advance toward perfection, a perfection that entails both sinlessness and the full development of that new life implanted in us in regeneration. Everywhere Warfield speaks of salvation as in progress and as experienced in successive stages.

---

[7]Westminster Confession of Faith 13.1.
[8]*SSW*, 1:223; *W*, 10:143.

This progressive experience of sanctification involves effort and struggle on the part of the believer. We are responsible at every step to work out that salvation which we have received. We must "cleanse ourselves" from all sin. It is not moment-by-moment surrender, as the higher life teachers advocate. It is moment-by-moment struggle.

Warfield emphasizes the various New Testament commands that we put sin to death, run the race, struggle, fight, and so on. Citing Watts's famous hymn, he reminds us that we are not to be carried to heaven on flowery beds of ease. If we would win the prize, we must fight. He understands Romans 7 as the portrayal of the constant struggle of the believer to "eradicate" sin. Far from "letting go," the Christian must fight his whole life long. Similarly, on 2 Peter 3:14–18 he notes that the apostle requires active engagement on the part of the believer in the advancement of the Christian life. He does not allow simply that we wait for God to give the increase. He commands us "to exert ourselves" or "to be diligent" (v. 14, cf. vv. 1–10, 15) and teaches that in this effort we are engaged in struggle toward our own sanctification.

But Warfield again reminds us that this is not mere self-help. Our responsibility is grounded in a thoroughgoing, gospel-centered supernaturalism. This is not *either–or*. It is not works *or* grace, effort *or* trust. Nor is it a mere abandonment of responsibility to Christ. Rather, it is the believer at work through liberating power rooted in regeneration and rewarded to him in justification. We take the armor provided us in Christ, certainly, but we fight with it nonetheless. Our struggle is rooted in a union with Christ in his death and resurrection and in the creative power of the Holy Spirit in us. God has not worked in us by persuasion only, Warfield insists. He has made the tree good so that the fruit also can be good. And so in this struggle there is every encouragement offered, for as in all aspects of salvation, God is the energizer of his people, himself bringing them both to will and to do according to his good pleasure (Phil. 2:12–13). We must indeed "work out our own salvation," but we do so in clear view of the great fact that the power within us to bring us to practical, realized righteousness is none other than God himself.

Warfield summarizes the apostle Paul's doctrine of sanctification as consisting in the following three propositions. First, in contradiction to the perfectionists, Paul insists "that to grace always belongs the initiative—it is grace that works the change." It is not in our turning to God, our trusting, or our "allowing" God to work that this change originates. It is of God. Second, "to grace always belongs the victory—grace is infinite power." There is no failure: God sanctifies all whom he justifies. And third, "the working of grace is by process, and therefore reveals itself at any given point of observation as conflict." Sanctification is, in short, a work of God in all his people by which they are certainly—even though only progressively—made holy.[9]

Final Sanctification

Third, and finally, Warfield speaks of sanctification in a final and perfected sense. Here he has his eye on glory and a degree of holiness not obtainable in this life. We will survey this more fully in due course, but we should at least note here the sustained emphasis in Warfield that this holiness we pursue at all costs in this life will one day be realized. We are not left in doubt as to the outcome of this struggle. Here we are "changed from glory into glory" but only "til in heaven we take our place." We may be sure: the glory we seek one day will be ours.

> Now may the God of peace himself sanctify you completely, and may your whole spirit and soul and body be kept blameless at the coming of our Lord Jesus Christ. He who calls you is faithful; he will surely do it. (1 Thess. 5:23–24)

> Beloved, we are God's children now, and what we will be has not yet appeared; but we know that when he appears we shall be like him, because we shall see him as he is. (1 John 3:2)

What a gospel this is! Are we commanded to pursue holiness? Yes, and in this pursuit we are given divine aid and every assurance that the goal will in fact be reached. And so we press on, in the certain knowledge of final victory.

---

[9] *W*, 8:584.

PART 3

ORIENTATION AND PERSPECTIVE

CHAPTER 9

RIGHTEOUS AND SINFUL

Miserable-Sinner Christianity

Mistaken Perfectionism

Warfield expended considerable effort (more than a thousand published pages!) analyzing and discrediting the several varieties of perfectionist teachings that had been popular in some Christian circles. Some of the perfectionists taught that the Christian, by definition, has reached perfection. Others considered perfection a higher stage of Christian experience attained by the most faithful. The claim was that the Christian is or at least ought to be sinless. On a more popular level today, even where a doctrine of perfectionism has not been taught, new Christians especially—but also older Christians—are sometimes puzzled and even surprised at the continued presence of sin. Haven't we been saved from sin? Shouldn't we be over this by now? Doesn't the apostle John say, "No one who abides in him keeps on sinning; no one who keeps on sinning has either seen him or known him" (1 John 3:6)?

In his massive response, Warfield argues many times over that perfectionistic thinking is mistaken on several levels and that it misses the entailments of some gospel essentials. Instead of a detailed exposition of Warfield's teaching, it will suffice here to highlight just a few of his general criticisms and then move on to Warfield's exposition of "miserable sinner Christianity."

First, in order to claim perfection, *perfectionist teachers inevitably and necessarily redefine sin and holiness.* How else could we claim to be perfect? Warfield often scoffs at the "imperfect perfection" of the perfectionists and finds it odd that "perfection" always means "perfection" except in "Christian perfectionism." More seriously, he finds the implications of such "adjustments" of God's law antinomian and even blasphemous. "Be perfect, as your heavenly Father is perfect" (Matt. 5:48) is still the standard, and we must not pretend otherwise.

Second, Warfield repeatedly charges that *perfectionist teachers are impatient.* He agrees with them that God has purposed for us to reach full perfection. But God nowhere says that this will be ours in this life. And it does God no honor "to demand, like greedy children, all the feast prepared for them in the first course" or to "chafe under the delay and require all their inheritance at once." The error of the perfectionists is that they gather together all of the biblical assurances of salvation and then demand of the Lord, "Give me all of it—now." It is good to be impatient with sin, Warfield counsels us, but "it is a different matter to show impatience with God."[1] We will see more of this later.

Third, *this teaching results in two classes of Christians*—"a lower and a higher variety," those who have reached perfection and the "ordinary" or "average" Christian. Warfield finds this unhealthful. On the one hand this teaching fosters pride in those who are professedly "perfect," and on the other hand it unnecessarily discourages the "ordinary" Christian who, humbly recognizing his sin, is made to feel inferior or not so blessed.

Finally, and closely related to this, Warfield judges that *these teachings constitute a hindrance rather than a help to the Christian life.* Neither deep repentance nor victorious ecstasy finds room here. With the law of God marginalized, an adequate appreciation of grace is lost. Warfield prefers the more realistic self-estimate engendered by traditional Reformed theology and expressed by Thomas Adam (1701–1784): sin is so deeply a part of who we are that not only do we sin inevitably, but "when we have done all we ever shall do, the very best state we ever shall arrive at, will be so far from meriting a reward, that it will need a pardon. . . . If I was to live to the world's end, and do all the good that man can do, I must still cry 'mercy!'"[2] This brings us to examine Warfield's exposition of "miserable sinner Christianity."

---

[1] *W*, 8:537.
[2] *W*, 8:571; 7:127–28.

Miserable-Sinner Christianity

Exposition

Warfield insists that the New Testament everywhere presents Christians as redeemed yet still sinning, and he provides extensive exegetical support. A few samples will suffice.

First, Warfield points out that in Romans 6—one of the classic expositions of the Christian life—the apostle Paul exhorts the believer to life "as if" alive from the dead (v. 13). Warfield notes that the apostle writes under the assumption that for these believers, sinning has not ceased. The whole force of the exhortation of Romans 6 rests on this assumption that sin yet occurs and that struggle against it is the ongoing responsibility of the Christian.

Again, Warfield argues that both sin and grace continue to be the experience of the believer, even if in increasingly contrasting proportion. Commenting on Romans 8:1 he remarks simply that the apostle does not say, "There is therefore now no sinning for those in Christ Jesus." Instead, Paul says, "'There is therefore no condemnation to those in Christ Jesus'; and on the face of it this means . . . that those in Christ Jesus live in an atmosphere of perpetual forgiveness."[3] The issue involved in justification is not past sins only but continued sins. This is an important point for Warfield, and he returns to it often in his treatment of "miserable sinner Christianity." Both sin and grace, sin and forgiveness, continue to be the experience of the believer.

Accordingly, when Paul warns of the problem of misbehavior at the Lord's Supper in Corinth (1 Cor. 11:17–34), he writes, "But if we judged ourselves truly, we would not be judged. But when we are judged by the Lord, we are disciplined so that we may not be condemned along with the world" (vv. 31–32). What is significant here is that not only does the apostle rebuke the sins of the Corinthian believers in this matter specifically, but in his change from the second person ("you") to the first person ("we") he broadens the exhortation as inclusive of all believers, himself included. His exhortation at this point applies not to the Corinthians only but to all Christians. The Corinthians had been guilty of the specific faults he rebukes. But all Christians are sinners, and thus all Christians alike—the apostle also—are responsible to "judge themselves."[4]

Likewise in Philippians 3:12, the apostle expressly declares that he has "not yet attained" and is "not yet perfect." Even elders in the church yet sin (1 Tim. 5:20). The repeated ethical imperatives of the New Testament

---

[3] W, 7:170.
[4] W, 7:258–59.

(e.g., 2 Cor. 7:1) all assume that the transformation of Christians was not yet complete. Similarly in 1 Corinthians 9:27, Paul admits to his own need constantly to struggle against sin. All this is in obvious keeping with the New Testament commands to Christians to cease rendering evil for evil (1 Thess. 5:15; Rom. 12:17), Jesus's instruction that we pray for forgiveness (Matt. 6:12, 14; Mark 11:25–26; Luke 11:4), the broader New Testament instruction for the treatment of the sinning brother (e.g., Gal. 6:1; Eph. 4:32; Col. 3:13; 1 Pet. 4:8; 1 John 5:16–18), and the general characterizations of Christians found throughout the New Testament (e.g., James 3:2; 4:8; 1 John 1:8). The whole tone of 1 John 1:8 and following, Warfield argues, "is not that Christians are sinless men who may possibly, however, be overtaken in a rare fault; but that Christians are sinful men, seeking and obtaining in Christ purification from their sins and striving day by day to be more and more delivered from them." And so Warfield does not find it surprising that the apostle Paul speaks of the forgiveness that believers enjoy in the present tense: "we *have* forgiveness of sins" (Col. 1:14; Eph. 1:7). Passages such as these demonstrate that the forgiveness of sins is a blessing continuously needed and continuously enjoyed by all Christians. This constant possession of divine mercy was foundational to the joy and assurance of the apostle Paul and his converts alike. It was "the fundamental blessing on which they rested their whole lives long."[5]

Warfield seems nearly stunned that one popular perfectionist teacher, Charles Finney (1792–1875), "challenged the world" to demonstrate any Scripture to support the notion that justified sinners continue to sin. Warfield responded, simply, that Paul might seem to have written a great part of his epistles just to answer Mr. Finney's challenge! Warfield then proceeds to cite Romans 3:21ff.—with its pointed emphasis on the freeness of divine grace given only to believing yet ill-deserving sinners—as ample demonstration of the Pauline teaching that God justifies *sinful* believers.[6] As Warfield summarizes elsewhere, it is just too plain to be denied that the Scriptures everywhere exhort men and women, assumed to be justified, to improve their walk in holiness. Justified men and women, therefore, are not yet perfect.

Finally, Warfield sees clear reason why we sin: the fruit is corrupt only because the tree itself is corrupt. Given our sinfulness, our sins inevitably follow. We are yet incapable of not sinning, simply because we are sinners.

---

[5] *W*, 7:258–59.
[6] *W*, 8:156–57.

Given all this, even the mighty apostle Paul is, in the fullest sense of the word, a "miserable sinner Christian."[7]

Application

The point of all this surely is not to excuse sin or to make the Christian comfortable in sin. But Warfield insists that a right understanding of this doctrine does have implications that are essential to Christian life and devotion.

For a perfectionist of any variety, the term "miserable sinner" cannot and must not be used in reference to the Christian, and this historic designation was mocked in Warfield's day. And in our own day many object to the traditional Christian characterization of the believer as a "sinner." But Warfield is quite prepared to accept this as an accurate and appropriate characterization of himself and of every Christian. Following Martin Luther's famous dictum that the Christian is *simul iustus et peccator* (at the same time just and a sinner), indeed, *semper iustus et peccator* (always just and a sinner), and in agreement with the traditional Reformed doctrine of remaining sin in the believer, Warfield glories in the fact that although he is a "miserable sinner" and, this side of heaven, will always be a "miserable sinner," he is nonetheless truly perfect in his status before God in Christ while awaiting his full transformation to perfection in the resurrection. He maintains no illusion that his transformation, although well under way, has yet been completed. He finds in the Scriptures, in the historic statements of the church, and in his own heart and life ample evidence that he is yet, to borrow Luther's words, a Christian "in the making." In short, our justification ensures both our sanctification and our glorification, but our sanctification is an ongoing process never completed in this life. Accordingly, the apostle Paul describes himself as "less than the least of all the saints" (Eph. 3:8) and "the chief of sinners" (1 Tim. 1:15).[8]

Moreover, this self-understanding is a necessary one. It "belongs to the very essence" of gospel Christianity. At the heart of the Christian gospel, Warfield insists, "lies the contrast of sin and grace," which drives the Christian to "feel himself continuously unworthy of the grace by which he lives." At no stage of Christian development are we acceptable to God by virtue of what is done by us.

---

[7] *W*, 7:221.
[8] *W*, 8:156–57.

Our need of Christ does not cease with our believing; nor does the nature of our relation to Him or to God through Him ever alter, no matter what our attainments in Christian graces or our achievements in Christian behavior may be. It is always on His "blood and righteousness" alone that we can rest. . . . We are always unworthy, and all that we have or do of good is always of pure grace. Though blessed with every spiritual blessing in the heavenlies in Christ, we are still in ourselves just "miserable sinners": "miserable sinners saved by grace to be sure, but 'miserable sinners' still, deserving in ourselves nothing but everlasting wrath."[9]

That is, we are always but pardoned criminals. "In fact and in act" we are continuously sinful and in need of "unbroken penitence throughout life." Our problem lies in what we are, not simply in what we do; sin, therefore, "is a quality which, entrenched in the heart, affects all of our actions without exception." It is not a question of which of our actions are sinful and which are not—everything we do is tainted. We will never be truly perfect "until our hearts are perfect."[10]

Given the indispensableness of this doctrine, it is not surprising that Warfield finds this aspect of Christian doctrine and devotion embedded in a long list of Protestant catechisms and confessions. Martin Luther's own conversion experience left him with the ineradicable conviction that he was a miserable sinner, deserving of wrath, yet alive and blessed only through the grace of God in Christ. Warfield refers to Luther's conversion as "his discovery of this bitter-sweet fact." After all his struggles he found that he was a sinner still, and yet he found the guilt entirely removed in Christ. And Luther never wearied of setting these two truths side by side. These two concepts are diametrically opposed, yet both are true: I am both bad and good, a sinner and a saint, deserving of God's wrath and yet free, unlovely and yet loved. "Thus the Christian remains in pure humility. . . . He remains also at the same time in pure and holy pride in which he turns to Christ and arouses himself through Him against this sense of wrath and the divine judgment," believing that his sins are not imputed to him and that he is loved by God on account of Christ.[11]

Reflecting all this, in his Large Catechism Luther incorporates a "full and searching exposition" of the fifth petition ("Forgive us our trespasses"), affirming that "we sin daily in words and deeds, by commission and omis-

---

[9] W, 7:113–14.
[10] W, 7:114; 8:457.
[11] W, 7:115–16.

sion," and warning us that "no one is to think that so long as he lives here below he can bring it about that he does not need such forgiveness." Indeed, "unless God forgives without cessation, we are lost." In his Short Catechism he teaches us to say that "God richly forgives me and all believers every day, all our sins," "for we sin much every day and deserve nothing but punishment."[12] And so we learn to pray, thoughtfully, "Forgive us our trespasses."

Another example Warfield points us to is the Articles and Prayers of the Church of England, most prominently its famous prayer of confession.

> Almighty and most merciful Father: We have erred, and strayed from thy ways like lost sheep. We have followed too much the devices and desires of our own hearts. We have offended against thy holy laws. We have left undone those things which we ought to have done; And we have done those things which we ought not to have done; And there is no health in us. But thou, O Lord, have mercy upon us, miserable offenders. Spare thou them, O God, which confess their faults. Restore thou them that are penitent; According to thy promises declared to mankind in Christ Jesus our Lord. And grant, O most merciful Father, for His sake; That we may hereafter lead a godly, righteous, and sober life, To the glory of Thy holy Name. Amen.

This, Warfield comments, is the very spirit of the "miserable sinner Christian." We recognize our sin and so make humble confession, and yet we rejoice in the provision of grace found in Christ and seek to honor him with our lives.[13]

Among his many samples from historical Protestant statements, Warfield also points us to Zinzendorf, who presents the Christian as "distinctively the pardoned criminal," whose preoccupation is therefore "less with the guilt from which he has escaped than with the deliverance which he has received." Warfield refers us specifically to Zinzendorf's famous hymn, "Christ's Blood and Righteousness," the cry of which reflects a sinner "who depends on the great Ransom alone" throughout life and even in the resurrection. Wesley's well-used translation of the hymn just barely conveys Zinzendorf's original.

> When from the dust of death I rise,
> To claim my mansion in the skies,
> Even then this shall be all my plea,
> Jesus hath lived and died for me.

---

[12] *W*, 7:115–16.
[13] *W*, 7:122–23.

Warfield's point in all this is to emphasize that the Christian must remain conscious at all times that "he has nothing to depend on but Christ." At the same time, he must keep in mind that "Christ is enough." The contrasting ideas of sin and grace form the center of our self-awareness always.[14]

We must not misunderstand. It would be a mistake to think that because the Christian is always sinful, he must therefore be marked by despair or depression and doubt. Warfield specifically disallows all such notions. The Christian, he insists, is not a person marked by a sour countenance, hanging his head and dejected, with a grumbling piety "which comes to nothing except the repetition of its dirges." To the contrary, miserable-sinner Christianity is a "joyous Christianity." The Christian is marked by assurance and "overmastering exultation." And for good reason.

> We are sinners and we know ourselves to be sinners, lost and helpless in ourselves. But we are saved sinners; and it is our salvation which gives the tone to our life, a tone of joy which swells in exact proportion to the sense we have of our ill-desert; for it is he to whom much is forgiven who loves much, and who, loving, rejoices much.[15]

Warfield then describes that Christian as one who lives in the experience of "'solaced contrition'—affliction for sin, yes, the deepest and most poignant remorse for sin, but not unrelieved remorse, but appeased remorse." And to this he adds, "There is no other joy on earth like that of appeased remorse." The Christian life is characterized, he insists, by a recognition of sinfulness and a contrasting joy in the awareness of rescue by divine grace. This type of piety, fostered in the Scriptures and brought into sharp focus by Augustine, was soon lost amid ideas of human merit so prominent in the Middle Ages. But "Luther brought it back. His own experience fixed ineradicably in his heart the conviction that he was a 'miserable sinner,' deserving of death, and alive only through the inexplicable grace of God." He found that although he could not think highly of himself, he could not think *too* highly of Christ. And so "it became his joy to be a 'miserable sinner,' resting solely on the grace of Christ."[16]

The Christian's continued recognition of sin and grace is all very important for Warfield, therefore, not only because it "belongs to the very essence" of the Christian gospel itself but also by reason of its indispensable useful-

---

[14] W, 7:124–25.
[15] W, 7:114, 125.
[16] W, 7:113–17.

ness in Christian devotion and worship. This concept of sin and grace has "moulded the piety of all the Protestant generations."[17] It informs for us the significance of that needed petition, "Forgive us our debts" (Matt. 6:12). The Christian's recognition of his own sinfulness and consequent reliance upon divine grace are attitudes that are fostered and made necessary by the very gospel they have embraced and continue to embrace. It is part and parcel of our continued reliance upon Christ.

> Sin and Christ; ill desert and no condemnation; we are sinners and saints all at once! That is the paradox of evangelicalism. The Antinomian and the Perfectionist would abolish the paradox—the one drowning the saint in the sinner, the other concealing the sinner in the saint. . . . It is a great paradox, but glorious truth of Christianity . . . that a good conscience may consist with a consciousness of evil. Though we can have no satisfaction in ourselves, we may have perfect satisfaction in Christ. . . . It is clear that "miserable sinner Christianity" is a Christianity which thinks of pardon as holding the primary place in salvation.[18]

And so there is contrition because of "a life of continuous dissatisfaction with self," but there is corresponding joy in a "continuous looking afresh to Christ as the ground of all our hope." Warfield argues passionately that "miserable sinner Christianity" is a necessary part of what drives the Christian to look continuously to Christ as the sole object of his faith. It incites continued appreciation for Christ as Savior and, therefore, a continued feeding upon him for life. "Thus in complete dependence on grace, and in never ceasing need of grace . . . the saint goes onward in his earthly work." Our "whole lives long" we rest on God's grace of forgiveness.[19]

Warfield stresses that we dare never lose the awareness of our sins, for "the moment we think that we have no sin, we shall desert Christ." This is the point. A continued sense of sin is necessary to a continued heart of reliance upon Christ. "On earth it is the great exercise of faith . . . to see sin and Christ at the same time, or to be penetrated with a lively sense of our desert, and absolute freedom from condemnation; but the more we know of both, the nearer approach we shall make to the state of heaven."[20] "It is only the saint who knows what sin is; for only the saint knows it in contrast with salvation, experienced and understood. And it is only the sinning saint

---

[17] *W*, 7:117.
[18] *W*, 7:130.
[19] *W*, 7:90, 219.
[20] *W*, 7:129–30; in both instances Warfield is quoting Thomas Adam.

who knows what salvation is: for it is only the joy that is lost and then found again that is fully understood."[21]

What encouragement this is to the struggling saint. Our sin, shameful and disappointing as it is, reminds us of Christ. We must live in light of the gospel. Miserable sinners we still are, but we are nonetheless safe in Christ forever. "Though we can have no satisfaction in ourselves, we may have perfect satisfaction in Christ." And again, "The ground of Paul's satisfaction was not in himself but in Christ. And that is precisely what 'miserable-sinner Christianity' means."[22]

---

[21] FL, 22.
[22] W, 7:130, 151.

CHAPTER 10

JESUS'S LITTLE ONES

Childship to God

One of Warfield's more famous themes, and one that in many ways best reflects the fervent devotion of his keen mind and tender heart, is that the Christian is a child of God. He treats this theme in a cluster of expositions, some of which he published more than once. In these expositions he explores what it is to belong to God—and to Christ—as his child both in terms of the blessedness that is ours in this relationship and in terms of what this expression tells us about the heart of God toward us. In this chapter I will reproduce Warfield's exposition somewhat fully so that Warfield's teaching can have its identity-shaping effect.

Childship to God

As Warfield notes, the apostle John presents the conception of the new birth as the root of the Christian life. Other New Testament writers also teach the doctrine of regeneration, but under other figures and terms, such as the new creation. But the expression "born again" or "born from above" is unique to John. By contrast, in keeping with his more "legal" or judicial point of view, Paul speaks of sonship as conferred by adoption; he emphasizes not the spiritual root of life that we have by the new birth but the privileges and inheritance that have become ours as sons of God, joined to Christ, the

Son par excellence. And so Paul prefers the word *sons*, while John prefers the word *children*. Paul and John do not disagree theologically, of course, but they do present a similar truth in different ways and under differing illustrations. Warfield explains:

> It will not do to say on its ground that John teaches that our sonship to God is due to regeneration and Paul that it is due to justification. It will not be accurate even to say that John emphasizes regeneration and Paul justification. What is true is that Paul has adopted the conception of sonship to illustrate the title to life and holiness which we obtain through justification, and John to illustrate the communication of a new principle of holy life to us in regeneration.[1]

Warfield observes further that Paul speaks more *objectively*, emphasizing our status, rights, and privileges as God's sons. John speaks more *subjectively*, emphasizing the experience of new life from above. Broadly speaking, Paul highlights what Christ has done *for* us, while John emphasizes what Christ has done *in* us.

Warfield uses 1 John 2:28–3:2 to expound his theme of childship to God, suggesting that perhaps no other Johannine passage better summarizes for us this apostle's viewpoint of this relationship "begun in regeneration and growing up in ever-increasing sanctification to its goal of likeness to God."[2] His primary focus is on 1 John 3:1: "See what kind of love the Father has given to us, that we should be called children of God; and so we are."

Warfield highlights the fact that this relationship to God as his child is not a natural one but one graciously and supernaturally conferred. Neither John nor Paul, nor any other New Testament writer, speaks of God as a universal Father. That is a heathen concept, a concept of a purely natural religion, reflecting the desire of God's creatures, made in his image, to know our Creator as something more than our Master and sovereign. But this relationship to God as his children is a saving relationship, freely given to us in grace. "What kind of love the father has *given* to us." "It is a matter of bestowment; it is a gift," Warfield reminds us. "See *what kind of love* the Father has given to us, that we should be called the children of God," John writes with exuberance. And nearly overcome with the wonder of such mercy, it seems, he adds, "and so we are." That is to say, "It is true! It is true! We are God's children! What a wonder!" This is not a natural relation to God as his creatures, merely. Nor is this relationship the result of our own endeavors

---

[1] *FL*, 449.
[2] *FL*, 450.

and achievements. This is a relationship born in sovereign love, granted to us by ineffable and indescribable grace.

> So the New Testament everywhere and under all its figures represents it; so John always represents it. And it is therefore that he sings paeans to God's love on account of it. "Behold!" "What manner of love is this!" "To seek us out and make us the sons of God!" Language could not convey more clearly, more powerfully, the conception of the absolute sovereignty of the gift of childship to God. Elsewhere it is conveyed more didactically, more analytically; here it is conveyed emotionally. Elsewhere we are told that it came not of blood, nor of the will of the flesh, nor of the will of man, but of God; here we have the answering thrill of gratitude of the human heart at this unexpected, undeserved gift. Elsewhere the sovereignty is asserted, explained; here it is acknowledged, honoured. Elsewhere it is claimed, here it is yielded, admired, glorified.[3]

Childlikeness

The Gospel passages that speak of Jesus's blessing the little children (Matt. 19:13–15; Mark 10:13–16; Luke 18:15–17) and in which Jesus describes believers as children (Matt. 11:25; 18:1–4; 21:15–16; Mark 9:33–35; Luke 9:46–48) are favorites for Warfield, and he finds them emotively illustrative of gospel truth that serves well to shape the Christian's perspective. We will take Luke's account as our sample.

> Now they were bringing even infants to him that he might touch them. And when the disciples saw it, they rebuked them. But Jesus called them to him, saying, "Let the children come to me, and do not hinder them, for to such belongs the kingdom of God. Truly, I say to you, whoever does not receive the kingdom of God like a child shall not enter it." (Luke 18:15–17)

Warfield remarks on the touching picture the Evangelists give us of Jesus when they relay to us the way he treats little children. Jesus "went about doing good," we are told, performing miracles and healing diseases of all kinds. And when he teaches, the people characteristically hear him gladly. Jesus clearly leaves a "beneficent impression" on the people of his world—the outcasts, afflicted, suffering, diseased, and disturbed of all kinds flock to him in search of blessing. And invariably we find them leaving blessed, with healing of both body and mind.

---

[3] *FL*, 453.

What we do not hear as much about, although it is prominent in the Gospels, is that mothers with equal anticipation bring their little babies to Jesus, and like all others coming to Jesus for blessing, they and their little children also go away blessed. Jesus not only welcomes the little children, and he not only blesses them, but he takes them up in his arms and blesses them. It's a tender scene indeed, and we find in it that Jesus's heart toward children is everything we would expect it to be and everything we would want it to be.

But for all the ink that has been spilled explaining from this scene Jesus's view of children, it is surprising to learn from Warfield that this passage is intended to teach us something else entirely. So far from teaching us something regarding children and their place in the kingdom, Warfield points out, Jesus simply uses children as an object lesson, an occasion to stress a truth that is essential to the Christian gospel. "Let the children come to me, and do not hinder them, for to such belongs the kingdom of God. Truly, I say to you, whoever does not receive the kingdom of God like a child shall not enter it" (Luke 18:15–17).

Jesus's disciples, who function like his gatekeepers, see no need for the little children to take his time or distract him from other things. Others have come to Jesus, but here the disciples draw the line. These children are not sick or in need of healing, and they are too young to benefit from Jesus's teaching. What good purpose can this distraction possibly serve? Jesus is already too busy and too burdened with too many important things, they think. And so, rebuking the mothers, they begin to shoo them away.

But they have misunderstood Jesus, and Jesus is not pleased. He is "indignant" (Mark 10:14) at the insensitivity of the disciples. So Jesus takes these small children up in his arms, embraces them, and blesses them. And mothers go away with their little ones, comforted and excited, no doubt, that Jesus has blessed them.

It is a wonderful picture of our Lord indeed. He *is* a busy man and no doubt feels tired in the pressing busyness of each day. But he is never so busy that he ignores those coming to him for blessing. He is much more than a teacher and a healer and a prophet. He is one who has come with blessing, even for helpless babes.

Who Is Jesus Talking About?

As wonderful as this is simply on a human level, this is not Luke's point. Jesus makes the point very clear in his remarks that follow. Again, "Let the children come to me, and do not hinder them, for to such belongs the kingdom of God. Truly, I say to you, whoever does not receive the kingdom of God like a child shall not enter it" (Luke 18:15–17).

Warfield stresses two details here that help us understand Jesus's point. First, these were not adolescents but "infants" (v. 15a), babies whom Jesus could hold in his arms. Second, Jesus does not say that the kingdom of God belongs to these infants. He does not say "*theirs* is the kingdom." He says, "*of such* is the kingdom." We must receive the kingdom "*like* a little child." Jesus's point is not that infants may inherit the kingdom but that the kingdom belongs only to those who are *like* infants. The little children brought to Jesus are illustrations, pictures of the point Jesus is emphasizing. Simply, if we would be saved, we must become like these infants. This, Warfield stresses, is the point. The passage says nothing about baptism or the salvation of little children. The passage insists, rather, that to enter the kingdom we must come like little babies. Childlikeness is the requisite characteristic of all who would be saved.

What Is the Childlikeness That Jesus Requires?

And what is the leading attribute of infants? Some have suggested that it is *innocence*, but of course our Lord nowhere suggests innocence as a requirement to the kingdom—he came to call sinners! Christianity is specifically a *sinners'* religion, as Luke's preceding paragraph regarding the Pharisee and the tax collector illustrates.

Many have suggested our Lord is commending *humility*, but Warfield remarks that at this stage of life we are perhaps more self-centered—"the most egotistic"—than any other!

So some have suggested that Jesus is commending the natural, even if gullible, *trustfulness* of a child. Warfield agrees that this is a step better than the other suggestions. But it only moves us closer to the specific point at hand. It is difficult to speak of infants as having a trusting state of mind. If they are trusting, it is only because they are *utterly dependent*. And this, Warfield insists, is the point—not a subjective state of mind but something objectively true about them: infants are *helpless* and *dependent*. Everything must be given to them, done for them, provided for them. They are helpless.

So our Lord is not commending any virtue as prerequisite; he is speaking of something more objective. What he commends is not their disposition of mind but their condition—*what they are*. To enter the kingdom, he says, we must stoop to become like them—utterly helpless and dependent, with no claim on anything but mercy, creatures for whom everything must be done, altogether dependent on the care of another. We come to Christ stripped of everything, as helpless and as dependent as a baby on his mother's breast, with nothing to contribute or commend ourselves. Just as a baby lies thoughtlessly secure in his mother's arms, so we cast ourselves wholly, helplessly, into the care of our great Savior.

When the Lord Jesus demands that we humble ourselves "like this little child" (Matt. 18:4), *this* is what he means. To be saved we adults must recognize that we are as helpless and dependent as a newborn baby. In other respects, relatively speaking, we are not helpless. But in this respect we are entirely helpless.

Warfield points to the scene of Jesus's triumphal entry to Jerusalem in this connection. The Jewish leaders are indignant of the high praises given to Jesus, and in response, Jesus asks, "Have you never read, 'Out of the mouth of infants and nursing babies you have prepared praise'?" (Matt. 21:16). Jesus's point is that the praises of the children are typical of the praises rising from the hearts of all his people, men and women who in childlikeness own their helplessness and complete dependence upon him. This is exactly the praise we give Christ, is it not? It is the praise of the helpless who have received from him all that is needed to enter the kingdom of God. Warfield also points to Matthew 11:25 in this connection: "At that time Jesus declared, 'I thank you, Father, Lord of heaven and earth, that you have hidden these things from the wise and understanding and revealed them to little children.'"[4] It is to these kinds of people, helpless babies, that the Lord Jesus sovereignly reveals his saving grace.

This, then, is the lesson our Lord would teach his disciples. These little children, they think, are too young and too helpless to profit from Christ. The disciples do not understand. "No," Jesus responds, "do not misunderstand. Bring the children to me! The kingdom of God belongs only to those who, like little children, are helplessly dependent upon me."

Here is the urgency of the gospel. We are indeed helpless, with nothing to contribute. We need a Savior! And the gospel invitation is just that: come to Christ just as you are, with your hands empty, stripped of everything, laying claim to nothing but his mercy.

But here is the great glory of the gospel also. Although we are helpless, our great Savior is all-sufficient. All by himself he gives us all that we need.

Warfield loves to quote the lines to a revival hymn, "Cast Your Deadly Doing Down." He mentions at one point that James Anthony Froude found

---

[4]Warfield points out here that the Greek term is *nēpios*, infant.

this hymn particularly offensive. We do not know the exact reference Warfield makes, but Froude was a one-time divinity student who washed out because of his rejection of orthodox Christian faith. Evidently he had expressed high thoughts of his own ability to contribute to his salvation. And of course such a man would find this hymn offensive. Warfield loved it all the more.

> Till to Jesus' work you cling
> By a simple faith,
> Doing is a deadly thing—
> Doing ends in death.
>
> Cast your deadly doing down—
> Down at Jesus' feet:
> Stand in him, in him alone,
> Gloriously complete!
>
> [Refrain]
> "It is finished!" Yes, indeed,
> Finished every jot.
> Sinner, this is all you need;
> Tell me, is it not?

So far from considering it an offense, Warfield gloried in this line of thinking. This is the whole ground of Christian joy. We come helpless, with nothing to contribute, to our wonderful Savior and enjoy in him all that God requires of us. To be told that our standing with God has nothing to do with us and everything to do with Christ is not bad news but good news! And so for Warfield this note of helplessness only enhances the notes of praise, and he exults in the overwhelming adequacy of Christ. Here, in him, the Christian heart may peacefully rest.

Christ's "Little Ones"

All this, in turn, helps inform us of the significance of those Gospel passages in which Jesus refers to his disciples as his "little ones" (Matt. 10:40–42; 18:10, 12–14; Mark 9:42; Luke 17:1–2; cf. Mark 9:33–37; Luke 12:32).

First, it is important for Warfield to point out—surprisingly to many—that Jesus is not referring in these passages to children specifically. The phrase "little ones" or "my little ones" is a designation Jesus uses for his disciples. Those who believe on Jesus come like little children, and, in turn, Jesus refers to them as "his little ones."

We will not take the time to exhaust Warfield's discussion here, but we should at least highlight his contention that in all of these passages it is not children specifically, but his disciples that are in view. Take Matthew 10:40–42 as an example.

> Whoever receives you receives me, and whoever receives me receives him who sent me. The one who receives a prophet because he is a prophet will receive a prophet's reward, and the one who receives a righteous person because he is a righteous person will receive a righteous person's reward. And whoever gives one of these little ones even a cup of cold water because he is a disciple, truly, I say to you, he will by no means lose his reward.

Warfield notes that no children are present here at all, nor are they even suggested. Jesus is sending his disciples out on their maiden voyage, their first apostolic mission and evangelistic tour, and he wraps up his exhortation and instructions with these words of encouragement: "Whoever receives you receives me." He identifies with his disciples, his ambassadors, and makes common cause with them.

Then Jesus encourages his disciples with two illustrations. First, "The one who receives a prophet because he is a prophet will receive a prophet's reward." That is, you link up with a prophet as one of God's spokesmen, and you will be treated by God accordingly. Similarly, when you welcome a righteous person because he is, in fact, a righteous person, then you identify with him, and again, you will share in his reward: "The one who receives a righteous person because he is a righteous person will receive a righteous person's reward." The broad principle here is that the one who receives these people will be rewarded by God on the same level as the ones they receive. By our reception of a prophet or a righteous person we take common ground with them and, thus, will share in their reward.

Finally, Jesus gives the application: "And whoever gives one of these little ones even a cup of cold water because he is a disciple, truly, I say to you, he will by no means lose his reward." Notice that Jesus specifically identifies "these little ones" as his disciples. He is not talking about giving water to little children but to his disciples. This is Jesus's point stated already in verse 40: "Whoever receives you receives me." Jesus so identifies with his disciples, so links with them in common cause, that to receive them is to receive him. And it is to be rewarded accordingly.

Certainly the point of all this, Warfield says, is that *Jesus's disciples are under the watchful charge of his jealous love.* The slightest good done for them, Jesus says, will be rewarded as if done for him.

Similarly, in the opening verses of Matthew 18, Jesus again uses little children as illustrations of his disciples, those who believe on him. And then in verses 5–6 he warns, "Whoever receives one such child in my name receives me, but whoever causes one of these little ones who believe in me to sin, it would be better for him to have a great millstone fastened around his neck and to be drowned in the depth of the sea." Again Warfield points out that Jesus is not warning about the right treatment of children. He is warning about the right treatment of his disciples. And again, he refers to his disciples as his "little ones," and he is pledging to them his own jealous, protective care. He does the same in Luke 17:2, and here, with no children anywhere in the context, the identification is unmistakable. "And he said to his disciples, 'Temptations to sin are sure to come, but woe to the one through whom they come! It would be better for him if a millstone were hung around his neck and he were cast into the sea than that he should cause one of these little ones to sin.'"

So also the "little ones" in Matthew 10:42 become simply "you" in Mark 9:41. And in the next verse Jesus explicitly identifies them as "little ones who believe in me." Warfield establishes his point well—Jesus refers to his disciples, those who helplessly trust in him for salvation, as "his little ones."

Next, Warfield finds some Old Testament precedent for this designation in Isaiah 8:18 (cited in Heb. 2:13) and especially Zechariah 13:7 (cf. Matt. 26:31; Mark 14:31). Here the Messiah refers to his followers as his children and his little ones.

Most to the point, Warfield explores the significance of this terminology. Why does Jesus use this language in reference to his disciples? On one level, as the Isaiah and Zechariah passages inform us, this language is charged with messianic implications. With this language Jesus is reminding his disciples that he is their long-awaited, heaven-sent King, and that they belong to him in that capacity. They are his disciples.

But more to the point, and what Warfield emphasizes at length, is that this designation is simply a *term of endearment.* Jesus's disciples are, first and foremost, just that—his *disciples*—and the Lord Jesus regularly speaks of them as such (Luke 22:11; John 8:31; 13:35; 15:8). As his disciples, they are also his *servants* (Matt. 10:24–25; John 12:26; 13:16). But then they are more than that: they are Jesus's *friends* (John 15:15), and no doubt this designation is a source of encouragement to them. But they are more than friends: they are his *"children"* (Mark 10:24; John 21:5). But then again, they are not just his children: they are to him his *"little children"* (John 13:33), tender and dear. With similar tenderness, they are his *"flock"* (Matt. 26:31; John 10:16) and his *"little flock"* (Luke 12:32). They are his *"sheep"* (Matt. 10:6) and even his *"little sheep"* (John 10:7, 16), indeed, *"his lambs"* (Luke 10:3) and *"his little lambs"* (John 21:15).

All these are simply terms of endearment, Warfield says—Jesus's pet names, if you will, for his disciples. These terms reflect Jesus's heart, how he *feels* toward his disciples. And most tender of all, they are *"his little ones."* They are not merely his friends or his children or even his little children—they are "his little ones." They have, after all, come to him "like little babies," helplessly to receive from him all that they need. And from his own standpoint, the Lord Jesus views them as his own—his own to save, his own to care for, to provide for, and to protect. If you receive them, you receive him. If you do good for them, you do it for him. But if you endanger them, you will come under his jealous wrath. As a loving father who would protect and even avenge his children at any cost, Jesus warns that it would be better for you to have a millstone tied around your neck and be thrown into the sea than to make one of "his little ones" stumble.

What is significant is that this term says almost nothing about Jesus's disciples themselves. Given Jesus's language elsewhere it implies their helpless dependence upon him, but it says nothing else about them. When Jesus refers to his disciples as "his little ones," it tells us, rather, about Jesus and his heart toward his disciples. Simply put, he loves them very fondly, tenderly, and he watches over them accordingly.

But need it say anything more? Surely it is enough to learn here that Jesus thinks of us with tenderness and passion and concern and love. When we hear him say of us that we are "his little ones," we are reminded that the Lord Jesus Christ loves us, and as for his tender little child he cares for us, watching over us with a loving, protective, jealous eye. He is our Savior, and as our Savior he has a fatherly, loving heart toward us. We need, then, never fear that we will perish, because he is very pleased to give the kingdom to his little ones. And we need never fear that he will ever do us anything but good.

Is there really anything else that matters? We need him desperately, and he loves us passionately. What difficulty, then, do we face? What uncertainty? No matter, for we are Christ's little ones.

Further Thoughts

It is important for the shaping of our own perspective that we understand that God sees us as his dear children. In fact, it is important to God himself that we understand this. As we have already seen, it is in order to assure us of this new, privileged, and joyous status as God's children that God has sent us his Spirit to bear witness with our spirit that we are his children (Rom. 8:16). It is not enough for him to *tell* us that we are his children. It is not enough for us to *hear* from Christ that we are his little ones. God has sent us his Spirit to make us *sense* his love shed abroad in our hearts, and thereby to give us assurance of his great love for us. We are God's dear children, and he treats us accordingly, taking every step to assure us of it and to see that we realize his fatherly affection.

This, for Warfield, is the rightful and healthful orientation of the Christian mind and heart. Yes, we are miserable sinners, but we are sinners rescued by divine grace, enjoying daily the deep comfort of "solaced contrition" and "appeased remorse." We have been reconciled to God and made through Christ to enjoy peace with him. We are at the same time sinners and righteous—*righteous* because we are joined to Christ. And because of our union with Christ, God's Son, we are also God's *children*, living under his sovereign and fatherly care. And in another sense we are Christ's little children, in that we have come to him, helplessly dependent upon him, to receive from him every needed grace. God the Father loves us as his children. God the Spirit ministers an awareness of this to our hearts. And God the Son tenderly and passionately cares for us also, out of a heart of deepest loving concern. We are the cherished delight of his great heart.

What more could we want than this? With these truths held firmly in place, we are well positioned to live faithfully and joyfully unto him, are we not? We need never doubt our standing with God, and we need never doubt his good purposes for us. There are countless other blessings and privileges the Christian enjoys, but none better than this. And none more treasured.

CHAPTER II

GOD OVER ALL

Resting in Divine Providence

The Christian life is one of trust. We come to God trusting in his Son to be for us all that God requires of us. We trust him for our salvation. We trust him to accomplish in us all the virtues and graces he has called us to manifest in our lives. We trust him for our eternity. The whole of our salvation lies in his hands, and we gladly trust him for it.

But what of trusting him in our daily lives? Warfield presses this question tellingly.

> Is it true that we can trust the eternal welfare of our souls to God and cannot trust to Him the temporal welfare of our bodies? Is it true that He has provided salvation for us at the tremendous cost of the death of His Son, and will not provide food for us to eat and clothes for us to wear at the cost of the directive word that speaks and it is done? Is it true that we can stand by the bedside of our dying friend and send him forth into eternity in good confidence in God, and cannot send that same friend forth into the world with any confidence that God will keep him there?[1]

Well of course we can. But our question here is *how*. On what ground can we trust God in all the affairs of daily living? There is much that goes into the

---

[1] *FL*, 45–46.

answer to this question. We trust God because of his love, his goodness, his faithfulness, his justice, and so on. But here we look to ultimate concerns: we may trust God because he is the sovereign governor of all things. We trust him, in short, because his providence is over all.

Exposition

The late nineteenth and early twentieth centuries were marked by a distinct optimism. It was a day of dramatic technological progress and epochal scientific and academic advance that bettered life and society in many ways. "Every day in every way we are getting better and better" was the slogan that characterized the era. And within this atmosphere of inevitable progress the relatively new theory of evolution fit very well. Pride in human potential reached an all-time high, which, in turn, raised serious questions concerning traditional Christian understandings. Just how necessary is God, after all? What role does he really play in human affairs? Did he create? And if so, how? Did he inspire the biblical writers? Does he govern all things? Bluntly put, just how much do we need him?

Inevitably this kind of thinking brought the historic doctrine of God's sovereignty into question. Such notions as an all-inclusive divine decree and an all-governing God just did not fit well in an atmosphere charged with such self-confidence. As one historian has said of the time, "Men could not forever bow as wretched sinners on Sunday and swell with self-confidence the other six days of the week."[2] The historic doctrine of God's sovereignty had come on bad times, and out of deep commitment to it Warfield addressed the issue at considerable length. But for him this theological issue was not merely theoretical and detached from life. It was essential to a life of trust.

Warfield often emphasizes that God is neither the god of the deist nor that of the liberal. The deist God is so transcendent that he is far removed from the affairs of this life. He created the world, but he has left it to operate according to its own laws and motions. The liberal God, Warfield charges, is so identified with the created order as to lose the distinction and lapse into virtual pantheism. But Christian theism recognizes that God is both *transcendent*, distinct from and above the created order, and *immanent*, ever present within his creation. He is a conscious, personal Spirit who acts sovereignly and according to purpose. He ordinarily works by means of second (created or "natural") causes, but he remains free always to intrude, whether miraculously or via second causes, to do the extraordinary. He is exalted over his creation, yet always working through

---

[2]Lefferts A. Loetscher, *The Broadening Church* (Philadelphia: University of Pennsylvania Press, 1954), 9.

it to his own purpose and glory. This, in a nutshell, is Warfield's understanding of the biblical revelation of God.

The necessary corollary of this is that God is almighty over all and stands behind all that is, ordering it according to his own eternal, wise, and good purpose. The world's history with all its complexity of events is not the result of accident or chance happenings, nor of blind fate or merely human designs. Everything that exists is but the orderly outworking of the purpose of God. To say "God," Warfield argues, is to say "predestination." God as a personal being acts always to purpose, and that is predestination. This is of the essence of theism, the very basis of prayer, and the whole foundation of order in the universe. In all things God acts with his own purpose in view.

Warfield traces this conception of God throughout the Old Testament, and he does so in a vivid and memorable way. He mentions the vocabulary of predestination, predetermination, decree, providence, God as the "almighty maker" and "irresistible ruler" of all that he has made, and so on. But at length he demonstrates in the biblical narrative itself that this conception of God was pervasive in the minds of his people, and it colored their understanding of all events. In even the most mundane of occurrences, the inspired writers maintain such a vivid sense of dependence upon God that they rarely speak abstractly of the rain or of famines and such: it is rather God who sends the rain, God who sends the famine, God who sends the wind and has his way in it, God who hurls the lightning to strike its intended mark, God who opens the womb, God who gives prosperity or calamity, God who directs the feet of men and even creates the thoughts and intents of the soul—and it is God who opens the heart and God who hardens hearts. Even the seemingly chance happening—the occasional "it happened that" (e.g., Ruth 2:3)—is not conceived as apart from God's direction and provision. Indeed, even the lot was understood to be at his disposal (Josh. 7:16; Prov. 16:33). All of heaven and earth are seen as the instruments of his hands working out his irresistible purpose. Nations, nature, individual experiences, all alike are the disposition of his will.

So pervasive and so specific is this kind of language about God that it might appear at times that God works in all things to the exclusion of second causes. That is not the case, as Warfield explains at length. Men are everywhere recognized as authors of their own actions and are therefore held accountable for those actions. But the language of God working in all things is so pervasive and constant that his use of secondary causes can sometimes be missed. God is at work in and by means of all that is, directing all things to accomplish his all-inclusive and perfect plan. It is evident on the very face of the pages of the Old Testament that this is the world in which the biblical writers lived and thought.

This conscious awareness of God's all-inclusive rule, in turn, prompted in the biblical writers an instinctive sense of absolute dependence upon God. God is God over all, and we are therefore utterly dependent upon him for all things. And this sense of dependence upon the all-governing God, in turn, renders faith—trust—the keynote of piety. We have no hope but in this God, who rules over all things and directs the affairs of the world to his own ends. And this God who rules over all has made gracious promises to his people, promises with which, precisely because he rules over all, nothing could possibly interfere.

Warfield emphasizes further that the New Testament presentation of the doctrine of predestination follows in the same vein. With the additional emphasis on God's fatherhood, God is "the great king" (Matt. 5:35) and "Lord of heaven and earth" (Matt. 11:25) who does all his pleasure. He rules and directs the rain, the flowers of the field, the birds of the air, the falling sparrow, and even the very hairs of our heads. In the minutest details of the course of the world's history God is directing all things toward his appointed goal in the world to come.

Against this larger backdrop the doctrine of election becomes very obvious. It is the God who works "all things" according to his own will who chose to save us (Eph. 1:1–12). Our very salvation itself is due only to a divine, gracious choice. Our salvation, and all of life with it, lies in the hands of our heavenly Father, the God who rules over all things. In several places in his writings Warfield makes the point that throughout the centuries this understanding of God has produced a distinctive piety: a firm understanding that God rules over all, that he has chosen to save us, that he is the source of every blessing, and that because he rules over all, his promises are unchangeably sure. This fosters a keen sense of dependence, trust, and devotion—a deep sense of grateful and worshipful dependence on our all-sovereign God.

Application

The shaping influence these truths are intended to have on our lives is obvious. First, it is basic to our worship to acknowledge that our salvation is due only to God's sovereign initiative. "We have not made the first step in knowledge of the salvation of God until we have learned, and made the very center of our thought of it, this great fact: that it is by the pure grace of God, by that and that alone, that we are saved." This is of the very heart of the gospel, that our salvation is his doing and his choice. We may wonder why God chose to save some and not others. But the truly puzzling question is

> how the holy God could get the consent of his nature to save a single sinner. If we know what sin is, and what holiness is, and what salvation from sin to

holiness is, this is what we shall feel. That is the reason why meditation on our eternal election produces such blessed fruits in our hearts and lives. That God has saved me, even me, sunk in my sin and misery, by the marvels of his grace, can only fill me with adoring praise. . . . This is the foundation of all my comfort, the assurance of all my hope.[3]

Moving forward we continue to acknowledge the same, that God rules over all and that our entire earthly sojourn is the outworking of his gracious plan for us. Christianity is not stoicism or a mere surrender to blind fate. It is a life of faith. It is a life of trust in the God who loves us and out of his all-inclusive providence cares and provides for us. As we become more acquainted with God in his Word, we are increasingly impressed with his all-embracing rule over all things. And with that we are increasingly impressed with the fact that our lives are at his disposal, that this God who has committed himself to us is the one in whose hands lie all the affairs of heaven and earth. Indeed, our comfort comes as we acknowledge that there is no more secure place for us to rest than where we are—at his disposal and in his care.

For Warfield it is of the essence of our religion, a distinct mark of a Christian, not only to acknowledge that God rules over all things but trustingly to *see* and *recognize* him in all things.

A glass window stands before us. We raise our eyes and see the glass; we note its quality, and observe its defects; we speculate on its composition. Or we look straight through it on the great prospect of land and sea and sky beyond. So there are two ways of looking at the world. We may see the world and absorb ourselves in the wonders of nature. That is the scientific way. Or we may look right through the world and see God behind it. That is the religious way.

The scientific way of looking at the world is not wrong any more than the glass-manufacturer's way of looking at the window. This way of looking at things has its very important uses. Nevertheless the window was placed there not to be looked at but to be looked through; and the world has failed of its purpose unless it too is looked through and the eye rests not on it but on its God. Yes, its God; for it is of the essence of the religious view of things that God is seen in all that is and in all that occurs. The universe is his, and in all its movements speaks of him, because it does only his will.[4]

This understanding on our part comes to its highest expression, Warfield goes on to observe, when we are on our knees, when prayerfully and gratefully we respond to the all-sovereign God by bowing before him, acknowledging

---

[3] *SSW*, 1:298.
[4] *SSW*, 1:108.

our dependence upon him, and calling upon him for his help in all the details of our experience and of the world. This is "religion come to its rights."[5]

Warfield also makes the crucial point that a "God" who did not control all things could not be trusted. It would be impossible to trust him. We might believe that he cares, but we could not *trust* him if he were not God over all—something beyond his control might interfere with his purpose for us! But precisely because he is God over all, we may trust him with full confidence and rest peacefully in his wise, loving, and sovereign disposition of all things. This is the ground of our comfort and assurance.

Warfield further addresses the question of providence as it relates to evil and the unpleasant and often dreadful things that happen to God's people. Unless we would dethrone God, we must acknowledge that all things are still at his disposal even though he does work through second causes and the responsibility for sin lies with the sinner who willfully does the evil in question. We cannot say that God did not see these things coming, for that would undo his rule also. And we cannot say that we deserve only the smiling providences. Like those on whom the tower fell (Luke 13:4), we cannot complain, as though God were unjust, when we also become victims of tragedy. We must acknowledge that what God does is always good and right, even if we do not understand how it is so at every given point. If this disappointment or injury did not serve his good and wise purpose, it would not have come. It is not always for us to understand fully what his purpose is in all things. It is ours simply to trust him, to acknowledge in humble dependence that all events are at his disposal, and to assure ourselves that he will neither make a mistake nor do us harm. We trust the God who rules over all, and we do not lean on our own weak understanding.

In this discussion it was important to Warfield to emphasize that providence is not fate, and that the Christian life is marked by trust in a sovereign God, not resignation to blind forces. To illustrate the difference, Warfield often repeated this story about a young Dutch boy, a story found in one of Warfield's published articles but often repeated in the classroom also:

> This little boy's home was on a dyke in Holland, near a great wind-mill, whose long arms swept so close to the ground as to endanger those who carelessly strayed under them. But he was very fond of playing precisely under this mill. His anxious parents had forbidden him to go near it; and, when his stubborn will did not give way, had sought to frighten him away from it by arousing his imagination to the terror of being struck by the arms and carried up into the air to have life beaten out of him by their ceaseless strokes. One day, heedless of their

---

[5] *SSW*, 1:108.

warning, he strayed again under the dangerous arms, and was soon absorbed in his play there—forgetful of everything but his present pleasures. Perhaps, he was half conscious of a breeze springing up; and somewhere in the depth of his soul, he may have been obscurely aware of the danger with which he had been threatened. At any rate, suddenly, as he played, he was violently smitten from behind, and found himself swung all at once, with his head downward, up into the air; and then the blows came, swift and hard! O what a sinking of the heart! O what a horror of great darkness! It had come then! And he was gone! In his terrified writhing, he twisted himself about and looking up, saw not the immeasurable expanse of the brazen heavens above him, but his father's face. At once, he realized, with a great revulsion, that he was not caught in the mill, but was only receiving the threatened punishment of his disobedience. He melted into tears, not of pain, but of relief and joy. In that moment, he understood the difference between falling into the grinding power of a machine and into the loving hands of a father.

"That," Warfield adds, "is the difference between Fate and Predestination. And all the language of men cannot tell the immensity of the difference."[6]

It is here Warfield finds the value of the doctrine of divine sovereignty and our understanding of it. The difficulties that arise from the doctrine of pre-destination arise chiefly from our natural "unwillingness to acknowledge our selves to be wholly at the disposal of another," he reminds us. But he is eager to point out that such unwillingness is misguided and not at all in our own best interests. Do we really not care "whether it be the everlasting arms or merely our own weak arms that we rest on in all our Christian life"? Do we really not care for the confident certainty of knowing that God works all things according to the counsel of his own will? What comfort can be derived from a God, infinitely caring though he may be, who stands impotent over the course of world and life events? Watching from all eternity things that he does not wish to happen, seeing them coming, ever coming, until at last they come, and he is unable to stop them? Would we really prefer chaos to order? To deny God's all-sovereign control over all things is to do away with God altogether and leave us to the uncertain fate of our own making.[7]

So much better this doctrine of the divine decree in which we can rest and which inevitably evokes in us a deep sense of grateful dependence upon God. And so much better this assurance that despite appearances, "there is stretched beneath us the everlasting arm of the almighty Father" working all things together for the good of those whom he has called according to his

---

[6]*SSW*, 1:395–96.
[7]*SSW*, 1:101, 103.

purpose. In this doctrine we have, provided for us, the whole ground of our trust and hope. It establishes "all that gives us a right as individuals to trust in the saving grace of God alone for the inception, continuance, and completion of our salvation" and all that gives us a right to trust in God, the governor of the universe. Commenting on Romans 8:28 he counsels:

> The fundamental thought is the universal government of God. All that comes to you is under His controlling hand. The secondary thought is the favour of God to those that love Him. If He governs all, then nothing but good can befall those to whom He would do good. The consolation lies in the shelter which we may thus find beneath His almighty arms.[8]

That is to say, here in the doctrine of the universal providence of God we learn that "all is well with the world," and in that realization we may rest confidently.

> The world may be black to us; there may no longer be hope in man; anguish and trouble may be our daily portion; but there is this light that shines through all the darkness: "We cannot be robbed of God's providence." So long as the soul keeps firm hold of this great truth it will be able to breast all storms.[9]

Here we learn with grateful adoration that our eternal salvation depends absolutely on "the infinite love and undeserved favor of God." And here we learn that every good thing we enjoy comes to us from the hand of the God who appoints all things according to his own will. And here we come to worship God aright. Contemplation of this doctrine enhances our conception of God and strengthens our fundamental confession, *soli Deo gloria*. A deep realization of this truth drives us to a firm dependence upon divine mercy and to that highest and purest expression of religion—prayer. Here is the very ground of the Christian's confidence and hope. "It is because we cannot be robbed of God's providence that we know, amid whatever encircling gloom, that all things shall work together for good to those that love him."[10]

Here, in a word, is "the solution of all earthly troubles."[11]

---

[8]*SSW*, 1:95; *SW*, 102; *FL*, 204.
[9]*SSW*, 1:111.
[10]*SSW*, 1:110.
[11]*SSW*, 1:111.

PART 4

LIVING RESPONSE

CHAPTER 12

LOOKING TO JESUS

Our Model and Forerunner

Our Christian life begins with looking to Jesus. We come to him helpless and empty, and we look to him to do for us all that God requires of us. This emphasis lies at the center of Warfield's theological understanding and at the center of his own perspective as a Christian also. But for Warfield the significance of Christ most certainly does not end with our conversion—that is just the beginning. And just as passionately he would want us to know that the Christian life continues just as it began—looking to Jesus. His writings everywhere are marked by an "adoring gaze" on our glorious Savior.

One of many examples of this in Warfield's works is provided in his sermon, "The Risen Jesus," taken from the words of 2 Timothy 2:8: "Remember Jesus Christ, raised from the dead, descended from David." Warfield describes the opening verses of 2 Timothy 2 as "a comprehensive exhortation to faithfulness."[1] Here Paul is exhorting Timothy to continue steadfastly in the work of the ministry despite the opposition, false teaching, and all that has been set to his discouragement. The apostle is not discouraged, nor do we sense that he is overly concerned for Timothy in this regard. He has found a source of strength that will more than suffice. And so he writes to Timothy, not so much by way of exhortation but to give encouragement. And

---

[1] *SW*, 191.

this encouragement culminates in this sentence pregnant with implications of Paul's gospel: "Remember Jesus Christ, raised from the dead, descended from David." Here is the citadel of Paul's strength. It is in a continued consideration of the glorified Jesus and his regal lordship that Paul urges Timothy to find courage for continued faithfulness. Jesus Christ, once dead, having died for sin, now risen and ascended as universal Lord—call to mind these things, he says, and our hearts will be strengthened.

This is very typical of Warfield's thinking. His focus is on the glories of Christ. This is his reference point always. His life is stamped by this note of worshipful adoration. And it is here that he urges us, his readers, to find all the incentive, drive, and strength necessary to our continued faithfulness. We must continue our pilgrimage as it began, looking to Jesus.

We saw something of this in chapter 2 also, in Warfield's exposition of the deity and two natures of Christ. Although it was a doctrine under stringent attack, demanding rigorous thinking, precise exegesis, and exact definition, Warfield maintains a worshipful tone throughout. He writes not merely as an academician but as a worshiper, one who adores his great Savior and loves to say so. Yet for Warfield, the value of the Lord Jesus does not end with the forgiveness of sins.

The Human Ideal

Humanity in Adam has fallen into sin, and in all of Adam's race there is but one who "committed no sin, neither was deceit found in his mouth" (1 Pet. 2:22). The Lord Jesus is the exception. True man he is—he became one of us! But sinful man he is not. And thus he stands as the model and pattern of ideal humanity.

Warfield expounds this idea at some length in "The Revelation of Man," a sermon on Hebrews 2:6–9.

It has been testified somewhere,

> "What is man, that you are mindful of him,
>   or the son of man, that you care for him?
> You made him for a little while lower than the angels;
>   you have crowned him with glory and honor,
>   putting everything in subjection under his feet."

Now in putting everything in subjection to him, he left nothing outside his control. At present, we do not yet see everything in subjection to him. But we see him who for a little while was made lower than the angels, namely Jesus, crowned with glory and honor because of the suffering of death, so that by the grace of God he might taste death for everyone.

Warfield points out that in chapter 1 of Hebrews the writer has exhausted language, seeking to exhibit the surpassing dignity of Christ our representative. In contrast with all the great prophets of the Old Testament he is God's *Son*, the Creator and sustainer of all that is, the one whom even the angels of heaven worship, the one who shares in the name of the almighty and eternal God, the Lord over all.

Then in chapter 2, Warfield remarks, the writer exhausts language yet again, now emphasizing the condescension of the Son in his complete identification with mankind. He took our very blood and flesh (2:14) and this, so that by death he might deliver his people from sin and its many entailments. "He shared with us our estate that we might share His merit with Him."[2]

The larger theme of the passage is that of redemption through Christ our representative, and Warfield notes this clearly. But in this sermon Warfield emphasizes also *Christ's perfect identification with man*, and *the consequent revelation of man* that we have in him. Christ is the revelation of God, to be sure, and Warfield emphasizes this at great length elsewhere. But he insists that it is equally true that because the Lord Jesus truly became one of us, he is, then, the revelation of humanity in its ideal perfection. As he summarizes:

> It behooves us to look with wondering eyes upon Him whom to see is to see the Father also, that we may learn to know God. . . . It may also behoove us to look upon Him who is not ashamed to call us brethren, that we may learn to know man—the man that God made in His own image, and whom He would rescue from his sin by the gift of His Son.[3]

Warfield demonstrates that this focus is demanded by the language of Hebrews 2. Here the writer is stressing the dignity of man, and to make his point he cites the words of Psalm 8 where the psalmist glories in the goodness of God in exalting man as king over his creation. God has made man but "a little lower than the angels" and "crowned him with glory and honor" (Ps. 8:5; Heb. 2:7). As God's vice-regent man is created to exercise dominion over all things—God has "put all things under his feet" (Ps. 8:6; Heb. 2:8). Such is the dignity God has given humanity.

---

[2]*SW*, 191.
[3]*PGS*, 6.

Yet there is an obvious problem in all this: "At present, we do not yet see everything in subjection to him" (Heb. 2:8). Man has sinned and fallen from his intended dignity, and he has failed to achieve the dominion for which he was created. And it is at this point that the writer to the Hebrews introduces Jesus as the ideal man: "But we see him who for a little while was made lower than the angels, namely Jesus, crowned with glory and honor because of the suffering of death" (2:9). Here, in the Lord Jesus, we see humanity in its ideal. In him we see "man as man, man in the possession and use of all those faculties, powers, dignities for which he was destined by his Creator." Christ is "the pattern, the ideal, the realization of man." In Jesus we have revealed to us man as he was intended to be.[4]

In "The Human Development of Jesus" Warfield explores this in reference to Jesus's boyhood. Here he examines the implications of Luke's unique characterizations of Jesus in his early life. Luke presents Jesus's human development successively as "infant" (Luke 2:16), "child" (2:40), and "boy" (2:43). The Evangelist also rather formally summarizes Jesus's entire growth and development from childhood to manhood: "And the child grew and became strong, filled with wisdom. And the favor of God was upon him" (2:40). Again, "And Jesus increased in wisdom and in stature and in favor with God and man" (2:52).

While the passage is charged with suggestions that Jesus was an extraordinary child, still this language expresses a normal human development. Luke draws attention to Jesus's physical, intellectual, and even moral or spiritual progress. Daily he grew and became strong, and as he grew in stature he correspondingly increased not only in knowledge but also in skill and the practical use of knowledge—"wisdom" and moral and spiritual insight. God's grace was upon him as he advanced "in favor with God." As he grew he advanced more and more in wisdom, and as the grace of God was given him, he increased also in character such that God looked on him with increasing favor. He was, in turn, a good child, a good boy, a good youth, and a good man; and with each new stage of development there was an accompanying increase in wisdom and in moral and spiritual power. "In a word, Jesus grew as steadily and rapidly in character and in holiness as he grew in wisdom, and as steadily and rapidly in wisdom as he grew in stature."[5] He advanced continually in favor with both men and God.

---

4 *PGS*, 8–9.
5 *SSW*, 1:159.

On one level, this is all very unremarkable. Because Jesus took the same humanity as ours, we would expect his human development to be a normal human development also. He too grew physically, and he too learned and increased in wisdom and understanding. But, Warfield points out, Jesus's development was nonetheless an exceptional development in that his was ideal. As a young child Jesus grew and improved steadily and without interruption. He progressed at equal pace in moral and spiritual character as well as in stature, spiritually as well as physically, in favor with God as well as with men. As he grew physically, he correspondingly grew in moral depth and character—extraordinary human development indeed! Yet it is "normal"—in fact

> the only strictly normal human development, from birth to manhood, the world has ever seen. For this child is the only child who has ever been born into the world without the fatal entail of sin, and the only child that has ever grown into manhood without having his walk and speech marred at every step by the destructive influences of sin and error.

This perfection has significance as far as humanity itself is concerned. "This is how men ought to grow up; how, were men not sinners, men would grow up." It is a great thing, Warfield goes on to explain, that human history has seen one such man, for it serves as an example for us. There has been one man who has reached his creaturely ideal, and this life stands before us "as an incitement and an inspiration." As we observe his perfect human development, we see that the Lord Jesus Christ provides, further, the model "for every age and for every condition of man"—he is the model child, the model youth, and the model man. From him we learn what humanity was meant to be and what humanity ought to be.[6]

What we see in Christ's humanity, specifically, Warfield says, is "perfection." "Christ Jesus has come into the world full of grace and truth; and he confronts us all with the spectacle of his perfect humanity." There was no sin in him. He was without moral blemish or spot. Those who accompanied him testified to his sinlessness, and even his enemies were frustrated by their inability to find fault with him (e.g., Mark 14:55–56; John 8:46). With him there was no confession of sin, no twinge of conscience, not the "slightest hint of inner conflict with sinful impulses." To be sure, such was the excellence of his perfection that we are unable to characterize it adequately. The excellences of the best of men, by contrast, are usually condensed to a most

---

[6]*SSW*, 1:160.

outstanding virtue by which he is specially known. "Thus we speak of the faith of Abraham, the meekness of Moses, the patience of Job, the boldness of Elijah, the love of John." But, by contrast,

> the perfection of Jesus defies such particularizing characterization. All the beauties of character which exhibit themselves singly in the world's saints and heroes, assemble in Him, each in its perfection and all in perfect balance and harmonious combination. If we ask what manner of man He was, we can only respond, No manner of man, but rather, by way of eminence, *the* man, the only perfect man that ever existed on earth, to whom gathered all the perfections proper to man and possible for man, that they might find a fitting home in His heart and that they might play brightly about His person. If you would know what man is, in the height of his divine idea, look at Jesus Christ.[7]

So also Jesus manifests the full range of human emotions, but never in excess and never in any manner that would belie other virtues. His anger, for example, did not inhibit his compassion. Nor did his love keep him from feelings of indignation against evil. And his joy was such that even in his sorrow he did not give way to despair. In every emotion and in every virtue he is the model. "The mark of his individuality was harmonious completeness: of him alone of men, it may be truly said that nothing that is human was alien to him, and that all that is human manifested itself in him in perfect proportion and balance," and whether in pity or grief or joy or even rage, he remained always in control. He teaches us not to eradicate our affections but to sanctify them.[8]

In Jesus we have the perfect embodiment of God's law, himself providing the measure of what humanity was intended to be. What a straight edge is to a carpenter's board, Jesus is to the human soul. He is the standard. In the passion narratives, for example, the shameful character of Pilate, the hypocrisies of the priests, and the fickleness of the mob are all thrown into prominence precisely because they were in the presence of perfection, humanity in its ideal. It is Jesus who shows us what it is we ought to be in contrast to what we are. In his life as it is recorded in the Gospels we see "the ever-growing glory" of his perfect life in contrast to the "ever-increasing horror" of human weakness and sin that he exposes. Next to him all classes of humanity are seen in contrast to what they ought to be. Jesus Christ alone is what man ought to be, and it is therefore "to Him that we are to look if we would see

---

[7]*PGS*, 12–14; *SSW*, 2:691, emphasis original.
[8]*PWC*, 141–43.

man as man, man in the possession and use of all those faculties, powers, dignities for which he was destined by his Creator." He is "the pattern, the ideal, the realization of man. Looking upon Him, we have man revealed to us." In that he was made one of us, "He reveals to us in His own life and conduct what man was intended to be in the plan of God." "When we turn our eyes toward Him, we see in the quality of His humanity God's ideal of man." In a word, Jesus Christ "exhibits to us what man is in the idea of his Maker," and to look on him is to elevate our ideals and raise our expectations.[9]

It is surely good for us, Warfield exclaims, that the world has seen one such man. Too easily we blame human nature for our faults, and too easily we set our expectations too low and settle for too little. Too easily we excuse ourselves from the ideal and even consider it vain to aspire to it. But when we see Jesus, Warfield reminds us, "the scales fall from our eyes." In Jesus we see what God intended for us to be, and what we must seek to become.[10] Certainly it is good for the world to have seen one such man.

In one of his sermons, Warfield summarizes all this in passionate and adoring terms.

> "Christ our Example." After "Christ our Redeemer," no words can more deeply stir the Christian heart than these. Every Christian joyfully recognizes the example of Christ, as, in the admirable words of a great Scotch commentator, a body "of living legislation," as "law, embodied and pictured in a perfect humanity." In Him, in a word, we find the moral ideal historically realized, and we bow before it as sublime and yearn after it with all the assembled desires of our renewed souls.
>
> How lovingly we follow in thought every footstep of the Son of Man, on the rim of hills that shut in the emerald cup of Nazareth, on the blue marge of Gennesaret, over the mountains of Judea, and long to walk in spirit by His side. He came to save every age, says Irenaeus, and therefore He came as an infant, a child, a boy, a youth, and a man. And there is no age that cannot find its example in Him. We see Him, the properest child that ever was given to a mother's arms, through all the years of childhood at Nazareth "subjecting Himself to His parents." We see Him a youth, labouring day by day contentedly at His father's bench, in this lower sphere, too, with no other thought than to be "about His father's business." We see Him in His holy manhood, going, "as His custom was," Sabbath by Sabbath, to the synagogue,—God as He was, not too good to worship with His weaker brethren. And then the horizon broadens. We see Him at the banks of Jordan, because it became Him to fulfil

---

[9] *SSW*, 2:688–92; *PGS*, 9, 11, 12, 15, 16–20.
[10] *PGS*, 15.

every righteousness, meekly receiving the baptism of repentance for us. We see Him in the wilderness, calmly rejecting the subtlest trials of the evil one: refusing to supply His needs by a misuse of His divine power, repelling the confusion of tempting God with trusting God, declining to seek His Father's ends by any other than His Father's means. We see Him among the thousands of Galilee, anointed of God with the Holy Ghost and power, going about doing good: with no pride of birth, though He was a king; with no pride of intellect, though omniscience dwelt within Him; with no pride of power, though all power in heaven and earth was in His hands; or of station, though the fulness of the Godhead dwelt in Him bodily; or of superior goodness or holiness: but in lowliness of mind esteeming every one better than Himself, healing the sick, casting out devils, feeding the hungry, and everywhere breaking to men the bread of life. We see Him everywhere offering to men His life for the salvation of their souls: and when, at last, the forces of evil gathered thick around Him, walking, alike without display and without dismay, the path of suffering appointed for Him, and giving His life at Calvary that through His death the world might live.

"Which of you convinceth Me of sin?" is too low a question. Who can find in all His life a single lack, a single failure to set us a perfect example? In what difficulty of life, in what trial, in what danger or uncertainty, when we turn our eyes to Him, do we fail to find just the example that we need? And if perchance we are, by the grace of God, enabled to walk with Him but a step in the way, how our hearts burn within us with longing to be always with Him,—to be strengthened by the almighty power of God in the inner man, to make every footprint which He has left in the world a stepping-stone to climb upward over His divine path. Do we not rightly say that next to our longing to be in Christ is our corresponding longing to be like Christ; that only second in our hearts to His great act of obedience unto death by which He became our Saviour, stands His holy life in our world of sin, by which He becomes our example?[11]

The Forerunner

But, thankfully, our Lord is more than our example. If he were only our example we would cry in despair and in utter frustration, for an example alone falls short of changing the heart and imparting new life. As an example alone he would show us what we ought to be but what we could never become. But the Son of God came into the world, Warfield reminds us, not to condemn it but to bring rescue. And he is not only our model and ideal—he is our life and our hope. He became all that we are in order to

---

[11] *PGS*, 15.

become our Sin-Bearer, and as perfect man he died in place of sinners and has purchased the sanctifying Spirit for us. By the enablement of his Spirit we are increasingly made like him until finally, when he returns for us, "we shall be like him" (1 John 3:2). In the Lord Jesus we see not only what we ought to be but what we shall be. As our forerunner he has run the race ahead of us and shown us what we shall become by his work for us and in us. "We shall be like him."[12]

Warfield points us to the words "not yet" in Hebrews 2:8. "At present, we do *not yet* see everything in subjection to him." Man is yet to realize his created glory. Jesus is there ahead of us as our forerunner—the earnest and pledge of what we shall also attain. When he passed through sufferings into glory it was "in bringing many sons to glory" with him (Heb. 2:10). He is our forerunner, and in the perfections of his humanity we are intended to see the revelation of what we too shall be when his work in us is complete.

Warfield presses the point to our encouragement. What wonderful assurances these are! Without them Jesus's example could only bring us to despair and condemn us. Surely we must thank God that Jesus is not only our example—he is our life, our hope, and our joy. An example of perfection alone can only show us what we ought to be but could never become, and "hopeless gloom would inevitably settle upon our souls."[13] But we need not look to the future with doubt or dismay. Because the Lord Jesus has come as one of us, and because he has offered himself on our behalf, purchasing our redemption, we have assurance that we will one day be like him.

> Oh, toil-worn pilgrim, weary with your burden, would you know the glory in store for you? Look at Jesus: you shall be like Him. Are you tempted to despair? Do you shrink from an endless future in which you shall remain for ever yourself? Look at Jesus: not as you are, but like what He is, you are to be. If we can but attain to such a hope, heaven bursts at once upon our souls. To be like Jesus! Is this not a glory, in the presence of which all other glories fade away by reason of the glory that is surpassing? When we look at Jesus, we may not—we cannot afford to—forget that we are looking at that which, by the grace of God, we may and shall become. . . . The one perfect man, the one perfect model of life, stands before us in Christ Jesus. And the voice comes to us—not the voice of an angel only, but God's own voice of power—proclaiming, Ye shall be like Him!

---

[12] *PGS*, 22–23.
[13] *PGS*, 22.

Could there be another proclamation of equal encouragement, of equal strengthening? Up, brethren, let us take Him, the perfect One, for our model; let us nurse our longing to be like Him; and let us go forth to the work of life buoyant with the joy of this greatest of hopes, this most precious of assurances—We shall be like Him; what He is, that shall we also become! In the strength of this great hope let us live our life out here below, and in its joyful assurance let us, when our time comes to go, enter eagerly into our glory.[14]

Jesus Christ the Same: Yesterday, Today, and Forever

There is another sense in which Warfield would point us to look to Christ. The Lord Jesus is our model and ideal, he is our forerunner, he displays for us what we *ought* to be and what we *will* be by his redemption—but there is more. It is the Lord Jesus who, providing for us and working in us, will see to it that we will, in fact, succeed in this pursuit of glory.

Hebrews 13:8 makes a statement about our Lord that is so simple and stated so briefly and abruptly that we might pass over it without noticing its intended implications for Christian living: "Jesus Christ is the same yesterday and today and forever." Warfield begins his exposition of this verse observing, simply, that its affirmation is that Jesus is today all he ever was. Yet the inspired writer is not intending to stress merely what Jesus is in himself. His intent is to encourage his readers by reminding them that there is nothing he has been to any past generation that he is not to this generation also, and that there is nothing he has ever been even to the greatest of his saints that he is not to the weakest one of us who believes in him today. He is the same throughout all generations of those who trust him.

The inspired author is encouraging his readers—including us—to maintain a right perspective in service for Christ, difficult and even filled with suffering though that service may be. He has exhorted them to remember those who had taught them and to "imitate their faith" (Heb. 13:7). Their teachers/leaders had served not only as formal instructors but as models of the faith. They had been faithful "examples to the flock" (1 Pet. 5:3). Just as truly as that "great cloud of witnesses" reviewed in Hebrews 11 had by their lives given witness to the trustworthiness of God, so these in their own church had been a model and inspiration to them in Christian living. They too were "heroes" of the faith. And so the writer exhorts his people to imitate their faith.

---

[14]*PGS*, 26.

And it is to encourage them in this pursuit that the writer "suddenly raises their eyes from the servants to the Master. 'Jesus Christ, yesterday and today the same—and forever!'"[15] The point, Warfield tells us, is that if we but repeat the faith of our teachers, we will surely repeat their victory also. We may be sure of this, because "Jesus Christ is the same yesterday and today and forever." This Christian life of service to which we are called may be beset with dangers and difficulties of all kinds, but the outcome is not uncertain. Jesus Christ remains the same, and he is as ready to help us as he has been to the faithful of all generations. He is accessible and as willing and able to provide for us as he has for all his people. The enablement and perseverance and comfort and strength he gave them he will surely give us, for he is the same. We have only to trust him, as others have before us, and we like them will not fail.

So the appeal, Warfield says, is to the faithfulness of Christ. But, he quickly reminds us, it is not merely Christ's faithfulness that is in view. It is surely something deeper. When we speak of a house built on a rock so that the house securely stands in a storm, we do not describe the rock as "faithful." Of course, in one sense the rock *is* faithful. But the point is that because the rock is so *permanent*, the house remains. So also, Warfield points out, Jesus Christ is faithful. But the point here is that he cannot but be faithful because he is *changeless*. The appeal, Warfield urges us to see, is to the *unchangeableness* of Christ.

But Warfield is still not done. The point of this verse is not abstract, merely affirming the immutability of Christ. The point is that he is "*unalterably constant* in his dealings with his people." The writer is appealing to the "immutable steadfastness" of Christ.[16]

Probing still deeper, Warfield says that "immutable steadfastness" is too impersonal, too cold, to capture the atmosphere of the verse. Having come this far we must still "pour more emotion" into these words, he says, in order to relate to them rightly. More than merely "immutable," we should say "unfailing," and rather than "steadfastness," we should say "trustiness." The writer's point of assurance to his readers is that Jesus Christ is "*unfailingly trusty*."[17] We may safely trust in him, for he both can and will be for us all he ever was for his people. Look back to the great saints who have gone before us. They found him trustworthy, and you will find him trustworthy

---

[15] *SSW*, 2:694.
[16] *SSW*, 2:694–95, emphasis added.
[17] *SSW*, 2:695.

also. Indeed, "Jesus Christ is the same yesterday and today and forever." He is the same "trusty" Lord to us he was to them.

So the appeal is to our Lord's "unfailing trustiness." But Warfield wants still to reduce this further. It is, at bottom, an appeal to Christ's *love*—his *changeless* love; no, his *almighty, changeless love*. Warfield insists that we must emphasize all three if we are to understand the force of the affirmation.

> What the writer was telling his readers is that the same Christ was theirs in whom their revered teachers had trusted—the same Christ in the same almighty changeless love; and therefore to trust in him would bring them to the same victory, the contemplation of which in their teachers filled them with mingled awe and rejoicing.[18]

Next Warfield leads us to notice that the inspired writer does not offer this encouragement to those ancient Hebrew Christians only. This encouragement is offered directly to us also. It is specifically worded in such a way that it cannot be confined to any specific time at all. It is expressly universal: "Jesus Christ is the same yesterday and today and forever." If the writer had said, merely, "Jesus Christ is the same yesterday and today," that would have established the point sufficiently for us also; it would be impossible to miss. But just in case someone might misunderstand, and in order to make sure no one will misunderstand, the writer adds, "and forever." It is specifically intended for universal application to all believers of all times. Those first-century readers could read it to their own encouragement, and we may as well.

Then Warfield conjectures further that this verse may have been something of a slogan or motto already known to the church. It is thrown into the passage suddenly and without introduction. It is compact and vivid, complete but without any connectives: "Jesus Christ, yesterday and today the same—and forever!" It is exclamatory in form and gives the appearance of a well-known, crisp, proverbial reminder, something already known and familiar to the readers, an already well-repeated crystallization of their faith.

Perhaps, Warfield wonders, it was a saying they were already accustomed to using for mutual encouragement. We find other such already well-known sayings in the New Testament, such as the "faithful sayings" of the Pastoral Epistles. It is compressed, like the Muslim's "No God but God," and like the Jew's "Jehovah our God, Jehovah One!" But "for depth of emotional appeal," Warfield says, this saying "passes far beyond either." "Jesus Christ, yesterday and today the same—and forever!" "Here vibrates a passionate assertion of

---

[18]*SSW*, 2:695.

the unfailing trustiness of Jesus Christ, the Christian's support and stay, the eternal refuge of his people."[19]

Now if this is the case, Warfield observes, then in claiming this great assurance for ourselves we do not so much apply to our needs words spoken first to Hebrew Christians of two thousand years ago, words intended merely to encourage their faith. Rather, the writer here "applies to their needs words put together first for us and by us—by the general Christian community, for every Christian of that and of every time reminding himself of the Rock on which he builds the house of his life." Warfield continues with application.

> And in that case the words must be taken in their most unlimited meaning, and come to us today, after all these years, as the embodiment of our common Christian assurance. They remind us that Jesus Christ is the strong Son of God who has come into the world to save sinners, and who, through all the world's life, as age passes on into age, abides the same strong Savior—yea, forever. In the midst of the trials of life and its perplexities, its temptations and its failures, its errors and its sins, what we want to know—what we want with all the strength of our hearts to believe—is that Jesus Christ is the same, yesterday, and today, and forever; that we can safely venture on him with our all—whether for this life or for the life to come. It is this assurance that this great Christian battle cry gives us.[20]

Do you ever think that you just cannot make it? That you will surely fail? Are you ever so caught in the grip of a sluggish heart, and does temptation seem so overpowering that you just cannot see how you could ever prove faithful to the end? Our confidence is in this: "Jesus Christ is the same yesterday and today and forever."

---

[19] *SSW*, 2:696.
[20] *SSW*, 2:697.

CHAPTER 13

CHRISTLIKENESS

Imitating the Incarnation

Because Warfield's leading legacy to the church is his massive defense and exposition of the doctrine of inspiration, it is surprising to many to learn that this was not the center of his attention in his theological writings. It was a leading area of attention, to be sure, for it was in many respects the issue of the day. And he devoted well over a thousand published pages to the theme. But his center of attention is found, rather, in the person and work of Christ. First and foremost, Warfield was a christologian.

His day was marked by a convinced anti-supernaturalism. The advance in the sciences and technology had made its impact, leaving Western society with a distinct sense of self-sufficiency and optimism. In such an atmosphere, men began to question what involvement God really had in human affairs. Did God create? Did he supernaturally inspire men to write his Word? And did he really invade humanity? Did he truly become incarnate? Is Jesus really God? And if so, in what sense?

This anti-supernatural atmosphere had made its way into professing Christianity, and now the very person of Jesus Christ was held under question also. And just as he did with the doctrine of inspiration, Warfield stood up to meet the attack and left the church with a massive defense of the historic Christian doctrine of the person of Christ also. Indeed, his writings on the

157

person and work of Christ significantly surpass (in volume at least) his work on the doctrine of inspiration. Both were fundamental issues. But here we reach the heart of the heart of Christianity: the incarnate Savior, the Lord from heaven come to the rescue of his people.

The specific question at issue is whether Jesus was both God and man, as Christians have affirmed from the beginning. And if we speak of him as God incarnate, did he retain his deity in his incarnate state? Or did he in becoming man leave his deity behind him? At stake in this question, for Warfield, was the gospel itself.

Within this context, Philippians 2:5–8 became the subject of endless discussion. Warfield treats the passage in many places in his published works, but perhaps most famously in his sermon "Imitating the Incarnation,"[1] in which he both expounds the doctrine of the incarnation with great theological precision and applies this doctrine to Christian living.

Let us keep the passage firmly in mind as we trace out Warfield's moving exposition.

> Have this mind among yourselves, which is yours in Christ Jesus, who, though he was in the form of God, did not count equality with God a thing to be grasped, but emptied himself, by taking the form of a servant, being born in the likeness of men. And being found in human form, he humbled himself by becoming obedient to the point of death, even death on a cross.

The apostle's intent is to exhort us to Christlikeness. Specifically, he would have us imitate the spirit that animated our Lord in the act of his incarnation. Our model is found in the One who though rich became poor for our sake.

Warfield begins his exposition by noting that the force of the apostle's exhortation stems from a consideration of the deity of Christ and the nature of his condescension. He reminds us somewhat fully—even if in only a few lively, compressed phrases—of who Christ was and the lengths to which he went for our salvation. Only with this fixed in our minds does Paul's exhortation gain its force. His purpose here is ethical, but his exhortation is given weight by a consideration of a rather robust summary of the doctrine of our Lord's person. It is our Lord's example we are called to follow. But just who is this Lord Jesus Christ?

First, Warfield carefully notes that the apostle declares that Jesus is none other than God himself. "Who was before in the form of God" are his words, unmistakably affirming his full deity. He was "in specific character" none

---

[1] SW, 245–70. All quotations in this chapter are from this source.

other than God. The apostle's affirmation is that Jesus "had all those characterizing qualities which make God God, the presence of which constitutes God, and in the absence of which God does not exist. He who is 'in the form of God' is God."

A clear understanding of the deity of Christ is essential to an appreciation of the action he took in his incarnation. "He took the form of a servant by coming into the likeness of men; and being found in fashion as a man, He humbled Himself by becoming subject even unto death, and that the death of the cross."

Warfield emphasizes that the act described here was no transformation of substance. The "form of God" is not said to have been changed into the "form of a servant." Rather, the apostle says simply that this one who was "in the form of God" took also to himself the "form of a servant." Nor was his act a deceptive one, a pretending to be man when he was not. He did not take the appearance of man or the mere state and circumstances of man. He took "the form of a servant." He took to himself, as Warfield describes it, "all those essential qualities and attributes which belong to, and constitute a being 'a servant.'" That is, he became what a servant is. "He took the form of a servant 'by coming into the likeness of men.'"

And so this one who was God took also to himself a real and complete humanity. Remaining God all the while, he assumed humanity also.

Moreover, having taken the form of a servant, as a man, Warfield says, "he became subject to obedience,—an obedience pressed so far in its humiliation that it extended even unto death, and that the shameful death of the cross." How can words adequately convey the depth of such humiliation? God has become man—indeed, a man subject to obedience until death, even the death of the cross. This, Warfield worshipfully reminds us, is what our Lord, "who was by nature in the form of God,—in the full possession and use of all the divine attributes and qualities, powers and prerogatives,—was willing to do for us."

Next, the inspired apostle describes for us the spirit in which our Lord performed this great act. "Although He was in the form of God, He yet did not consider His being on an equality with God a precious prize to be eagerly retained, but made no account of Himself, taking the form of a servant." As Warfield graphically describes it, it was

in a spirit of pure unselfishness and self-sacrifice, that looked not on its own things but on the things of others, that under the force of love esteemed others more than Himself,—it was in this mind: or, in the apostle's own words, it was

159

as not considering His essential equality with God as a precious possession, but making no account of Himself,—it was in this mind, that Christ Jesus who was before in the form of God took the form of a servant.

This was the spirit that animated our Lord in his infinite condescension. He was not forced. Nor did he act for personal gain. Nor out of fear of loss. It was pure, selfless, self-sacrificing love.

At this point Warfield pauses to emphasize that God is not woodenly "impassible" as some have described him. He is not unmoved by considerations outside himself. He is touched by our need, and out of love gave himself for us. Making nothing of himself and surrendering self-interest, he came to our rescue. This is our God, and this self-sacrificing condescension is part of his glory.

This, in turn, is the apostle's point of exhortation, and Warfield expounds it famously.

> A life of self-sacrificing unselfishness is the most divinely beautiful life that man can lead. He whom as our Master we have engaged to obey, whom as our Example we are pledged to imitate, is presented to us here as the great model of self-sacrificing unselfishness. "Let this mind be in you, which was also in Christ Jesus," is the apostle's pleading.

To be Christlike, to imitate our Lord as we ought, we must learn from him the grace of self-abnegation for the sake of others. And yet Warfield is careful to note that what the example of our Lord calls us to is not self-depreciation. It is self-abnegation that he models for us. Humility, yes. Lowliness, yes. But not lowness. If we would follow our Lord, we will "not degrade ourselves but forget ourselves, and seek every man not his own things but those of others." Self-sacrifice for others—this is the model our Lord has left us.

In a world driven by arrogance, self-assertion, self-promotion, and conquest we need reminding of this ideal. The very Son of God "made no account of himself." He did not look upon his equality with God as "a possession to be prized when He could by forgetting self rescue those whom He was not ashamed, amid all His glory, to call His brethren." Surely there is great glory in this condescension. And surely here we find a model of grace that we must strive to imitate.

Are there those whom we are ashamed to call our brother? Are there those we are slow to help because they do not deserve it? Would it be too great a condescension for us? Could we stoop so low? Our Lord's example tells us that we surely can.

Indeed, following our Lord's example, what limits can we possibly set? Is there anything too beneath us if, in doing so, we would help our brothers and sisters? Are we called to give ourselves? What is that when compared with our Lord's condescension—God from the glories of heaven to the shameful cross. Are we called to endure wrongs? Did he not endure more? Must we surrender our rights? Our Lord did not retain his. What possible limits could we set when we see another in need? Our Lord's condescension was infinite.

Warfield carefully emphasizes that this self-abnegation to which we are called is not for its own sake. *Our Lord's* self-abnegation was not for its own sake. It is for the sake of others. "And thus it is not to mere self-denial that Christ calls us, but specifically to self-sacrifice: not to unselfing ourselves, but to unselfishing ourselves." The apostle Paul here makes no virtue of asceticism. He is not calling us to be monks. He is calling us to be like Christ, who, taking no account of himself, served the needs of others. As Warfield expands:

> Self-sacrifice brought Christ into the world. And self-sacrifice will lead us, His followers, not away from but into the midst of men. Wherever men suffer, there will we be to comfort. Wherever men strive, there will we be to help. Wherever men fail, there will be we to uplift. Wherever men succeed, there will we be to rejoice. Self-sacrifice means not indifference to our times and our fellows: it means absorption in them. It means forgetfulness of self in others. It means entering into every man's hopes and fears, longings and despairs: it means manysidedness of spirit, multiform activity, multiplicity of sympathies.

And yet, Warfield reminds us, this life of self-sacrifice we will not find morbid and distasteful. Rather, here we will find the promise true, that he who loses his life shall find it.

> Only, when, like Christ, and in loving obedience to His call and example, we take no account of ourselves, but freely give ourselves to others, we shall find, each in his measure, the saying true of himself also: "Wherefore also God hath highly exalted him." The path of self-sacrifice is the path to glory.

Jesus Christ—the Lord from heaven, has come to our rescue. At great cost to himself he has redeemed us. Ironically, then, in his condescension we find him all the more glorious. God to the rescue—the Lord our help, at a cost that is only his. This is the gospel. And this is the pattern we are called to follow.

CHAPTER 14

THE RELIGIOUS LIFE
Cultivating Practical Piety

Learning and Living

Speaking to the students at Princeton Seminary Warfield labored to emphasize that the religious life was the very most important subject to which they could give attention, and by "religious life" he meant communion with God and the improvement of practical piety. He acknowledged that the purpose of the seminary was for learning, education. He emphasized at length that learning is indispensable to all whose calling is "to teach" (1 Tim. 3:2) and that there is no possibility of Christian ministry, rightly understood, apart from learning. But even so, he insisted that the cultivation of the religious life was of greatest importance—for ministerial students as for every Christian. "Before and above being learned, a minister must be godly."[1] And not ministers only, of course, but for every Christian the cultivation of godliness must be the highest priority.

But Warfield is very careful to discount the false disjunction that is prevalent in much of Christian thinking. Learning is not godliness, to be sure. But *as a means to godliness*, learning plays a major role.

Sometimes we hear it said that ten minutes on your knees will give you a truer, deeper, more operative knowledge of God than ten hours over your books.

---

[1] *SSW*, 1:412.

"What!" is the appropriate response, "than ten hours over your books on your knees?" Why should you turn from God when you turn to your books, or feel that you must turn from your books in order to turn to God? If learning and devotion are as antagonistic as that, then the intellectual life is in itself accursed, and there can be no question of a religious life for a student, even of theology.[2]

There is no "either–or" here, Warfield insists. Godliness comes in large part *by means of* learning—learning God's Word.

Do we wish to grow in grace? It is the knowledge of God's truth that sanctifies the heart. . . . There is no way so potent for awakening a craving for personal holiness or for arousing a love of souls in our hearts, as to fill the mind with a knowledge of God's love to man as revealed in his Holy Book.

Our learning itself, therefore, ought to be both a means to and therefore an exercise of godliness.

Religious knowledge and religious living go hand in hand. "It might be instructive to inquire," writes good Dr. A. Bonar, "why it is that whenever godliness is healthy and progressive we almost invariably find learning in the Church attendant on it: while, on the other hand, an illiterate state is attended sooner or later by decay of vital godliness." We deceive ourselves if we think we can give a portion of our being only to God. If we withhold the effort requisite to learn to know the truth, we cannot hope to succeed in any effort to do his will. Unknown truth cannot sanctify the soul; and it is by the truth that we are to be sanctified.[3]

There doubtless have been men who are great in learning and yet useless in Christian ministry, and such men have lent credibility to the notion that much learning can be detrimental to the religious life. Warfield acknowledges this. But he will not allow learning to be blamed. "There is not a too muchness in the case at all, but a too littleness somewhere else." The problem is "not that their head has received too much attention, but that their heart has received too little."[4] So Warfield counsels that we must be careful not to misunderstand. Certainly, we are deficient until and unless we are learning God's Word. But it does not quite follow that the religious life is all it must be simply because we are learning God's Word. "It is possible to study—even

---

[2]*SSW*, 1:412.
[3]*SSW*, 2:472, 494.
[4]*SSW*, 2:470.

to study theology—in an entirely secular spirit."[5] Every branch of biblical and theological studies has as its end the knowledge of God, but of what value is our study apart from worship? What does it say of a man who studies daily the things of God with a cold and impassive heart? If our learning of Scripture is merely academic and secular and not a specifically religious exercise, we will not only cease to grow—we will harden. Our study and learning of God's Word are indeed a means of godliness. But if it is to be so, it must be an exercise of godliness also, our heart's pursuit of God.

That is to say, as Warfield exhorted his students, there must be both learning and devotion. It is not enough to study the Word of God—we must study it *as* the Word of God, approaching each line of it with utmost reverence.

> Keep in mind whose word it is we are dealing with, even when we are merely analyzing its grammatical expression. And when, done with grammar, we begin to weigh the meaning, O let us remember what meaning it has *to us!* Apply every word to your own souls as you go on, and never rest satisfied until you feel as well as understand.[6]

Corporate Worship

Still there is more. It is not only the pursuit of God in his Word, individually, that is necessary to the cultivation of godliness. Corporate or community life is essential also. Warfield speaks to this point emphatically: "No man can withdraw himself from the stated religious services of the community of which he is a member, without serious injury to his personal religious life."[7] It is surely significant, Warfield says, that the apostolic writer links closely the two exhortations, to "hold fast the confession of our hope without wavering" (Heb. 10:23) and "not neglecting to meet together" (v. 25). When he commands us not to neglect the common meetings, he plainly has in mind the formal, stated meetings of the church community of which his readers were a part. The intention of the inspired writer, Warfield argues, is to urge upon the conscience of his readers their duty both to the church and to themselves. Moreover, the writer adds a kind of lash to his words when he says, "as is the habit of some": "We can see his lip curl as he says it. Who are these people, who are so vastly strong, so supremely holy, that they do not need the assistance of the common worship for themselves;

---

[5]*SSW*, 1:415.
[6]*SSW*, 2:479, emphasis original.
[7]*SSW*, 1:418.

and who, being so strong and holy, will not give their assistance to the common worship?"[8]

Warfield's observation is telling. In the mind of the inspired biblical writer, godliness simply cannot be realistically pursued alone. "Nothing can take the place of this common organic worship of the community as a community, at its stated seasons, and as a regular function of the corporate life of the community."[9]

Warfield belabors this point emphatically. There can be no religious life in isolation. Neither is Warfield content with "going to church," merely.

> You will observe that I am not merely exhorting you "to go to church." "Going to church" is in any case good. But what I am exhorting you to do is go to your own church—to give your presence and active religious participation to every stated meeting for worship of the institution as an institution. Thus you will do your part to give to the institution an organic religious life, and you will draw out from the organic religious life of the institution a support and inspiration for your own personal religious life which you can get nowhere else, and which you cannot afford to miss—if, that is, you have a care to your religious quickening and growth. To be an active member of a living religious body is the condition of healthy religious functioning.[10]

Corporate worship, Warfield insists, is not optional, nor is involvement in the fellowship of the church. It is "the condition" of godliness.

But still Warfield is not done. It is not mere attendance at stated meetings that is necessary. Just as individual study of God's Word must be accompanied by faith and a heart pursuit of God himself in his Word, so also our attendance to the stated meetings of the church. To attend the meetings is one thing. To attend the meetings seeking God is quite another.

Here Warfield addresses himself to those who find the church meetings boring and of little interest. He acknowledges that the church leaders ought to take such comments to heart, but he is not at all willing to leave the blame with them. "No man can fail to meet with God in the sanctuary if he takes God there with him."

> And let me tell you straightout that the preaching you find dull will no more seem dull to you if you faithfully obey the Master's precept: "Take heed how ye hear"; that if you do not find Christ in the [preaching hall] it is because you

---

[8] *SSW*, 1:418.
[9] *SSW*, 1:419.
[10] *SSW*, 1:419.

do not take him there with you. . . . If there is no fire in the pulpit it falls to you to kindle it in the pews. No man can fail to meet with God in the sanctuary if he takes God there with him.[11]

Doubtless Warfield assumes that the church in question is one in which the truths of Scripture are upheld. And he assumes also the responsibility of the minister to learn God's Word and proclaim it faithfully, as we have already noted. But he will not leave the Christian to be spoon-fed forever. We are responsible to attend and hear God's Word eagerly and prayerfully. And Warfield assures us that as we do, we will not fail to find profit for our souls that is found nowhere else.

Finally, to drive his point with greatest force, Warfield points us to the example left for us by our Lord.

Have we not the example of our Lord Jesus Christ? Are we better than he? Surely, if ever there was one who might justly plead that the common worship of the community had nothing to offer him it was the Lord Jesus Christ. But every Sabbath found him seated in his place among the worshiping people, and there was no act of stated worship which he felt himself entitled to discard. Even in his most exalted moods, and after his most elevating experiences, he quietly took his place with the rest of God's people, sharing with them in the common worship of the community. Returning from that great baptismal scene, when the heavens themselves were rent to bear him witness that he was well pleasing to God; from the searching trials of the wilderness, and from that first great tour in Galilee, prosecuted, as we are expressly told, "in the power of the Spirit"; he came back, as the record tells, "to Nazareth, where he had been brought up, and"—so proceeds the amazing narrative—"he entered, as his custom was, into the synagogue, on the Sabbath day." "As his custom was!" Jesus Christ made it his habitual practice to be found in his place on the Sabbath day at the stated place of worship to which he belonged. "It is a reminder," as Sir William Robertson Nicoll well insists, "of the truth which, in our fancied spirituality, we are apt to forget—that the holiest personal life can scarcely afford to dispense with stated forms of devotion, and that the regular public worship of the church, for all its local imperfections and dullness, is a divine provision for sustaining the individual soul." "We cannot afford to be wiser than our Lord in this matter. If anyone could have pled that his spiritual experience was so lofty that it did not require public worship, if any one might have felt that the consecration and communion of his personal life exempted him from what ordinary mortals needed, it was Jesus. But he made no such

[11] *SSW*, 1:420.

plea. Sabbath by Sabbath even he was found in the place of worship, side by side with God's people, not for the mere sake of setting a good example, but for deeper reasons. Is it reasonable, then, that any of us should think we can safely afford to dispense with the pious custom of regular participation with the common worship of our locality?" Is it necessary for me to exhort those who would fain be like Christ, to see to it that they are imitators of him in this?[12]

Prayer

Vitally important as all this is, Warfield contends, it is not enough. The greatest source of "growth in religious power" is found elsewhere.

Not even with the most assiduous use of the corporate expressions of the religious life of the community have you reached the foundation-stone of your piety. That is to be found, of course, in your closets, or rather in your hearts, in your private religious exercises, and in your intimate religious aspirations.[13]

As no one can give you intellectual training except at the cost of your own strenuous effort, so no one can communicate to you spiritual advancement apart from the activities of your own eager souls. True devoutness is a plant that grows best in seclusion and the darkness of the closet; and we cannot reach the springs of our devout life until we penetrate into the sanctuary where the soul meets habitually with God. If association with God's children powerfully quickens our spiritual life, how much more intimate communion with God himself. . . . Above all else that you strive after, cultivate the grace of private prayer.[14]

For Warfield it is in prayer that we come to the very center of the religious life. All the stated means of grace are essential, and we cannot neglect any. But here the soul of man finds immediate communion with God, and for this there simply can be no substitute. "There is no mistake more terrible than to suppose that activity in Christian work can take the place of depth of Christian affections."[15] And so he exhorts his students:

Above all else that you strive after, cultivate the grace of private prayer. It is a grace that is capable of cultivation and that responds kindly to cultivation; as it can be, on the other hand, atrophied by neglect. Be not of those that

---

[12]*SSW*, 1:421–22.
[13]*SSW*, 1:422.
[14]*SSW*, 2:481–82.
[15]*SSW*, 1:424.

neglect it, but in constant prayer be a follower of Paul, or rather of our Lord himself, for, God as he was, our blessed Lord was a man of prayer, and found prayer his ceaseless joy and his constant need. Of course the spirit of prayer is the main thing here, and the habit of "praying without ceasing," of living in a prayerful frame, is above all what is to be striven for. But let us not fall into the grave error of supposing this prayerful habit of mind enough, or that we can safely intermit the custom of setting apart seasons for formal prayer.[16]

Because of the supreme importance and value of prayer, Warfield warns against the lightheartedness and busyness of modern life, characteristics that tend to its neglect.

This is the reason why many good men are shaking their heads a little today over a tendency which they fancy they see increasing among our younger Christian workers to restless activity at the apparent expense of depth of spiritual culture. Activity, of course, is good: surely in the cause of the Lord we should run and not be weary. But not when it is substituted for inner religious strength. We cannot get along without our Marthas. But what shall we do when, through all the length and breadth of the land, we shall search in vain for a Mary? Of course the Marys will be as little admired by the Marthas today as of yore. "Lord," cried Martha, "dost thou not care that my sister hath left me to serve alone?" And from that time to this the cry has continually gone up against the Marys that they waste the precious ointment which might have been given to the poor, when they pour it out to God, and are idle when they sit at the Master's feet. A minister, high in the esteem of the churches, is even quoted as declaring—not confessing, mind you, but publishing abroad as something in which he gloried—that he has long since ceased to pray: he *works*. "Work and pray" is no longer, it seems, to be the motto of at least ministerial life. It is to be all work and no praying; the only prayer that is prevailing, we are told, with the same cynicism with which we are told that God is on the side of the largest battalions—is just work. You will say this is an extreme case. Thank God, it is. But in the tendencies of our modern life, which all make for ceaseless—I had almost said thoughtless, meaningless—activity, have a care that it does not become your case; or that your case—even now—may not have at least some resemblance to it. Do you pray? How much do you pray? How much do you love to pray? What place in your life does the "still hour," alone with God, take?[17]

---

[16]*SSW*, 2:482.
[17]*SSW*, 1:424–25.

Private prayer—the prayerful spirit and regular seasons of prayer—is first and most basic to the cultivation of godliness.

Meditation

Next, Warfield says, is "the habit of reverent meditation on God's truth."[18] As many others have also, Warfield complains that in the contemporary hurried life this practice seems to have become extinct. In our "nervous fussy times," as he calls them, if we must read, we would rather read while running, and we certainly have little time for meditation.

But again, what substitute can there be for this? How else will the truths of God's Word sink deep into our minds and hearts? If we do not think at length on the teachings of Scripture, how will its truths have their intended influence on our lives? If we do not meditate on God's self-revelation, how shall we know him? "Life close to God's Word is life close to God."[19]

Warfield defines meditation as "an exercise which stands somewhere between thought and prayer." It is not mere reasoning, nor must it degenerate into mere daydreaming. "It is reasoning transfigured by devout feeling."[20] It involves not merely analysis but a "brooding dissolving" of truth in the mind and heart. And in order to prevent mere daydreaming, we meditate with our Bible in our hands—perhaps not actually, always, but always with its truths in direct focus. It entails prayer on the one hand and devotional Bible reading on the other.

To strengthen his exhortation Warfield enlists C. H. Spurgeon, quoting from his famous devotional book, *Morning by Morning.*

> We ought to muse upon the things of God, because we thus get the real nutriment out of them. Truth is something like the cluster of the vine: if we would have wine from it, we must bruise it; we must press and squeeze it many times. The bruiser's feet must come down joyfully upon the bunches, or else the juice will not flow; and they must well tread the grapes, or else much of the precious liquid will be wasted. So we must, by meditation, tread the clusters of truth, if we would get the wine of consolation therefrom. Our bodies are not supported by merely taking food into the mouth, but the process which really supplies the muscle, and the nerve, and the sinew, and the bone, is the process of digestion. It is by digestion that the outward food becomes assimilated with the inner life. Our souls are not nourished merely

---

[18]*SSW*, 2:483.
[19]*SSW*, 2:485.
[20]*SSW*, 2:484.

by listening awhile to this, and then to that, and then to the other part of divine truth. Hearing, reading, marking, and learning, all require inwardly digesting to complete their usefulness, and the inward digesting of the truth lies for the most part in meditating upon it. Why is it that some Christians, although they hear many sermons, make but slow advances in the divine life? Because they neglect their closets, and do not thoughtfully meditate on God's Word. They love the wheat, but they do not grind it; they would have the corn, but they will not go forth into the fields to gather it; the fruit hangs upon the tree, but they will not pluck it; the water flows at their feet, but they will not stoop to drink it. From such folly deliver us, O Lord, and be this our resolve this day, "I will meditate in Thy precepts."[21]

Devotional Reading

Warfield emphasizes that there can be no substitute for reading Scripture itself. God inspired one book only, and we must give our prayerful meditation to it directly. But he acknowledges that God's people have produced other helps that are of use and value also, and he urges his students to take advantage of them. He recommends books of devotional reading, commentaries, and books that are intended to help us interpret the Bible ourselves. Spurgeon, Matthew Henry, the Puritans, Archibald Alexander's *Thoughts on Religious Experience*, Charles Hodge's *Way of Life*, J. C. Ryle's *Holiness*, Philip Doddridge's *Rise and Progress of Religion in the Soul*, Thomas à Kempis's *Imitations*, Augustine's *Confessions*, Jonathan Edwards's *Treatise Concerning Religious Affections*, Faber's *Hymns*, *The Olney Hymns*, and Philip Schaff's *Christ in Song*—all these and more receive Warfield's mention. But once again he urges us never to use them as a substitute for our own reading of Scripture.

Warfield gives special recommendation of the reading of Christian biographies, underlining the value of learning from the challenges and faithfulness of those who have gone before us. Here he mentions Augustine's *Confessions* (again), Blaikie's *Life of David Livingstone*, Brown's *Life of Rabbi Duncan*, Bonar's *Memoirs of McCheyne*, J. G. Paton's *Autobiography*, Bunyan's *Grace Abounding*, Edwards's *Life of David Brainerd*, and others. Warfield repeatedly emphasizes that it is by the truth that we are sanctified, but his focus here is on the benefit derived from the understanding and experience of truth in the lives of other believers.

Warfield also recommends the reading of published sermons, hymn books, and the creeds of the church. He mentions the creeds at some length: "First,

---

[21]*SSW*, 2:484.

because it is ever true that it is by the truth that sanctification is wrought. And next, because the truth is set forth in these Creeds with a clearness and richness with which it is set forth nowhere else." And here he specifically recommends Schaff's three-volume *Creeds of Christendom*, especially the second and third volumes, which are "'more directly, richly, and evangelically devotional'—than any other book, apart from the Bible, in existence."[22]

Summary

These are the means of grace that Warfield recommends, and he urges us to be diligent in their use: God's Word, corporate worship, prayer, meditation, and devotional reading. And he reminds us again that "Religious knowledge and religious living go hand in hand. . . . Unknown truth cannot sanctify the soul; and it is by the truth that we are to be sanctified."[23] We cannot strive to be like God unless we first strive to know what he is like. And so we must make the effort to learn and, by this learning, cultivate holiness of heart and life.

---

[22]*SSW*, 2:493.
[23]*SSW*, 2:484.

CHAPTER 15

PRAYER

A Practice of Piety and a Means of Grace

We have seen that Warfield presses the matter of prayer as a means to the cultivation of the religious life, underlining its central importance. But Warfield has more to say about prayer—prayer as a practice, prayer as a means of grace, and incentive to prayer—and here we turn our attention to this more directly.

Prayer as a Practice

Here we will survey Warfield's broader discussion of prayer in which he seeks to provide a general overview of the doctrine of prayer. Taking James 5:16 as his text, he prefers the Revised Version: "The supplication of a righteous man availeth much." This passage, Warfield says, may not quite tell us all we need to know about prayer, but it does present the general doctrine in a most vivid way.

Prayer as Petition

Warfield begins by affirming the value of prayer.

Men ask, What is the use of praying? Above all, What is the use of bringing specific petitions to the throne of the Almighty? "To crave boons you know

173

little of, from a God of whom you know nothing at all, save that you have made him in your own image—of what profit can that be?" That is the language of unbelief.

Much, however, which passes for belief asks practically the same thing in somewhat more chastened forms of speech. This half belief also asks, What is the use of praying? We must have a very low conception of God, it suggests, to suppose that He does not know how to govern His universe without our telling Him. Do we really think He will subordinate His wisdom to the demands of our folly? Cannot we leave the direction of affairs to Him? If He be, indeed, a good and wise God, must we not leave it to Him? Why rush hysterically into His presence and demand that the universe be ruled according to our notions? Are we competent to give Him advice? Do we fancy that we know what is best even for ourselves, as He does not? He cannot hear us unless He be God; He certainly ought not to hearken to us if He be God. If He is "mighty enough to make laws," why should we think Him "weak enough to break them" at our request? Prayer is in effect an attempt to undeify the Deity and substitute our will for His will. It is not only foolish and immoral, therefore, but supremely self-contradictory. We cannot attempt it save on the supposition that it is God whom we are addressing; we would not attempt it if we really believed that He whom we are addressing is God. Of one thing, at least, we may be assured, that it is of no use to pray.[1]

These are the questions to which James speaks, and Warfield draws out the implications of his answer at some length. James does not speak here of prayer generally but of prayer *as petition*. And James seeks to assure his readers that such prayer is of great use and value: "The prayer of a righteous person has great power as it is working." "The one main thing asserted," Warfield notes, "is that a righteous man's prayer is of high value; that it is strong to obtain its end; that it is fully worth offering up."[2]

But James is not content with this answer only, and so he strengthens it with an illustration from the life of Elijah. His purpose here is to encourage his readers to pray for one another in the case of both sickness and soul-sickness. In the case of sickness, he says, call the elders of the church to pray, and James assures us that "the prayer of faith" will heal the sick (James 5:15). Moreover, if this one who is sick has any sin on his conscience, prayer will be effective for that also (v. 16). "And all of you—why, confess your sins to one another—and pray for one another, and the prayer will bring healing. Take everything to God. If you are suffering go in prayer; if you are in joy go

---

[1] *FL*, 428–29.
[2] *FL*, 430.

in praise. But in any and every case, go." The counsel James gives is strong, repeated, and very clear, Warfield continues. "Go continually, go always, to God. Go, go, because prayer is not of no profit; but, on the contrary, the 'prayer of a righteous man profiteth much!'"[3]

It is at this point that James supports his argument with an example from the life of Elijah. Elijah was a man just like us. He prayed, and when he prayed, God gave what he asked. And it was no little request—drought and then rain! But this, James tells us, is the value and usefulness of prayer. God hears our petitions and answers our requests.

Taking encouragement from this passage from James regarding prayer as petition, Warfield backs up to view prayer from its larger perspective also.

The General Idea of Prayer

Warfield describes prayer in its most general sense as, simply, conscious communion with God. It is the "state of mind" that is "consequent on the apprehension of God."[4] But of course it entails much more. It is not petition only. Every Godward expression of the soul is a form of prayer. In 1 Timothy 2:1 the apostle Paul provides a summary description of prayer, four terms that highlight the various purposes in approaching God: "I urge that supplications, prayers, intercessions, and thanksgivings be made for all people." Warfield identifies these as adoration, petition, urgency, and thanksgiving, and he counsels that all of these aspects of prayer ought to characterize our prayer. "When we come before God, we should come with adoration in our hearts and on our lips, with thanksgiving suffusing all our being for His goodness to us, and making known our desires with that earnestness which alone can justify our bringing them to Him."[5]

The Presuppositions of Prayer

Presupposed in prayer, Warfield says briefly by way of reminder, is the existence of God, his personality, his accessibility, and his active involvement in the world. Prayer allows no sense of self-sufficiency. It is our appeal to God, grounded in our conviction "that he exists and that he rewards those who seek him" (Heb. 11:6). Scripture assures us throughout of God's involvement in the world—indeed, his rule over all things—but it does not explain in detail just how he answers prayer. Nor does it explain precisely how in

---

[3]*FL*, 430–31.
[4]*FL*, 431–32.
[5]*FL*, 432.

answer to prayer God may act in miracle or merely in special providence. But it assures us plainly that he hears us and answers the prayers of his people.

The Conditions of Acceptable Prayer

Warfield asserts that there are but two conditions of acceptable prayer, and these two are so closely related that they may be reduced to one. There is an objective condition and a subjective condition. Objectively, we must have access to God. Subjectively, we must have faith. Because it is only in Jesus Christ that we have access to God and because it is only through faith that we are in Christ, these two conditions are one. Those without Christ have no access to God. They may go through the motions of prayer, but they have no access to him. The only prayer that is acceptable to God and that therefore reaches his ears is prayer that is conveyed to him through Jesus Christ. And we have Christ through faith. It is by his work that we have access to God, and it is through faith that we have him.

Warfield emphasizes, then, that in Scripture God promises repeatedly and emphatically that the prayer of faith is effective. The one who prays in faith will be heard and will receive. "Faith can no more fail in prayer than in salvation."[6]

Warfield is aware of the questions raised by his exposition. Will *all* prayer in faith be answered? Yes, Warfield insists, but he directs us to consider what faith is and where it comes from. Faith is as much the gift of God in prayer as in justification. And so, Warfield reasons, if God gives us faith, surely he will not mock us by denying it. Would his Spirit work faith in us with no intention of providing the corresponding blessing? Of course mere man-made faith may fail, for that is not faith at all. But "God-inspired faith, as it is God within you working, so is it sure to find God without you hearkening."[7]

And so Warfield equates this with the teaching of Paul in Romans 8:26–27.

> Likewise the Spirit helps us in our weakness. For we do not know what to pray for as we ought, but the Spirit himself intercedes for us with groanings too deep for words. And he who searches hearts knows what is the mind of the Spirit, because the Spirit intercedes for the saints according to the will of God.

So also in James 5:16 the apostle speaks of an "energized prayer" that is effective. A Spirit-wrought prayer is a Spirit-wrought prayer of faith, and this prayer of faith will be heard.

---

[6] *FL*, 436.
[7] *FL*, 436.

Warfield does not expand at this point, but he is clearly seeking to cut the knot of our question as to why many of our prayers seem to go unheard when God has promised to answer. Not all prayer is the prayer of faith, he says. But God works in us by his Spirit to ask him, in faith, for that which is according to his will. And all such prayer is answered.

Warfield speaks further of "characterizing qualities" of prayer, such as sincerity, reverence, humility, persistence, and submission. These are necessary also to answered prayer, but Warfield will not call them conditions. They are "characterizing qualities, which are always present where faithful prayer is."[8]

The Effects of Prayer

Warfield also summarizes the effects of prayer as both objective and subjective. Most prominently, he says, prayer has an objective effect in that it terminates on God. It is not mere verbiage that bounces back from the ceiling onto our heads. Prayer is not a boomerang, as Warfield graphically states it. Especially in petition but also in adoration, prayer terminates on God. It is directed to and reaches the ear of God.

But prayer also has subjective effects—we receive that which we have requested! And Warfield stresses this at length. But he argues that the sheer joy of communion with God is of greater value to us than any other subjective effect of prayer.

> If we seek to enumerate the benefits obtained by prayer, then, I think we must say that they are, at least, threefold. There are the objective blessings obtained by means of the prayer in the answer to its petitions. There is the blessing that consists in the very act of prayer, that communion with God which is the highest act of the soul. There are the blessings that arise from the assumption in prayer of the proper attitude of the creature, especially of the sinful creature, towards God. Perhaps these last alone can be strictly called purely subjective. The first we may speak of as purely objective. It is the second in which the highest value of prayer is to be found.
>
> We must not undervalue the purely subjective or reflex effects of prayer. They are of the highest benefit to us. Much less must we undervalue the objective effects of prayer. In them lies the specific meaning of that exercise of prayer which we call petition. But the heart of the matter lies in every case in the communion with God which the soul enjoys in prayer. This is prayer itself, and in it is summed up what is most blessed in prayer. If it be man's chief end to glorify God and enjoy Him for ever, then man has attained his end,

---

[8] *FL*, 436–37.

the sole purpose for which he was made, the entire object for which he exists, when he enters into communion with God, abides in His presence, streaming out to Him in all the emotions, I do not say appropriate to a creature in the presence of his Maker and Lord, apprehended by him as the Good Lord and Righteous Ruler of the souls of men, but appropriate to the sinner who has been redeemed by the blood of God's own Son and is inhabited by His Spirit and apprehends his Maker as also his Saviour, his Governor as also his Lover, and knows the supreme joy of him that was lost and is found, was dead and is alive again,—and all, through the glory of God's seeking and saving love. He who attains to this experience has attained all that is to be attained. He is absorbed in the beatific vision. He that sees God shall be like Him.[9]

Prayer as a Means of Grace

In his sermon entitled "Prayer as a Means of Grace" Warfield examines the implications of the Lord's words to Ananias in Acts 9:11: "Rise and go to the street called Straight, and at the house of Judas look for a man of Tarsus named Saul, for behold, he is praying." Warfield finds it noteworthy that what we first read of Saul of Tarsus upon his conversion is that he was praying. The suggestion that prayer is the appropriate and even instinctive expression of the renewed sinner's heart is obvious.

But Warfield passes over this observation with only brief mention in order to investigate instead what this passage has to tell us of prayer *as a means of grace*. Warfield points out that the Lord's words are intended to convince Ananias of Saul's readiness to meet him. This was needed, of course, because of Saul's fearful reputation. And so the Lord does not simply tell Ananias to go meet Saul. He gives him reason to go: "Go," the Lord commands Ananias, "*for* he is praying." Warfield surmises from this that Saul's readiness for the reception of grace is evidenced by his being in prayer, and so from this he draws the broader observation that "the passage thus represents prayer as the state of preparedness for the reception of grace; and, therefore, in the strictest sense as a means of grace."[10]

Warfield's exposition from this point simply explores the ways in which prayer is, in fact, a means of grace. He begins with the simple observation that the attitude taken in prayer is one that necessarily "softens the soul and lays it open to gracious influences." The posture of prayer is a humbling one. To pray is already to break down pride, for it is by its very nature a

---

[9] *FL*, 438–39.
[10] *FL*, 147.

confession of weakness, need, and dependence, and a cry for help. Prayer is "a reaching out for something stronger, better, more stable and trustworthy than ourselves, on which to rest and depend and draw." Such a posture before God cannot but have effect on our character, and "no one can take it habitually without being made, merely by its natural, reflex influence, a different man, in a very profound sense, from what he otherwise would have been." Prayer, by its very nature

> an act of self-abnegation, a throwing of ourselves at the feet of One recognized as higher and greater than we, and as One on whom we depend and in whom we trust, is a most beneficial influence in this hard life of ours. It places the soul in an attitude of less self-assertion and predisposes it to walk simply and humbly in the world.[11]

In prayer, then, we take our place as dependent creatures before the God who rules over all. We acknowledge his rule and his gracious provision, and we make petition accordingly. As Warfield describes it,

> The soul in the attitude of prayer is like the flower turned upwards towards the sky and opening for the reception of the life-giving rain. What is prayer but an adoring appearing before God with a confession of our need and helplessness and a petition for His strength and blessing? What is prayer but a recognition of our dependence and a proclamation that all that we dependent creatures need is found abundantly and to spare in God, who gives to all men liberally and upbraids not? What is prayer but the very adjustment of the heart for the influx of grace?[12]

Prayer, then, Warfield says, is the epitome of a truly Christian attitude and posture before God. He remarks further that as every kind of religious teaching will foster a corresponding kind of religious life and experience, so also that teaching that most clearly recognizes divine sovereignty and grace and calls us to depend wholly on God will be marked—chiefly, at least in its ideal—by this posture of prayer. Do we believe that God is God over all? Do we believe that he is all-loving as well as all-powerful? Do we believe that he is free to exercise his grace at his will? Do we recognize our utter dependence upon him? Insofar as we do, our life will take this posture of prayer.

---

[11]*FL*, 147–48.
[12]*FL*, 149.

That is to say, for us Calvinists the attitude of prayer is the whole attitude of our lives. Certainly this is the true Christian attitude, because it is the attitude of dependence, and trust. But just because this is the attitude of prayer, prayer puts the soul in the attitude for receiving grace and is essentially a means of grace.[13]

Further, Warfield says, prayer is by its very nature a means of grace, "because it is a direct appeal to God for grace." At its very heart prayer is petition for help—that is, a plea for grace. The most appropriate means of receiving help from a superior is, simply, to ask for it, and this is what God has called us to do—ask him for grace out of recognition of our dependence upon him for it. Moreover, prayer is more than petition, to be sure. Prayer is all communication and communion with God, "the meeting of the soul with God, and the holding of converse with Him," conscious communion with him who is the source of all grace. Thus, Warfield concludes, "When the soul is in contact with God, in intercourse with God, in association with Him, it is not only in an attitude to receive grace; it is not only actually seeking grace; it is already receiving and possessing grace."[14]

And so Warfield surmises that it would be impossible to conceive of a praying man—like Saul of Tarsus—destitute of grace. To pray is to draw near to God with our hearts open to receive grace, humbly depending on him for that grace. And the man who thus draws near to God for grace will surely receive it.

Dr. Charles Hodge used to startle us by declaring that no praying soul ever was lost. It seemed to us a hard saying. Our difficulty was that we did not conceive "praying" purely enough. We can, no doubt, go through the motions of prayer and not be saved souls. Our Saviour tells us of those who love to pray on the street corners and in the synagogues, to be seen of men. And He tells us that they have their reward. Their purpose in praying is to be seen of men, and they are seen of men. What can they ask more? But when we really pray—we are actually in enjoyment of communion with God. And is not communion with God salvation? The thing for us to do is to pray without ceasing; once having come into the presence of God, never to leave it; to abide in His presence and to live, steadily, unbrokenly, continuously, in the midst of whatever distractions or trials, with and in Him. God grant such a life to every one of us![15]

---

[13]*FL*, 151.
[14]*FL*, 151–52.
[15]*FL*, 152–53.

Incentive to Prayer

In an article in *The Princeton Review* Warfield finds incentive to pray in Philippians 4:4–7.

> Rejoice in the Lord always; again I will say, Rejoice. Let your reasonableness be known to everyone. The Lord is at hand; do not be anxious about anything, but in everything by prayer and supplication with thanksgiving let your requests be made known to God. And the peace of God, which surpasses all understanding, will guard your hearts and your minds in Christ Jesus.

Warfield's attention here is focused on the brief expression of verse 5, "The Lord is at hand," or, as he translates it, "The Lord is near." The question that Warfield considers is whether this statement should be understood temporally or spatially. Does the apostle mean "the Lord is near" *in time*, or "the Lord is near" *in space*? Very often this is taken in the former sense: that the Lord's *coming* will be soon. In defense of this view, appeal is made to James 5:8, where the apostle exhorts us to "be patient. Establish your hearts, for the coming of the Lord is at hand." But Warfield questions whether this interpretation makes sense of the words James uses. If we mean near in time, we may say an event or action is near, or a person's coming is near (James 5:8). But when we say that a *person* is near, we naturally mean near in terms of space, that he is close by.

Searching for biblical indicators elsewhere, Warfield observes that there is no New Testament example to be found in which this language—a person is near—is to be understood in terms of time. The meaning is consistently that of space. However, the biblical writers do provide somewhat parallel expressions that are surely to be understood in terms of space.

> The LORD is near to the brokenhearted
>   and saves the crushed in spirit. (Ps. 34:18)

> The LORD is near to all who call on him,
>   to all who call on him in truth. (Ps. 145:18)

> They draw near who persecute me with evil purpose;
>   they are far from your law.
> But you are near, O LORD. (Ps. 119:150–51)

In all these, the sense is that God is nearby to protect and provide for his people and that his immediate presence is their encouragement. The parallel with Philippians 4:5 is so close that Warfield wonders whether Paul here is actually citing or at least alluding to these verses. It is certain at least that Paul is acquainted with them, and they may well be the influence behind the apostle's statement. At any rate, Warfield is satisfied that Paul's statement is to be understood in terms of space: "The Lord is nearby."

Which person of the Trinity is specifically in view is impossible to decide with confidence. "Lord" in Paul's writings usually refers to Christ, except when he is quoting Old Testament Scripture, in which case God the Father is often in view. And of course the apostle may even be referring to the triune God himself, although that is not his normal use of "Lord."

In any case, Warfield then proceeds to decide the meaning of the phrase in context. What is the connection with what precedes and follows? The reminder that "the Lord is near" (v. 5b) must be associated either with "Let your reasonableness be known to everyone" (v. 5a) or with "do not be anxious about anything, but in everything by prayer and supplication with thanksgiving let your requests be made known to God" (v. 6). If it is to be taken with verse 5a, then the sense of the reminder, "the Lord is near," would need to be taken as a kind of threat, a warning. This seems hardly likely. And so Warfield takes it in connection with verse 6, in which case "the Lord is near" is intended as an encouragement, a reminder of the Lord's presence to help. Hence, Warfield argues, Paul's reminder of the Lord's presence is an incentive to pray and to roll our cares on him who is with us to help. This is surely Paul's point. The Lord is near to his people to help; therefore, do not be anxious. As Warfield summarizes, "The Lord [God] is near [and can therefore hear and help]. Therefore, in nothing give way to worry, but in everything by prayer and petition let your wants be made known to God."[16] This, in turn, informs verse 7 also: "And the peace of God, which surpasses all understanding, will guard your hearts and your minds in Christ Jesus."

Warfield finds parallel with this verse, then, not in James 5:8 but in Matthew 6:25–34, where our Lord assures us of God's providential care for his children. God is not distant, far removed from his people. He is nearby, with his people always, able and ready to come to their aid.

Here, then, is incentive to prayer. It is indeed a means of grace, and our Lord is never far away.

---

[16]"Exegetical Note on Phil. iv. 5: ὁ κύριος ἐγγύς," *PR* 3 (January 1882): 163.

CHAPTER 16

MATTERS OF THE HEART

Motives, Goals, and Values

We have seen that the Christian life is grounded in the redemptive work of Christ, which issues in a transformation of the believer himself. Initially there is a radical break with sin. We were bound in sin and bound therefore to live for sin. But liberating us from sin's grip, Christ has freed us to live unto God. He has cleansed us and reshaped our affections. Simply, he has put it in our hearts to live for him. It is not rescue from hell alone that he has accomplished for us. He has saved us from sin itself. He has so renovated our being and transformed our appetites that we now find ourselves pursuing a new goal—falteringly, yes, but a new goal and a new ambition nonetheless. Living to please God is now the drive that animates us.

The *Summum Bonum*

Simply stated, what is this new goal? What is it we now live for? Does Scripture provide for us a system of ethics? What is the highest good that we can pursue?

Warfield takes up this question and stresses its vital importance, for this question (and its answer) defines everything about us. It defines virtue, duty, motive, and character, as well as life. If we think wealth is the highest good, then this will be the center around which everything about us will revolve.

And while many do consider wealth the highest good, all human systems of ethics reduce to one common factor: they seek to find the highest good in something human. They may differ vastly in their opinion of what that human factor is—whether individual pleasure, the pleasure of humanity, or whatever. But they are alike in that they define the highest good in human terms. According to them all, we need look no higher than ourselves to find the supreme ideal.

In Scripture, however, God directs us to find the highest good in something vastly superior. "It takes man out of himself, and bids him seek the highest good in the glory, not of his pitiful self, but of his all-glorious God."[1] In lifting our sights above ourselves to our great Savior and Creator, the whole notion of virtue and ideals and ambition is transformed; life itself is made holy and made to be lived on an infinitely higher plane.

"Whether you eat or drink, or whatever you do, do all to the glory of God" (1 Cor. 10:31). Warfield directs us to notice that this summary of the Bible's ethic is not a scientific statement carefully worded for philosophical analysis. It is simply a command. It does not come to us coldly encouraging us to consider, "On the whole, here is the best thing." Rather, it comes to us with an authoritative command: "Do this! Above all else, in all you do, do it to the glory of God."

This "highest good" is reflected in the famous first question of the Westminster Shorter Catechism: "What is the chief end of man?" Answer: "Man's chief end is to glorify God and to enjoy him forever." The catechism begins on the very highest plane. It withdraws our eyes from ourselves and bids us seek our highest blessedness in God. There just cannot be a higher motive, incentive, or goal. All things exist for his glory, and we as redeemed join to direct our lives accordingly.

This command is shaped in such a way that it gathers into itself everything about us. Tomorrow morning you will leave for your business. For what purpose? To make money? Well, of course. But are you in this consciously seeking to glorify God in the obtaining and use of that money? If you are a Christian, Warfield says, you must think of this carefully. "What God commands is—let us face it unflinchingly—that we shall do nothing without taking absolute care to see that we are trying to glorify God in the doing of it."[2] And we must not allow ourselves to think something too small to be governed by this consideration. Even our choice of food and drink,

---

[1] *SSW*, 1:132.
[2] *SSW*, 1:134.

the inspired apostle tells us—indeed, "whatever you do"—must be done to the glory of God.

This is the highest good, the ideal to which God calls us. God has called us to serve him, and he has called us to honor him in every detail of our lives. This, now, is the goal of our life. Our Lord taught us this exactly, that we must desert the world and all our own self-interests and follow him. This was the demand laid down for us at the very outset. "You cannot serve God and money" (Matt. 6:24). "Whoever does not take his cross and follow me is not worthy of me" (Matt. 10:38). And as the apostle John says, "If anyone loves the world, the love of the Father is not in him" (1 John 2:15).

But here we find not only the highest good but our highest joy also. Turning from ourselves to serve the glory of God we do not find ourselves repressed but fulfilled. This highest good is the end for which we were created. "Man's chief end is to glorify God and to enjoy him forever." Our chief end is not to enjoy God without glorifying him, to be sure, "for how can He to whom glory inherently belongs be enjoyed without being glorified?" But just as surely, our chief end is not to glorify God without enjoying him, "for how can He whose glory is His perfections be glorified if He be not also enjoyed?"[3]

Can you see how this serves to elevate everything we do? "Do all to the glory of God."

Warfield often speaks of the Protestant doctrine of vocation, and he speaks of it in this connection also. All that we are called to do is made holy by our doing it to his glory. It used to be under the Mosaic economy that there were holy places, holy things, holy days, holy people, holy activities, and so on. But in this gospel age every believer is a priest, and every activity of life is made holy. Doing "all to the glory of God," every place is made holy, every day is made holy, and every activity of life is made holy. "All" we do is unto him, and in this way every moment of every day is sanctified, and every act becomes an act of worship.

Here is the highest good, the supreme ideal that shapes our appetites and directs our lives. There can be no greater good, and there can be no good reason for living for anything less. "Whatever you do, do all for the glory of God."

For Christ's Sake

Warfield unpacks this theme in the context of Jesus's Sermon on the Mount also. He begins by characterizing Jesus's description of the nature of the king-

---

[3] B. B. Warfield, "The First Question of the Westminster 'Shorter Catechism,'" *PTR* 6, no. 4 (1908): 587.

dom he came to establish. Although Israel had for centuries been taught by Moses's law to look to Christ, and although Jesus's forerunner, preparing his way, called the people to repentance while emphasizing the spiritual nature of the kingdom, still our Lord found the majority of the people cherishing kingdom hopes that were this-worldly only. And so when he spoke to them, he set out to teach them regarding the spiritual nature of his kingdom. His sermon, then, opens not with a call to arms, and not even with a rebuke for their carnal concerns. He rather speaks "gently and winningly, wooing the hearers to the higher ideal" by describing in the most attractively simple language the blessedness of those who are "the true children of his kingdom."[4]

> Blessed are the poor in spirit, for theirs is the kingdom of heaven.
> Blessed are those who mourn, for they shall be comforted.
> Blessed are the meek, for they shall inherit the earth.
> Blessed are those who hunger and thirst for righteousness, for they shall be satisfied.
> Blessed are the merciful, for they shall receive mercy.
> Blessed are the pure in heart, for they shall see God.
> Blessed are the peacemakers, for they shall be called sons of God.
> Blessed are those who are persecuted for righteousness' sake, for theirs is the kingdom of heaven.
> Blessed are you when others revile you and persecute you and utter all kinds of evil against you falsely on my account. (Matt. 5:3–11)

Here we learn what the followers of Christ must be.

> They are not of lofty carriage—but "poor in spirit"; nor are they of gay countenance—they "mourn" rather, and "hunger and thirst" eagerly "after the righteousness" which they lack within themselves; they are "merciful, poor in heart, peacemakers." Surely then, they are well-esteemed among men! Nay, this is another of their characteristics. They are supremely lovable; but men hate them. They are persecuted for their very righteousness' sake.[5]

Warfield focuses on the ninth and final beatitude.

> Blessed are those who are persecuted for righteousness' sake, for theirs is the kingdom of heaven.
> Blessed are you when others revile you and persecute you and utter all kinds of evil against you falsely on my account. Rejoice and be glad, for your

---

[4]*FL*, 32.
[5]*FL*, 34.

reward is great in heaven, for so they persecuted the prophets who were before you. (Matt. 5:10–12)

The persecuted are blessed. They do not go unrewarded. Though reproached and persecuted by men, they have great reward in heaven. And their reward in heaven vastly outweighs the pain and the shame of their persecution on earth. "The more suffering for Christ here, the more glory with Christ there."[6] Hence, though persecuted, they rejoice.

Next Warfield is careful to point out that we are not rewarded for affliction merely. There is no virtue in affliction, itself considered. It is affliction *for Christ's sake* that issues in reward. This phrase, "for Christ's sake," is the key. This alone is what makes it a glory to endure persecution.

And here again is the great defining motive of the Christian life: "for Christ's sake." Scripture knows no higher motive, Warfield reminds us, than this. Here is the spring of all Christian service and endurance. When we endure hardship *for Christ's sake*, we are blessed indeed. This passage tells us, first, that "for Christ's sake" is the highest motive that could be brought to govern our conduct. And second, "for Christ's sake ought and must be our motive in *all* our conduct. In other words it is the grandest and most compelling, and we should make it our universal and continual motive, in all our conduct of life."[7]

Warfield exhorts us, then, to consider the greatness of this motive, "for Christ's sake," and he directs our thinking to three considerations. First, *the greatness of this motive is made evident by the great cost we are called to incur on its account.* Reproaches and persecutions and all kinds of evil all are sweetened by this single consideration: it is for Christ's sake. Scourging, imprisonment (Matt. 10:18), hatred (10:22), slander (Luke 6:22), death itself (Matt. 10:39), even of the most cruel and shameful kind—dreadful as all these are, we hesitate before none of them if it is for Christ's sake. For all the centuries of the church, Christian men and women have met these with praise on their lips, simply because it was done for Christ's sake. And they all testify together that it was this consideration alone that bore them with joy through it all.

Second, Warfield tells us that *the greatness of this motive, "for Christ's sake," is seen in the great promises that are attached to it.* To endure persecution for Christ's sake is to inherit great reward in heaven! "Everyone," our Lord

---

[6] *FL*, 35.
[7] *FL*, 36.

assures us, "who has left houses or brothers or sisters or father or mother or children or lands, for my name's sake, will receive a hundredfold and will inherit eternal life" (Matt. 19:29). We may deny Christ for the applause of men, but it is utter folly to do so—men and their applause will pass away. But if we deny men for Christ's sake, our Lord repays a hundredfold, both in this life and in the life to come. "Whoever finds his life will lose it, and whoever loses his life for my sake will find it" (Matt. 10:39). Indeed, there is no limit to the reward that is promised: "great is your reward in heaven" (Matt. 5:12, NIV). And so we see the greatness of this motive when we measure it by the greatness of the reward given us for living by it. "As high as heaven is above earth, as long as eternity is beyond time, as great as perfection is above lack, as strong as stability is above that which endureth but a moment; so high is the heavenly reward above the earthly suffering and so strong is the motive to act for Christ's sake."[8]

Third, Warfield says, *the greatness of this motive is evident in that God himself acts in keeping with it in his great works of redemption.* "He not only asks us to do for Christ's sake what is hard for us, but He Himself for Christ's sake does what is hard for Him." What could be more difficult, Warfield inquires, than for a just God to pardon sin and receive the sinner into his loving fellowship? Yet this is what God does—for Christ's sake.

> I am writing to you, little children,
> because your sins are forgiven for his name's sake. (1 John 2:12)

All the instrumentalities of grace are set at work in the world, only for Christ's sake. It is for His sake that we are accepted by God, that we have the gift of the Spirit, that we are regenerated, adopted, justified, sanctified, glorified. Nay, even the little things of life are for His sake. It is not only for His sake that we are received by God, but for His sake that we are treated even here and now while yet sinners as God's children, allowed freedom of access to the Throne of Grace, and have all our petitions (little and great alike) heard and answered. "Verily I say unto you," says the Saviour, "whatever ye shall ask in my name, that will I do" (John 14:13).[9]

Finally, Warfield stresses that *the greatness of this motive rests on the greatness of Christ's own work for us.* Just as our Lord stopped at nothing for our sakes, even so we, Warfield exhorts us, must stop at nothing for him. He

---

[8] *FL*, 39.
[9] *FL*, 39–40.

has given himself for us; so also we now gladly give ourselves for him. That is to say:

> Behind the phrase "for thy sake" lurks thus all the motive power of a great love, the fruit of a great gratitude. As we can never repay Him for our redemption, so there is nothing that we can pause at, if done for His sake. Is not this the core of the whole matter? What difference will it make to us what men may judge or what they will do? Need we hesitate because they consider us beside ourselves? If this is lunacy, it is a blessed lunacy! Nay, shall we not rather say with the Apostle of old, "whether we be beside ourselves it is to God. . . . For the love of Christ constraineth us." And why should the love of Christ constrain us? "Because we thus judge, that if one died for all then all died; and He died for all that those that live should no longer live unto themselves, but unto Him who for their sakes died and rose again." Yes, here it is: for our sakes He died and rose again. And because He died for our sakes, we shall live for Him, yea, and if need be, for His sake also die. Is there, can there be asked, a stronger motive than this?[10]

Surely there is no cause so great that this motive should not dominate it, no task so small that this should not govern us in it. We have been bought with a price, and we are called to give ourselves to our Redeemer (1 Cor. 6:20).

"For Christ's sake!" Could we wish to live by anything less?

This-Worldliness and Otherworldliness

Warfield turns to this theme again in his exposition of Matthew 6:33, only here he stresses the value and benefits of pursuing God above all things. "Seek first the kingdom of God and his righteousness, and all these things will be added to you." We will not trace out his exposition in detail, but we should at least sketch his train of thought.

This verse serves as a kind of summary of the whole point of Jesus's Sermon on the Mount. He begins with a description of the children of the kingdom, his people, and highlights that above all else they are otherworldly. They do not live for this world but for another. He then pronounces the law of the kingdom, a law that requires a genuine holiness that manifests itself in all the various dimensions of life. Beginning in Matthew 6:19 our Lord appeals to us to give our attention to heavenly things, the kingdom of God, and in doing so to lay aside our cares for earthly things. This culminates in Matthew 6:33: "But seek first the kingdom of God and his righteousness,

---

[10]*FL*, 40–41.

and all these things will be added to you." This, Warfield says, is the point of the whole sermon. He brushes aside earthly cares and calls us to live for the interests of the kingdom.

Warfield points out further that our Lord does not call us to monkery or a Buddhist-like retirement from normal life. Jesus presupposes that we continue in the normal circumstances of daily living, and it is in this busyness of life that he calls us to seek and serve God's kingdom above all other considerations.

On one level, Warfield notes, this is our Lord's protest against practical atheism. It is entirely possible, of course, to acknowledge fully that God exists and yet live as though he does not exist, or as though he makes no difference. This is not formal or dogmatic atheism, but it is practical atheism. "Formal atheism denies God; practical atheism is guilty of the possibly even more astounding sin of forgetting the God it confesses," Warfield says. "How many men who would not think of saying even in their hearts, There is no God, deny Him practically by ordering their lives as if He were not?"[11] It is against all this that our Lord protests in this verse and in this sermon.

But Warfield is quick to point out that the verse does not take the form of a rebuke. It is an appeal, "an appeal to make God's kingdom and righteousness the prime objects of our life." Moreover, it is an appeal with a promise attached to it. We are to seek first God's kingdom and righteousness, and as we do, our Lord assures us, "we shall more surely secure the earthly things we need."[12] "Seek first the kingdom of God and his righteousness, and all these things"—all the things of daily living that concern us, such as food, shelter, clothing—"will be added to you."

And so our Lord's words serve as a corrective to our priorities. We are to seek otherworldly things first, and we may do so with the assurance that God faithfully cares for his children.

Warfield next spends time stressing how much better it is for us to live for the kingdom in the assurance of God's provision of earthly things than to live in pursuit of those earthly things ourselves. Surely, as we live for God's kingdom we are better off in this world also.

But Warfield notes that all this misses the point. Our Lord is not calling us to live for God's kingdom as a means to obtaining earthly things. He does not say, "Seek first the kingdom of God and his righteousness *because* or *in order that* all these things shall be added to you." The obtaining of "all these

---

[11] *FL*, 44.
[12] *FL*, 46–47.

things" is not given as the reason for pursuing the kingdom first. Indeed, the word "added" is not the word for pay or reward but, as Warfield describes it, "the small gratuitous addition to the promised wages, given as we should say 'in the bargain.'"[13] That is, the worldly goods we may need for this life are described here as something "added" to the real benefit of pursuing the kingdom of God first. And so what our Lord implies is that we are to seek the kingdom of God first for its own sake.

> Herein resides the "lift" of the passage. It places the highest good before us— God and His righteousness—fellowship with God; and pries at our hearts with this great lever of, Who will seek earthly food and drink when they can seek the kingdom of God and His righteousness? In the restitution of the harmony between man and God thus involved, every blessing is included. Here is something worth losing all earthly joys for. Here is something worth the labour of men, the very end of whose being is to glorify God and enjoy Him forever. Would we not purchase it with loss of all earthly—if we can speak of loss in the exchange of the less for the greater? Will we not take this for our seeking when in addition to this great reward, we shall have also "all these things added to us"?[14]

Warfield's point has to do with the value of the kingdom itself considered. As when the laborer sold all he had to obtain the field, and the merchant sold all he had in order to purchase that most exquisite of pearls (Matt. 13:44–45), what is it to give up our pursuit of "all these things" when in pursuit of the kingdom we have fellowship with God?

At the bottom of all this is a sense of the value of the kingdom. We pursue God's kingdom, after all, out of love. But it is a love not for the kingdom, merely. It is a love for God himself that drives us to turn aside from all things and pursue "his kingdom."

And here Warfield follows an alternate reading of the Greek text of Matthew in order to stress his point, a point, he shows, carefully made by our Lord himself. The verse should not read, "Seek first the kingdom of God and his righteousness," but "Seek first his kingdom and his righteousness." The "his," Warfield reminds us, refers to "your heavenly father" (Matt. 6:26, 32). The kingdom in view is not simply "the kingdom of God," abstractly considered. And it is not merely "God's righteousness" we are called to seek. It is precisely *our heavenly father's* kingdom" and "*our heavenly father's*

---

[13]*FL*, 50.
[14]*FL*, 51.

righteousness" we are called to pursue above all else. The appeal is shaped in the tender tones of deepest love.

> Here our Lord is tugging at our hearts. "For your heavenly Father knoweth that ye have need of all these things. But seek ye first His kingdom and His—your heavenly Father's—righteousness; and all these things shall be added unto you." Did we say the passage is a protest? Did we say it is a command? Do we not now see that it is rather a pleading? O, the subtlety of love! Love speaks here to us; will not love respond in us? Under such pleading what can we do but seek first our heavenly Father's kingdom, our heavenly Father's righteousness? And because He is our Father, we are sure both that we shall find it, and with it—how comparatively little it seems now!—whatever else we need, added to us.[15]

Summary

Our Lord has redeemed us from sin and has transformed us from the core of our being outward. The entire nature and direction of our lives have been radically changed. We live now for him. We seek God's glory in all we do. We live, at all costs, for Christ's sake. We seek our heavenly father's kingdom and righteousness above all else. And as we do, we are thrilled with the honor of fellowship with God, knowledge of the King, and all else besides. What a God our God is! No wonder we cannot but love him and live for him.

---

[15]*FL*, 52.

CHAPTER 17

THE GOOD FIGHT, I

Faithfulness to Christ

We have seen repeatedly that Warfield views the Christian life as the outworking of the gospel. This means, in the context of this chapter, that faithfulness in service to Christ is not an optional extra. Nor is it something reserved only for "super saints." Faithfulness in serving Christ is of the essence of Christian salvation itself. We have been saved from sin and unto Christ, and this is not a mere theoretical truth. It *is* the Christian life.

Warfield finds this expressed in Paul's words to Timothy,

The saying is trustworthy, for:

If we have died with him, we will also live with him. (2 Tim. 2:11)

This "faithful saying" was already well known to that early Christian community, evidently often repeated by them. And understandably so: it sounded a note familiar to any who had heard the apostle Paul preach or who had read his letters. It expresses a sentiment that is Pauline to the very core, and reminds us immediately of such passages as Romans 6:8 and 2 Corinthians 5:14–15.

Now if we have died with Christ, we believe that we will also live with him. (Rom. 6:8)

193

> For the love of Christ controls us, because we have concluded this: that one has died for all, therefore all have died; and he died for all, that those who live might no longer live for themselves but for him who for their sake died and was raised. (2 Cor. 5:14–15)

The "dying" that the apostle speaks of here is clearly judicial. Paul is speaking in terms of our union with Christ, Warfield explains. This is the ground of our justification—Christ our substitute, Christ bearing our sin, Christ our stand-in, Christ our surety. Joined to Christ, we died with him so that God's justice is satisfied and we are set free.

But the apostle continues. "Now if we have died with Christ, we believe that we will also live with him." We died with Christ, and consequently, we live. Nor will it do justice to this "faithful saying" to understand this "living" only in terms of final resurrection. The saying makes it clear that it is living for Christ, a faithful endurance to the end, that is in view.

> The saying is trustworthy, for:
>
>> If we have died with him, we will also live with him;
>> if we endure, we will also reign with him;
>> if we deny him, he also will deny us;
>> if we are faithless, he remains faithful—
>
> for he cannot deny himself. (2 Tim. 2:11–13)

Stress is laid here on Christian perseverance. We shall be raised with Christ in the final resurrection, to be sure, but we live with Christ here and now. The power of his resurrection is at work in us already. The Son of God works powerfully in his people, causing them to live for him.

> The pregnancy of the implication is extreme, but it is all involved in the one fact that if we died with Christ, if we are His and share His death on Calvary, we shall live with Him; live with Him in a redeemed life here, cast in another mould from the old life of the flesh, and live with Him hereafter for ever.[1]

Warfield comments on this again in reference to Colossians 3:1–4 (and context). We have died with Christ, and now we have been raised with Christ. To speak in these terms in any meaningful sense, Warfield insists,

---

[1] *FL*, 422–23.

must have implications not in regard to our judicial standing before God only but in regard to Christian experience also.

> If we be Christians at all, we are such only in virtue of the fact that when He died, He died for us, and we, therefore, died as sinners with His death; and that when He rose again for our justification, we rose again into newness of life with Him,—the life that we now live is a new life, from a new spring, even the Spirit of Christ which He as the risen Lord has sent down to us. This is the great fact of participation in the saving work of Christ, with all that it involves. And what we have here is an assertion that such a participation involves seizing of us bodily and lifting us to another and higher plane. We were sinners, and lived as sinners; we lived an earthly life, in the lowest sense of that word. But now we have died with Christ as sinners and can live no more as sinners; we have been raised together with Him and can live only on the plane of this new life, which is not in sin, not "in the earth," but in heaven. In a high and true sense, because we have died to sin and been raised to holiness, we have already passed out of earth to heaven. Heaven is already the sphere of our life; our "citizenship is in heaven"—we are citizens of the Kingdom of Heaven, and have the life appropriate thereto to live.[2]

Warfield stresses this point often. We who are in Christ live for Christ. This in large measure is what salvation is.

Surrender and Consecration

Despite whatever details surrounding the conversion of Saul of Tarsus that may be unique, Warfield emphasizes that in its essentials it is not unique at all. It is simply a model of Christian conversion. When Saul was stricken to the ground on his way to Damascus by the glory of the risen Christ, he had just two questions: "Who are you, Lord?" (Acts 9:5), and "What shall I do, Lord?" (Acts 22:10). In the first question he acknowledged the majesty and lordship of Christ, before whom he now lay prone. And in the second question he quickly and willingly enlisted in his service. This, Warfield says, is just the experience of all who come to Christ.

> No one can call Jesus Lord save by the Holy Ghost; but when the Holy Ghost has moved with power upon the soul, the amazed soul has but two questions to ask: Who art thou, Lord? and What shall I do, Lord? There is no question in its mind as to the legitimacy of the authority claimed, as to its extent and

[2]*FL*, 351–52.

limitations, as to its sphere, as to its sanction. He whose glory has shone into the heart is recognized at once and unquestioningly as Lord, and is so addressed no less in the first question than in the second. Who art thou, Lord? is not a demand for credentials; it is a simple inquiry for information, a cry of wondering adoration and worship. And it is, therefore, followed at once with the cry of, What shall I do, Lord?[3]

Warfield explains further that in the second question are united two elements that are essential to all true religion, namely, *surrender* and *consecration*. Here, he says, are combined both the passive and the active aspects of faith. Here is faith's self-abnegation, the casting of ourselves wholly onto Christ, a firm entrusting of ourselves and our future to Christ, and the placing of ourselves at his disposal. This is the position faith in Christ always takes—and must take, not with absolute purity, for our faith in this life is not absolutely pure, but this is the position taken by faith nonetheless. "What shall I do, Lord?"

An Attending Humility

This position of surrender and consecration is marked by an unmistakable humility. How different is Paul the Christian from Saul the Pharisee! Saul the Pharisee was very certain as to his course of life. He was a man of decision and energy, a man who knew very well what he should do. He was decisive and somewhat self-sufficient, Warfield writes. He was not simply a man of impulse. He was a man of deep religious heart, intent on serving God, and very clear as to how that service should be rendered. Headstrong and opinionated, perhaps he felt himself capable of defining that service to God himself. God had certainly not directed him to persecute the saints. But Paul, a self-directed man, confidently charted his own course.

And so Warfield notes that Saul the Pharisee possessed elements of great character. He was ready to serve God even daringly. What he lacked was humility. This was the change he underwent on the Damascus road, and that change was as immense as it was immediate.

It was a totally new note which vibrated through his being, that found expression in the humble inquiry, "What shall I do, Lord?" It is no longer a question directed to himself: "What shall *I* do?—what shall *I*, in my learning and strength and devotion—what shall *I* do to the glory of God?" It is the final and utter renunciation of self and the subjection of the whole life to the guidance

[3] *FL*, 154.

of another. "What shall I do, *Lord*?" Heretofore Paul had been, even in his service to God, self-led; hereafter he was to be, even in the common affairs of life, down to his eating and drinking, God-led.

This, Warfield stresses, is "the characteristic change" that makes a man a Christian. In Christ we are no longer self-led but Spirit-led (Rom. 8:14). "And as the Christian more and more perfectly assumes the attitude of a constant and unreserved 'What shall I do, Lord?', he more and more perfectly enters into his Christian heritage, and lives out his Christian life—the very keynote of which is thus easily seen to be humility."[4]

An Attending Dignity

There is more than humility in consecration to Christ, however. There is dignity also. When Paul surrendered to Christ, he did not step down. It was a step up. Warfield counsels that there is within us all the feeling that our dignity consists in our self-government, self-sufficiency, and self-dependence. There is a place for all this, to be sure, and Warfield encourages the virtue of industry. Being self-motivated or a "self-starter" is a good thing in its own place. This is a good gift of God. But there is a place for authority also, and "as liberty must not be allowed to lapse into licence, so independence must not be permitted to degenerate into self-assertion."[5]

The dignity of surrender and consecration is found only in the object of our submission. "He who hitches his chariot to a star is not thereby sinking to a lower status," Warfield quips. And the man who is consecrated to Christ, led by his Spirit, is surely the man of highest dignity. Again he quotes his favorite lines from Rudyard Kipling.

> The 'eathen in 'is blindness bows down to wood an' stone;
> 'E don't obey no orders unless they is 'is own.

The Christian is a man under orders. We are not as the heathen or the hoodlum, devising our own way. We are under orders from the great King himself.

> And what is the characteristic of the Christian man but just this: that he has found his Captain and receives his orders from Him? "What shall I do, Lord?"— that is the note of his life. And is it not clear that it is the source of an added dignity and worth to his life? Just as the soldier is nothing but the hoodlum

---

[4]*FL*, 157–58.
[5]*FL*, 159.

licked into shape by coming under orders—under the establishing and form-ing influence of legitimate and wise authority—so the Christian is nothing but the sinner, come under the formative influence of the Captain of us all.[6]

An Attending Power

Still there is more to this that Warfield would have us see. There is in sur-render and consecration to Christ an attending power also. In setting out to serve Christ we do so as people "under orders" and as members of his body—part of a great army of soldiers enlisted in Christ's service and with strength and armor supplied by the Lord himself.

Summary

Here then is Warfield's snapshot of Christian faithfulness. Faithfulness to Christ is an entailment of saving faith. We have surrendered to him and consecrated our lives wholly to him. Coming to Christ we have found a new reason for being, a new defining note for life. And as we give ourselves to Christ and his cause, we do so both with a sense of the honor that is ours in serving him and with an assurance that he will supply for us all that is needed to serve him aright, keeping us faithful until he comes.

Faithfulness to the Truth

Heresy and Concession

As we have already seen, the foundational and controlling thought in War-field's doctrine of Scripture is that it is the very word of God. It was given by God through human agency, but it is God's word nonetheless. This, in turn, settles all questions regarding Scripture's authority, truthfulness, iner-rancy, and so on. As God's word it comes to us with supreme authority, and because it is his word, we may trust it at every point and rely on its direction for both faith and practice.

One aspect of Christian faithfulness, then, is continued adherence to Scrip-ture in all it teaches. Warfield makes much of this. By very definition the Christian believes the Bible to be true, for it is God himself speaking. We are happy to learn truth from any source, and precisely because God is the God of truth, we never fear the advancement of genuine knowledge in any field of study. All truth is God's truth, and we are certain that all truth will lead back to him. But there is no source of knowledge that for us holds authority

---

[6]*FL*, 161.

above that of the written Word of God. "It is a mark of the Christian man that the Word is his source and norm of truth, and wherever it has spoken he asks no further evidence, nor can he admit any modification whatever of its deliverances, no matter from what quarter they may be drawn." Very simply, we read in the Bible what God has spoken, and so when we read it, we do not question its truthfulness. The very condition of orthodoxy, Warfield insists, is that we look out upon the world's thinking "from the safe standpoint of the sure Word of God."[7] We may be sure that here, in God's written Word, is truth.

The world is very confident in its own thinking, independent of God, Warfield remarks, and it dignifies its conclusions with such impressive names as "philosophy," "science," "learning," "scholarship," or "consensus of scholarship." And of course the world never offers its findings to the Christian for testing. With supreme confidence it simply thrusts its conclusions on us with the expectation that we accept them as final. But Warfield warns that it is the very essence of heresy that it takes its starting point outside Scripture. The Christian, by contrast, because he is Christian, takes his starting point in the safety of the sure Word of God.

> In the sphere of science, philosophy, and criticism alike, it is the conjectural explanations of phenomena which are put forward as the principles of knowledge. It is as depending on these that men proclaim science, philosophy, and criticism as the norm of truth. We are "orthodox" when we account God's declaration in his Word superior in point of authority to them, their interpreter, and its corrector. By this test we may each of us try our inmost thought and see where we stand—on God's side or on the world's.[8]

In John 10:35 Jesus declared his conviction that "Scripture cannot be broken." His view was that it could never fail at any point. And Warfield loves to argue from this that if Jesus accepted God's Word as true, then we who call ourselves his followers must also. We cannot have the Jesus of the Bible and at the same time reject the Bible of Jesus. Simply put, trusting God's Word and unhesitatingly accepting it as true is a necessary expression of faithfulness to our Lord.

Faithfulness in Proclaiming the Truth

For Warfield, faithfulness to the truth demands more than quiet faith. It demands that we proclaim that truth to others also, even if in the face of

---

[7] *SSW*, 2:674–75.
[8] *SSW*, 2:679.

unbelief. One place Warfield treats this theme is in connection with his exposition of 1 Timothy 6:20–21: "O Timothy, guard the deposit entrusted to you. Avoid the irreverent babble and contradictions of what is falsely called 'knowledge,' for by professing it some have swerved from the faith." Here the apostle Paul as he comes to the conclusion of his letter to Timothy intends to sum up his counsel regarding his pastoral ministry. He has counseled Timothy regarding many specific issues related to Christian ministry, provided instruction, and encouraged him to fulfill his responsibilities as a minister of Christ. And concluding it all he says, "Hear the sum of the whole matter, Be faithful to the Gospel committed to you and shun all the pretentious show of superior learning which is proving a snare to many."[9] The assault of the world against the truth of Scripture is nothing new. Its bold presumption of truth is not new. All this was in Paul's day also, and because of it many had strayed from the faith. And so the apostle urges Timothy to guard the truth of God that has been entrusted to him in order that he also can faithfully pass it on to others. As Warfield describes the responsibility, expanding the translation of the verse, it is "'to keep the deposit inviolate' and to shun the worldly inanities and contradictions of falsely so-called knowledge, by making profession of which so many in every age, and in our age too, have gone astray with respect to faith."[10]

The word that Warfield translates "the deposit" he finds elsewhere in the Pastoral Epistles as a kind of technical term. The Authorized Version expands it further as "that which is committed to thy trust." It is not a word that occurs often, but it is used frequently enough, Warfield observes, for us to see that it was a common designation for the gospel, that body of truth revealed to us by Christ and his apostles and entrusted to the care of the church. It is related to the term *witness*. The gospel is a "deposit," and the duty of the church and its ministers is to bear witness to it. The two ideas are obviously related.

Warfield explains that this is given in order to define the responsibility of the Christian minister. He is to bear witness to the truth deposited into his care. He is not to produce or invent anything. He is not to come up with anything new. He is not an originator. He is not the author of the message he is given to proclaim. He is just to bear witness to it, to transmit it faithfully. It is not his own message but a message committed to his trust, deposited to his care. It is not a matter of human genius but simply a matter of instruc-

---

[9] *FL*, 385.
[10] *FL*, 385.

tion. Divine truth has been entrusted to him, and he is obliged faithfully to pass it along to others. Independent speculation is exactly the opposite of the minister's responsibility. "O Timothy, keep the deposit inviolate!"

Keeping the deposit is accomplished precisely by "avoid[ing] irreverent babble and contradictions of what is falsely called 'knowledge.'" Any proposition that contradicts the Scripture entrusted to us is not real knowledge but falsely so called.

> Any speculation, any philosophizing, any form of learning, any scientific theorizing which sought to intrude itself, in the way of modifying it in the least respect, upon the Gospel of Christ,—which is a sacred deposit committed to its ministers not to dilute or to alter or to modify, but to learn, hold, guard and preach,—would be characterized by Paul without hesitation as among the profane inanities and contradictions of knowledge falsely so called.[11]

Warfield clarifies that the apostle Paul is not condemning knowledge as such. Nor is he condemning new knowledge. But if that so-called knowledge presumes to contradict or demand any alteration of that which has been entrusted to us, we may be sure that it is shown by that very fact to be mistaken.

> A practical lesson imposes itself upon us. Preach a full-orbed, a complete Gospel. The deposit is not yours to deal with as you will; it is another's entrusted to your care. The deposit is not your product to be treated as you will; it is the creation of another placed in your keeping. You are but its witnesses. Bear your witness truly and bear it fully. Keep the deposit inviolate.[12]

Warfield also treats this theme in connection with his exposition of 2 Corinthians 4:13, which he entitles "The Spirit of Faith." The apostle Paul writes, "Since we have the same spirit of faith according to what has been written, 'I believed, and so I spoke,' we also believe, and so we also speak." Here is the ground of Paul's courage and faithfulness in preaching the gospel. He tells us in the previous verses something of the trying circumstances of his ministry and the persecution he endured for Christ's sake. Everywhere he went, his gospel was met with disbelief and opposition, and often the opposition was extreme. Still he continued undaunted. He remained faithful in the proclamation of the gospel at all costs, and by his labors men and women came to Christ and were saved.

---

[11] *FL*, 388.
[12] *FL*, 392.

Paul sees in this, Warfield explains, a kind of reenactment of Christ's saving work. Just as our Lord died and by his death secured life for the world, so in the apostle's suffering and faithfulness and gospel success we see again life coming by means of death. This is the power of God at work both in the "earthen vessel" or "jars of clay" (v. 7) and in those who believe.

For his part, Paul says, his faithfulness stems from his firm conviction that God is powerfully at work through the gospel: "Since we have the same spirit of faith according to what has been written, 'I believed, and so I spoke,' we also believe, and so we also speak, knowing that he who raised the Lord Jesus will raise us also with Jesus and bring us with you into his presence" (vv. 13–14). Here, Warfield says, is the source of the apostle's strength: he believed in the gospel he preached. With less a faith he would long ago have fallen beneath the physical and emotional stress his service to Christ had brought upon him. With less a faith he would have become silent. But he believed, and therefore he spoke. He believed that God works to the salvation of the lost through this message, bringing men to faith. And believing this, Paul said, he continued preaching even in the face of determined opposition.

Warfield then presses this point at some length. Do we believe that God works powerfully through the gospel to bring men and women to faith in Christ? Of course we do—this is what explains our own conversion! And if we do believe this, then how can we not speak? How can we not bear continued witness for Christ?

When we really believe the Gospel of the Grace of God—when we really believe that it is the power of God unto salvation, the only power of salvation in this wicked world of ours—it is a comparatively easy thing to preach it, to preach it in its purity, to preach it in the face of a scoffing, nay, of a truculent and murdering world. Here is the secret. . . . Believe this Gospel, and you can and will preach it. Let men say what they will, and do what they will,—let them injure, ridicule, persecute, slay,—believe this Gospel and you will preach it.

Men often say of some element of the Gospel: "I can't preach that." Sometimes they mean that the world will not receive this or that. Sometimes they mean that the world will not endure this or that. Sometimes they mean that they cannot so preach this or that as to win the respect or the sympathy or the acceptance of the world. The Gospel cannot be preached? Cannot be preached? It can be preached if you will believe it. Here is the root of all your difficulties. You do not fully believe this Gospel! Believe it! Believe it! and then it will preach itself! God has not sent us into the world to say the most plausible things we can think of; to teach men what they already believe. He has sent us to preach unpalatable truths to a world lying in wickedness; apparently absurd truths to men, proud of their intellects; mysterious truths to men who are carnal and cannot receive the things of the Spirit of God. Shall we despair? Certainly, if it is left to us not only to plant and to water but also to give the increase. Certainly not, if we appeal to and depend upon the Spirit of faith. Let Him but move on our hearts and we will believe these truths; and, even as it is written, I believed and therefore have I spoken, we also will believe and therefore speak. Let Him but move on the hearts of our hearers and they too will believe what He has led us to speak. We cannot proclaim to the world that the house is afire—it is a disagreeable thing to say, scarcely to be risked in the presence of those whose interest it is not to believe it? But believe it, and how quickly you rush forth to shout the unpalatable truth! So believe it and we shall assert to the world that it is lost in its sin, and rushing down to an eternal doom; that in Christ alone is there redemption; and through the Spirit alone can men receive this redemption. What care we if it be unpalatable, if it be true? For if it be true, it is urgent.[13]

Our Faithfulness and His

We began this chapter glancing at Warfield's comments on 2 Timothy 2:11–13, and we highlighted his emphasis that we who are in Christ characteristically live for him. But there is more to Warfield's exposition of this passage that we should see before we move on. Again,

The saying is trustworthy, for:

If we have died with him, we will also live with him;
if we endure, we will also reign with him;
if we deny him, he also will deny us;
if we are faithless, he remains faithful—

for he cannot deny himself.

The apostle's intention here, very obviously, is to give warning and encouragement. The point is that the Christian must remain faithful. The warning is severe—the most severe imaginable. Yet Warfield sorts through the details of the passage to demonstrate that the encouragement stands more prominently in the thought of the passage.

The saying consists of four conditional ("if") clauses, which stand in a certain parallel relation. The first clause tells us that sharing in Christ's death entails sharing in his life, as we have seen. "If we have died with him, we

---

[13] *FL*, 241–42.

will also live with him." This is the inevitable experience of every Christian. Having died with him we now shall live in and through him. The appeal is to our union with Christ and its abiding effects.

The second and third clauses present a contrast of possibilities. "If we endure, we will also reign with him; if we deny him, he also will deny us." In the first of these the thought is that of Romans 8:16–17, where the apostle declares that if we are God's children, then we are heirs, joint heirs with Christ, "provided we suffer with him in order that we may also be glorified with him." The general thought is that if we abide in Christ, we will inherit the kingdom with him.

The next clause presents the opposite possibility and its dreadful consequence: "If we deny him, he also will deny us." This recalls the solemn words of our Lord in Matthew 10:33: "Whoever denies me before men, I also will deny before my Father who is in heaven."

Thus in the first three clauses, Warfield says, "a fitting pause is reached." We have covered all possibilities and reached a kind of climax, solemn as it is. Warfield summarizes:

> "If we died with Him we shall also live with him; if we steadfastly endure we shall also reign with him; but if we shall ever, by any possibility, deny Him, He, too, will deny—us!" The thought is complete with this. Both alternatives are developed. And the effect of the whole is a powerful incentive to abide in Christ. Patient endurance—nay, bold, steadfast, brave endurance—has its reward—reigning with Christ. But if we fall from this and disown Christ, do we not remember His dreadful threat: "He, too, can and will disown—even us!"[14]

So it would seem, Warfield observes, that we have said all there is to say. The appeal is to faithful endurance with Christ, and to further this appeal the apostle offers both a note of hope for those who are faithful to the end and a note of warning for those who are not. Surely there is nothing needed to add to this.

But the apostle is not done. There is a closing word of encouragement yet to be given, one especially needed for the weak and faltering Christian. What if we are to fall? Is there hope for us? In light of such a severe warning, and knowing as we do the failures of our own hearts, how can we possibly expect to persevere to the end? Is there hope for the lapsed Christian? The fourth clause is given to just this question: "If we are faithless, he remains

---

[14]*FL*, 425.

faithful—for he cannot deny himself." We may prove faithless at times, but not our Lord. He cannot deny himself.

> If this be the construction, the whole closes on a note of hope. The note of warning throbs through even the note of hope, it is true, for He who cannot deny Himself must remember His threats also; and no Christian holding this wonderful "faithful saying" in his heart will fail to note this. But the note of hope is the dominant one, and I take it this last clause is designed to call back the soul from the contemplation of the dreadfulness of denying Christ and throw it in trust and hope back upon Jesus Christ, the faithful One, who despite our unfaithfulness, will never deny Himself—will never disown Himself,—but will ever look on His own cross and righteousness and all the bitter dole He has suffered, and will not let anything snatch what He has purchased to Himself out of His hands.
>
> In this view of the matter, then, the arrangement of the clauses is not in a straightforward quartet—two by two—but rather this:

> If we died with Him we shall also live with Him;
>   If we endure we shall also reign with Him;
>   If we shall deny, He too will deny us.
> If we are faithless, He abideth faithful, for Himself He cannot deny.[15]

And so Warfield closes with a theme eagerly repeated and emphasized all through his works: God gives us in Christ all that he requires of us. Faithfulness is the mark of the Christian. We have died with Christ, and now we live for him. And we *must* live for him. Thankfully, however, the Lord Jesus is more faithful than we are. He is "the same yesterday and today and forever" (Heb. 13:8), and we may be sure that despite our lapses he will not cast us off. He will keep us to the end for which he has saved us.

Here is not only comfort and encouragement, but also incentive inflaming our hearts to persevering, loving, and thankful service.

---

[15] *FL*, 427.

CHAPTER 18

THE GOOD FIGHT, 2

In Pursuit of Perfection

Remarks taken from the introduction to Warfield's sermon "Entire Sanctification" will serve well to frame the theme of this chapter.

There is no feature of Christianity more strongly emphasized by those to whom its establishment in the world was committed, than the breadth and depth of its ethical demands. The "salvation" which was promised in the "Gospel" or "Glad Tidings" which constituted its proclamation, was just salvation from sin and unto holiness. In other words, it was a moral revolution of the most thoroughgoing and radical kind. "Sanctification" is the Biblical word for this moral revolution, and in "sanctification" the very essence of salvation is made to consist. "This is the will of God" for you, says the Apostle to his readers in this very epistle, "even your sanctification." A great part of the epistle [1 Thessalonians] is given, accordingly, to commending the new converts for the progress they had already made in this sanctification, and to urging them onward in the same pathway. No moral attainment is too great to be pressed on them as their duty, no moral duty is too minute to be demanded of them as essential to their Christian walk. The standard the Apostle has before him, and consistently applies to his readers, falls in nothing short of absolute perfection, a perfection which embraces in its all-inclusive sweep the infinitely little and the infinitely great alike.[1]

---

[1] *FL*, 361–62.

When we speak of faithfulness to Christ, practical godliness, the Christian race, the fight of faith, or "the Christian life" generally, this is ultimately what we have in view. We seek nothing less than likeness to the Lord Jesus Christ—complete moral and spiritual perfection.

Working Out Salvation

Although the apostle Paul was unceasingly insistent that salvation is "not of works" (Eph. 2:8–9, KJV), he was equally insistent that salvation is *unto* good works (v. 10). Warfield remarks that in large measure it is in good works that our salvation is realized. Not only does salvation entail holiness of life, but holiness of life is of the very essence of salvation. Our good works are rooted in the saving work of Christ, and it is only on the ground of Christ's saving work that we can hope to achieve practical godliness. It is to good works that God has destined us, and it is for good works he has prepared us in Christ (Eph. 2:10; cf. Rom. 6:2; 2 Cor. 5:14; Phil. 1:21; 2:12–13; Col. 1:10; 1 Thess. 2:12; 2 Thess. 2:13–15; 2 Tim. 2:19).

Warfield finds perhaps the most precise expression of all this in the words of the apostle Paul to the church at Philippi. "Therefore, my beloved, as you have always obeyed, so now, not only as in my presence but much more in my absence, work out your own salvation with fear and trembling, for it is God who works in you, both to will and to work for his good pleasure" (Phil. 2:12–13). "Here the saint is exhorted to 'work out his own salvation,'" Warfield comments, "just because 'it is God who is the worker in him of both the willing and the doing, in pursuance of His good pleasure.'"[2]

Warfield notes that this command is addressed not to sinners but to saints (cf. Phil. 1:1) and that it has to do not with entrance to the Christian life but with the pursuit of the goal of the Christian life already entered. It concerns the life that is "worthy of the gospel of Christ" (1:27). The apostle is not here calling us to work *in* our salvation—everywhere Paul insists that this is God's doing alone. He is calling us to "work *out*" our salvation, to bring our salvation to its completion and see it to its earthly end. Now that we, like Paul, have entered the Christian race, we are commanded to run to the finish line and work this salvation completely out in life. Just as in Philippians 1:6 the apostle expresses his confidence that God, having begun this good work, will bring it to completion, so now he exhorts us to strive

---

[2]*FL*, 299.

to attain the same goal. "Work out your own salvation"—that is, "work it completely out, advance it to its accomplishment, bring it to its capstone and crown it with its pinnacles."[3]

Again Warfield notes that the apostle is not calling us here to continued faithfulness merely. What he is calling us to is nothing less than "the attainment of ethical perfection." There is little question that there is an eschatological goal in view. From the beginning of this passage Paul has envisioned the "day of Christ," at which time God's work in us will have been perfected: "I am sure of this, that he who began a good work in you will bring it to completion at the day of Jesus Christ" (Phil. 1:6). God will complete his work in us, and we may be sure of this glorious truth. But this must not obscure the fact that "the pathway that leads to the eschatological goal of salvation is that walk in good works unto which Christians have been created in Christ Jesus." It entails the "fruit of righteousness" realized through Christ *in view of* the day of Christ.

> And it is my prayer that your love may abound more and more, with knowledge and all discernment, so that you may approve what is excellent, and so be pure and blameless for the day of Christ, filled with the fruit of righteousness that comes through Jesus Christ, to the glory and praise of God. (Phil. 1:9–11)

And so Warfield comments, that

> when [the apostle] exhorts his readers at the close of this paragraph "to work out their own salvation," he obviously has the same thing in mind which he had at its beginning, when he exhorted them to "let their manner of life be worthy of the gospel of Christ"; and the same thing which he explains in the course of it to include steadfastness in testimony to the gospel, love to the brethren, humility of mind and the like Christian virtues. In the acquisition and cultivation of such graces they would be "working out their salvation," realizing in life in its ever-growing completeness what is involved in "salvation" as its essential contents.[4]

Here is the goal of the Christian life, the object of pursuit in the Christian race. What we must strive to achieve is nothing less than complete moral and ethical perfection. How could we set our sights on anything less?

---

[3] *FL*, 300.
[4] *FL*, 300–301.

New Testament Puritanism

Warfield emphasizes this often. His argument against the "perfectionists" is not that they pursue perfection. His argument, in part, is that the "perfection" to which they strive is considerably less perfect than what is demanded. He emphasizes this at length in his sermon on 2 Corinthians 7:1.

> Let us cleanse ourselves from every defilement of body and spirit, bringing holiness to completion in the fear of God (2 Cor. 7:1).
>
> It is perfection, we perceive, that the Apostle is after for his followers; and he does not hesitate to raise this standard before the eyes of his readers as their greatest incitement to effort. They must not be content with a moderate attainment in the Christian life. They must not say to themselves, O, I guess I am Christian enough, although I'm not too good to do as other men do. They must, as they have begun in the Spirit, not finish in the flesh; but must go on unto perfection.

Establishing his point, Warfield continues:

> What are they to cleanse themselves from? *Every* defilement—every *kind* of defilement—not only of the flesh but of the spirit. Aiming at what? At the completion of holiness in the fear of God! The Apostle does not tell them they are already holy—except in principle. They obviously were not already holy—except in principle. . . .
>
> No, they were not perfect—except in principle. But in principle, they were perfect; because they had within them the principle of perfection, the Spirit of the Most High God. Let them walk in accordance with their privileges, then, on a level with their destiny. Hear God's great promise. And having these promises, cleanse yourselves; O, cleanse yourselves, the Apostle cries; cleanse yourselves from every defilement whether of flesh or spirit, and so perfect—complete, work fully out to its end—holiness in the fear of God. Let your standard be the holiness of the indwelling Spirit whose temples you are. Let your motive be, not merely regard to the good of others, much less to your own happiness, but joy in God's gracious promises. Let your effort be perfect sanctification of soul and body, cleansing from all defilement. Let your end be, pleasing God, the Holy One.[5]

This, Warfield says, is "New Testament Puritanism." We are called to cleanse ourselves from every kind of moral and ethical flaw. We are called to strive for absolute perfection.

---

[5] *FL*, 255–57.

God's Holiness and Ours

Warfield addresses this calling yet again in his sermon on 1 Peter 1:15: "As he who called you is holy, you also be holy in all your conduct." Here Warfield finds the entire argument stated succinctly. First, there is the command to be holy. Second, we are exhorted to become holy in every way—"in all your conduct." Third, the degree of holiness to which we are called is infinite, for we are called to be as holy as God himself is. This is the standard. "God exhibits His glory to us for our imitation and expects the sight of the beauty of holiness in Him to beget in us an inextinguishable longing to be like Him."[6] God intends to share his highest attribute with us, and he calls us to strive to attain nothing less.

That God calls us to strive for complete moral and ethical perfection is a familiar note in Warfield. It is not simply assumed, for he emphasizes it often. But it is for him a virtual given: what else could the standard be? How could we possibly be called to strive for anything less? God has purposed to make us like his Son, and this purpose he has determined to fulfill. And this is precisely the pursuit of our earthly struggle—to be like Jesus, to be holy as God himself is holy.

> It is not unadvisedly that we say that His holiness is here exhibited as the goal to which we must seek to attain. For not only is it in the text the incitement, but also the standard of the holiness for which we are to strive. We are to become holy as God is holy. Of course the finite cannot attain the infinite. But as the asymptote of the hyperbola ever approaches it but never attains, so we are eternally to approach this high and perfect standard. Ever above us, the holiness of God yet is ever more and more closely approached by us; and as the unending aeons of eternity pass by we shall grow ever more and more towards that ever-beckoning standard. That is our high destiny and it is not unfitly described as partaking in the Divine Nature.[7]

Entire Sanctification

For those who are acquainted with Warfield's severe and extended critique of the various perfectionist teachers it comes as a bit of a surprise to learn that he gives such sustained emphasis to the point that we are called to be perfect. It may be surprising further to learn that he titled his sermon on 1 Thessalonians 5:23–24 "Entire Sanctification." And for several pages into

---

[6] *FL*, 445.
[7] *FL*, 447.

that sermon the surprise is sustained, even heightened, as Warfield expounds the implications of the apostle Paul's prayer for the Thessalonians: "Now may the God of peace himself sanctify you completely, and may your whole spirit and soul and body be kept blameless at the coming of our Lord Jesus Christ. He who calls you is faithful; he will surely do it." I cited the opening paragraph of his sermon at the top of this chapter. Now let us follow his exposition.

As in all his letters the apostle Paul writes to the Thessalonians with a prominent ethical bent. The gospel that the Thessalonians have embraced teaches the believer to turn from idols and sin and to serve the living and true God (1 Thess. 1:2–10). Paul's gospel is a gospel that transforms life. And so in chapters 4 and 5 of his letter, his exhortation is heavily ethical. Believers must demonstrate the reality of their faith ethically in the way they live and behave privately, publicly, and in the relations of the church. All this Paul brings solemnly to the attention of the Thessalonian believers.

Then as Paul approaches the end of his letter, Warfield remarks, he seeks to expand their horizon further. Yes, there are all these particular duties, he says. But keep in mind that this is only to look at the small pieces of a larger picture. And so Paul prays, "Now may the God of peace himself sanctify you completely, and may your whole spirit and soul and body be kept blameless at the coming of our Lord Jesus Christ" (5:23). Here, Warfield says, we have the classical passage on what we may call "entire sanctification."

Warfield first takes up the question of the *degree* of sanctification the apostle has in view, and he labors carefully and at length to establish that it is, in fact, an entire sanctification. To the point almost of overkill, he notes, the apostle piles up terminology to stress exactly this point. "May the God of peace"—the God who has removed every obstacle to bring us to be at peace with him—"sanctify you completely"—wholly, making us perfect, with nothing that hinders the full realization of the goals of our salvation. Still there is more. "And may your whole spirit and soul and body be kept blameless at the coming of our Lord Jesus Christ"—that is, with a standing and character incapable of being accused, such that no one can bring charge of failure at any point to measure up to the perfect ideal.

Still further, Warfield points out, Paul speaks in both collective and distributive terms. He prays for the complete sanctification of the "whole spirit and soul and body"—all that we are generally, and every part of us specifically. Warfield acknowledges that this use of terminology is a rhetorical device and not a scientific analysis of the various constituent parts of man. But the accumulation of the terms—as Jesus's command to love God "with all your heart and with all your soul and with all your mind"—serves to stress the point. He is describing a sanctification that is entire, complete in every way, and affecting every compartment of our humanity. He prays, in effect, "that the God of peace would sanctify every part of you, and that completely." His plain meaning is "that there is no department of our being into which he would not have this perfection penetrate, where he would not have it reign, and through which he would not have it operate to the perfecting of the whole." He continues:

> By this double mode of accumulation, we perceive, the Apostle throws an astonishing emphasis on the perfection which he desires for his readers. Here we may say is "Perfectionism" raised to its highest power, a blameless perfection, a perfection admitting of no failure to attain its end, in every department of our being alike, uniting to form a perfection of the whole, a complete attainment of our idea in the whole man. There is certainly no doctrine of "entire sanctification" that has been invented in these later days which can compare with Paul's doctrine in height or depth or length or breadth. His "perfectionism" is assuredly the very apotheosis of perfectionism. The perfection proposed is a real perfection (which is not always true of recent teachings on this subject) and the man who attains it is a perfect man—every part of his being receiving its appropriate perfection (and this is seldom or never true of recent teachings). A perfect perfection for a perfect man—an entire sanctification for the entire man—surely here is a perfection worth longing for.[8]

Warfield next takes up the question of the *attainability* of this degree of sanctification. Very obviously, Warfield argues, the apostle Paul is not holding up this entire sanctification as a mere unattainable ideal. It is not to him a degree of moral perfection that lies hopelessly beyond us. He prays very seriously, and he exhorts his readers to keep this as their aim. Clearly, he presents entire sanctification as something that is within our reach, and so he prays that God will grant it.

Warfield does not for a moment imply in all this that this complete sanctification is something that we are able of ourselves to attain. He stresses that it is a gift of God. This, he says, is the drift of the whole passage: "Do this, do not do that, you must strive to attain," and so on, "*but may God himself sanctify you completely.*" The responsibility is ours, to be sure, and Warfield stresses this also. But it is in God alone that we have hope of attaining such great things.

---

[8]*FL*, 365.

This, in turn, raises yet another question: Can God really do that for us? Well, of course he can. But will he? Warfield here is as insistent as ever—of course he will! The whole thrust of the apostle's prayer is that God indeed will do this for us. Paul does not pray this to mock God, and he does not write this to mock us. Manifestly, his conviction is that God can and will do exactly this for his children. Indeed, it is something promised: "He who calls you is faithful; he will surely do it" (1 Thess. 5:24). Here the apostle appeals to the faithfulness of God and pledges that he will actually accomplish this entire sanctification for which Paul prays. God is faithful—of course he will do this!

Paul's reasoning here seems to be from the very nature of God. Has not God called us into his fellowship? Has he not, then, purposed just this for us? Do we think now that having called us he will mock us and deprive us, in the end, of that to which he has called us? No—this God who calls is the one who performs the work. He is the caller and the doer. And because God always works according to purpose, and because his purpose remains always certain, and because he is ever faithful, his very call is his pledge that he will finish the work he has begun. He will bring it to completion. "He who calls you is faithful; he will surely do it."

> The accomplishment of this our perfection then does not hang on our weak endeavours. It does not hang even on Paul's strong prayer. It hangs only on God's almighty and unfailing faithfulness. If God is faithful, He who not only calls but does—then, we cannot fail of perfection. Here you see is not only perfection carried to its highest power, but the certainty of attaining this perfection carried also to its highest power. Not only may a Christian man be perfect—absolutely perfect in all departments of his being—but he certainly and unfailingly shall be perfect. So certain as it is that God has called him "not for uncleanness but in sanctification" as the very sphere in which his life as a Christian must be passed, so certain is it that the God who is not merely a caller but a doer will perfect him in this sanctification. Such is the teaching of the text. And assuredly it goes in this, far, far beyond all modern teaching as to entire sanctification that ever has been heard of among men.[9]

What a wonderful promise this is! The attaining of the goal to which we are called does not hang on our weak efforts. Daily we struggle, and daily we fall. But our attainment of perfection is nonetheless certain, for God himself is faithful, and he will see to it that we attain this holiness to which he has called us. And so the apostle writes to encourage us in this very pursuit and

---

[9] *FL*, 368.

in this anticipation. We as the called of God not only may be perfect, but shall inevitably be perfect. God will see to it himself.

Finally, then, Warfield addresses the question of the *timing* of this entire sanctification. When will we finally experience this? If this is a matter of divine promise, why have we not yet attained it?

Warfield points out that the apostle Paul is not speaking of all this as something the Thessalonian believers already hold in possession. He is not congratulating them. He is not rejoicing with them in their attainment of it. Indeed, throughout the letter he exhorts them to it! Nor yet is he scolding them here for not having attained it. Clearly, for Paul entire sanctification is the object of hope. And it is in light of this hope that he pledges the faithfulness of God.

When shall we reach this goal? Paul tells us: "at the coming of our Lord Jesus Christ" (1 Thess. 5:23). Notice again his prayer. He does not pray only that we would be sinless. He prays that our "whole *body* and soul and spirit" will be sinless and blameless. He is directing his readers to think of the day of resurrection. Just as the body cannot and will not be perfect until the resurrection of the dead at the coming of Christ, so the entire perfection of soul and body must await that day also. Until then we continue in this life in our struggle with sin, moving ever upward, "from glory to glory" (2 Cor. 3:18, KJV), until we see him as he is and, so, shall be like him (1 John 3:2). We move today to glory, yet with glory in view. We have reached glory, but a greater glory is to come. And to that day God will safely bring us, for he is faithful.

Today, then, is a day of continued struggle. But it is a struggle borne by hope. We fight. We run the race. But we do so with the prize in view and in certain expectation of its attainment.

Certainly the gradualness of this process ought not to disturb us. It may be inexplicable to us that the Almighty God acts by way of process. But that is revealed to us as His chosen mode of operation in every sphere of His work, and should not surprise us here. He could, no doubt, make the soul perfect in a moment, in the twinkling of an eye; just as He could give us each a perfect body at the very instant of our believing. He does not. The removal of the stains and effects of sin—in an evil heart and in a sick and dying body—is accomplished in a slow process. We all grow sick and die—though Jesus has taken on His broad shoulders (among the other penalties of sin) all our sicknesses and death itself. And we still struggle with the remainders of indwelling sin; though Jesus has bought for us the sanctifying operations of the Spirit. To us it is a weary process. But it is God's way. And He does all things well. And the weariness of the struggle is illuminated by hope. After a while!—we may say; after a while! Or as Paul puts it: Faithful is He that calls us—who also will do it. He will do it! And so, after a while, our spirit, and soul and body shall be made blamelessly perfect, all to be so presented before our Lord, at that Day. Let us praise the Lord for the glorious prospect![10]

Here again is a familiar theme in Warfield's teaching on the Christian life. Not only must we pursue perfection, but we must do so in certain anticipation of success and a deep appreciation of the greatness of God's grace at work in us. Be encouraged, he says. This race will not end in failure. God has redeemed us for himself, and his purpose for us will surely be fulfilled in our experience. Press on, and do so in the knowledge of his reward.

---

[10]*FL*, 372.

CHAPTER 19

A BRIGHT HORIZON

The Christian Hope

We have seen that Warfield understands salvation as something given not all at once but progressively in stages. Redemption consists first in deliverance from guilt and issues in the emancipation from the power of sin and, finally, the complete removal of sin and all its attending ills. Warfield argues that God has set out to restore the world in this same way. He is reclaiming the world, saving representatives from every nation and tribe until all the nations will come to worship him. And the individual experience of salvation, Warfield reasons, is somewhat parallel. We are rescued from the guilt of sin and from its power, and throughout life we struggle by the enabling power of the Spirit of God to eradicate sin until finally we reach the goal of our salvation, perfect holiness, in the intermediate and then the final state, in the resurrection. The completion of our salvation, Warfield often reminds us, awaits the return of Christ. And so just as our life began by looking to Christ, so it continues by our looking for Christ, and it will be complete when at last we see him.

Although this is a familiar note in Warfield's writings, he seldom develops it in full. We will note here only a few of his briefer statements in this regard and conclude with his fuller treatment of the theme in his sermon "The Christian's Attitude Toward Death."

Glimpses of Glory

In his sermon "The Glorified Christ" Warfield expounds Hebrews 2:9, which speaks pointedly to the honor that the Lord Jesus achieved in his saving work. Jesus, having become incarnate and having suffered death for sin, was "crowned with glory and honor." The verse speaks of the glory of Christ in his session, his heavenly rule as the exalted Lord and King. Warfield sees in this not only what it means for Christ—his successful work and consequent glory—but a glimpse of what awaits the Christian also.

> Had He only died for us, perhaps salvation might have consisted solely in relief from this penalty of sin which He bore for us. That He ascended out of death to the throne, conquers the throne itself for us. When we behold Jesus on the throne for us, we may see how great a salvation He has wrought for us. For on that throne we too shall sit, not merely in Him but with Him. It has always been the Father's good pleasure to give us the Kingdom; not apart from the Son but along with that Son who is not ashamed to call us brethren. And because this has always been and still is the Father's will, it behoved Him who orders all things for His own glory, in leading many sons into glory, to bring the leader of their salvation through sufferings to the full accomplishment of His great task.[1]

Warfield's point, of course, is that the Christian's future is bound up with Christ. Just as we are united with him in his death and resurrection, so we are united with him in his glory. The glory he has achieved shall be ours. The apostle Paul teaches this often. "If we endure, we will also reign with him" (2 Tim. 2:12). If we are children of God, then we are heirs of God—"fellow heirs with Christ, provided we suffer with him in order that we may also be glorified with him" (Rom. 8:17). It is a happy and encouraging prospect indeed, and Warfield loves to emphasize it. We who belong to Christ will share with him in his glory.

Our final salvation will bring us to complete moral perfection also, and Warfield highlights this theme often. God is faithful, and having called us he will surely bring us to the entire sanctification he has purposed for us (1 Thess. 5:23–24). We saw this in the previous chapter.

Paul speaks in different terms to this same end in Ephesians 3:19, where he prays that his readers would be "strengthened" to know the unsearchable love of Christ and so "be filled to the whole fullness of God." Paul's language

---

[1] *SW*, 166.

is fascinating, even if puzzling. How could we be "filled to the whole fullness of God"? Warfield comments:

> Of course it does not mean that we are to be transmuted into God, so that each of us will be able to assert a right to a place of equality in the universe with God. Of course, again, it does not mean that God is to be transfused into us, so that we shall be God, part of His very essence. It means just what it says, that God presents the standard towards which we, Christian men, are to be assimilated. We are to be made like Him, holy as He is holy, pure as He is pure. Our eyes, even in the depths of eternity, will seek Him towering eternally above us as our unattainable standard towards which we shall ever be ascending, but we shall be like Him; He and we shall belong to one class, the class of holy beings. We shall no longer be like the Devil, whose children we were until we were delivered from his kingdom and translated into the kingdom of God's dear Son. No more shall we be what we were as men in this world, still separated from God by a gulf of moral difference, a difference so great that we are almost tempted to call it a difference of kind and not merely of degree. Nay, we shall, perhaps, be more like God than even the holy angels are; in our head, Christ Jesus, we shall be in Him who in a pre-eminent sense is like God. The process of the "filling" may take long; it is but barely begun for most of us in this life; but that is the standard and that the goal—"we shall be filled unto the fullness of God"; and it shall never cease. Such is the goal of the spiritual strengthening spoken of in our text.[2]

The Christian's Attitude toward Death

More warmly and at more length than anywhere else in his writings Warfield gives us in his sermon "The Christian Attitude Toward Death" a sustained look at his perspective on the bright future that awaits the Christian. This sermon is an exposition of 2 Corinthians 5:1–10, and before tracing out his lines of thought we should remind ourselves of the passage in full.

> For we know that if the tent that is our earthly home is destroyed, we have a building from God, a house not made with hands, eternal in the heavens. For in this tent we groan, longing to put on our heavenly dwelling, if indeed by putting it on we may not be found naked. For while we are still in this tent, we groan, being burdened—not that we would be unclothed, but that we would be further clothed, so that what is mortal may be swallowed up by life. He who has prepared us for this very thing is God, who has given us the Spirit as a guarantee.

---

[2]*FL*, 278.

So we are always of good courage. We know that while we are at home in the body we are away from the Lord, for we walk by faith, not by sight. Yes, we are of good courage, and we would rather be away from the body and at home with the Lord. So whether we are at home or away, we make it our aim to please him. For we must all appear before the judgment seat of Christ, so that each one may receive what is due for what he has done in the body, whether good or evil.

In the opening chapters of 2 Corinthians the apostle Paul describes in some graphic detail the trials and distresses that attended his life as an ambassador for Christ. His faithfulness to Christ had led him to endure physical and mental distresses of virtually all kinds. But in it all, the apostle is upheld and encouraged by the greatness of his hope in Christ.

So we do not lose heart. Though our outer self is wasting away, our inner self is being renewed day by day. For this light momentary affliction is preparing for us an eternal weight of glory beyond all comparison, as we look not to the things that are seen but to the things that are unseen. For the things that are seen are transient, but the things that are unseen are eternal. (2 Cor. 4:16–18)

Paul's courage and faithfulness draw their force, Warfield comments, from his confidence of his coming reward. "It is because he looks not at the things that are seen, which are temporal, but at those that are not seen, which are eternal, that he can bear all things." Like Moses and Abraham before him, who looked to that which is invisible, so Paul looks beyond this life to what lies ahead for us in Christ beyond the grave. And it is this consideration that renders his trials "light affliction," severe though they are in themselves. "What are earthly sufferings to one who looks upon his very bodily frame as but a tent, in which he sojourns for a time, and expects the laying of it aside to be merely a step toward entering into a mansion prepared for him by God himself."[3]

But Warfield clarifies that the apostle Paul has no death wish, as such. He is not longing for death. He longs for relief from present sufferings, but it is not the thought of death that encourages him. Like us all, he shrinks from death. To be "naked," without a bodily tent, soul separated from body, is not a welcome thought (2 Cor. 5:3). He would prefer to be alive to greet the Lord in his coming, at which time this "tent" would give way to "the heavenly dwelling" (v. 2), the glorified body of the eternal state. In this life

---

[3] *PrS*, 318–19.

he is in "deaths" often (2 Cor. 11:23); indeed, he "dies daily" (1 Cor. 15:31). And yet his natural shrinking from death recedes as he considers God and the blessedness God has promised him.

> So we are always of good courage. We know that while we are at home in the body we are away from the Lord, for we walk by faith, not by sight. Yes, we are of good courage, and we would rather be away from the body and at home with the Lord. So whether we are at home or away, we make it our aim to please him. (2 Cor. 5:6–9)

Thus, Warfield remarks, faith overcomes the fear of death. "As much as he fears it, he longs for the Lord more, and the most direct path that leads to his side, however painful or even unnatural it may be, he will joyfully take."[4]

And so here is the heart of the apostle. He longs to be with Christ. What he would want is not to die but to greet the Lord at his coming. But if this is not to be, his desire is to go, even in nakedness of soul and even though it be through that dreaded and unnatural portal of death, to be with Christ. And here, Warfield tells us, is the model of the Christian's attitude toward life, death, and life after death. And from this he draws the following lessons.

First, Warfield instructs us to learn from this that *for the Christian this life cannot be satisfactory.* We long for something better. "In this tent we groan, longing to put on our heavenly dwelling," Paul says (2 Cor. 5:2). Then he repeats the same: "For while we are still in this tent, we groan, being burdened—not that we would be unclothed, but that we would be further clothed, so that what is mortal may be swallowed up by life" (v. 4). Warfield clarifies further that this is not the state of mind of a great apostle only. All who belong to Christ feel the same. We also, "who have the firstfruits of the Spirit, groan inwardly as we wait eagerly for adoption as sons, the redemption of our bodies" (Rom. 8:23). This is characteristic of all Christians. This, he says, is the whole drift of Romans 7 also, which climaxes in the exclamation, "Wretched man that I am! Who will deliver me from this body of death?" (Rom. 7:24). If ours is "a body of humiliation" (Phil. 1:21), how can we not long for deliverance?

And so Warfield emphasizes again that part of the Christian attitude is a dissatisfaction with the life we live in the flesh. We are content in Christ and with whatever difficulties we must endure for his sake. This is part of the Christian attitude also. We are content with the dispositions of divine providence, and we do not despise his chastening. Our dissatisfaction "is

---

[4]*PrS*, 321.

with self and the meagerness of our Christian attainment."[5] Some years after writing to the Corinthians Paul would write again that his desire still was "to depart and be with Christ, for that is far better" (Phil. 1:23). And yet he was content to remain in this life and fulfill the work Christ would have for him here. But so long as we are in this life, we will never be all that Christ has designed us to be, and for this reason, although we are content with Christ in any state, we are not fully satisfied.

Second, Warfield instructs us to learn from this passage that *even to the Christian, death remains undesirable*. The apostle Paul groans in his earthly body and therefore longs to pass out of this life. But he does not want to die. What he longs for is the coming of his Lord so that he might "go to him without dying."[6] That is to say, he shrinks from death. Death is an unnatural and terrifying intrusion, and it is not the Christian attitude to long for it. But because our Lord stands now behind death, we can tolerate it. Christ has died and, having risen, has conquered death and broken its sting. And yet its gloom still hangs over us as a dreaded enemy.

Third, and very closely tied to the second, Warfield comments that *death is an undesirable state because it constitutes an unnatural separation of those lifelong companions, the soul and the body*. It is an unnatural state that comes only as the result of sin in humanity. And the object of Paul's hope in this passage is not a deserted body. He is appalled at this. The "unclothing" of his soul is a horror, and the condition of the "naked" soul (2 Cor. 5:3) is not the final or perfect state to which we have been redeemed. Yet the condition of the "naked" soul (v. 3) Paul finds undesirable in this sense only. For although this "intermediate" state is yet imperfect in the sense that it is unnaturally separated from its body, it is a state of happiness nonetheless. "Away from the body" the soul is "at home with the Lord" (v. 8). So far as the soul itself is concerned it is then in the state of "completed salvation, finished sanctification, entire holiness."[7] There is no room for purgatory here, no suffering for the purification of sins, no period of time at all between death and going home to be with the Lord. This "wicked invention," as Warfield calls it, is contrary to every statement of Scripture. The souls of the righteous are at the time of their death, as the Westminster Confession affirms, "made perfect in holiness, and are received into the highest heavens, where they behold the face of God in light and glory, waiting for the full redemption of their bodies" (32.1). At death the soul of the believer passes immediately into

---

[5] *PrS*, 324.
[6] *PrS*, 325.
[7] *PrS*, 327.

heavenly bliss where, still united to Christ, it awaits the fullness of salvation to be enjoyed in the resurrection at the return of Christ.

Given this knowledge, is there any wonder why Christians face death so well? Dreaded as death is, there is glory on the other side. Sin will then be gone forever, and there we will rest "at home" in the presence of Christ. Christ has "brought life and immortality to light" (2 Tim. 1:10), and it has forever changed our perspective on death.

So our outlook is one of hope. We fear death still, but on another level we do not. In death we will enjoy the immediate presence of our Lord while we wait the day of his glorious return, when our souls shall be reunited with their old companion, the body.

All this leads Warfield to his fourth point, which by now his exposition has already anticipated. It remains only to be stated more positively and at length *"that this intermediate state of the blessed dead, although imperfect when compared with their final state, when the whole man shall partake of the divine glory, is, apart from that comparison, unspeakably blissful, and to be infinitely desired and longed for by every Christian soul."*[8] Paul understands very clearly the appalling unnaturalness of the separation of soul and body. Despite this he still prefers to be absent from the body, since it is in that state that he will be at home with the Lord (2 Cor. 5:8). This, he says, is "far better" (Phil. 1:23). He is repulsed by death. But recalling that to be away from home in the body is to be at home with Christ, he desires to be at home with the Lord.

Warfield comments here that a wonderful blessedness awaits us in heaven if it is so intensely desired, even if it can be gained only through such an unnatural and fearful experience as death. There are other considerations, to be sure, not least of which is the will of Christ for us to remain to serve him in this life until he takes us. And there are the needs of others. But Paul says that for himself the blessedness of being with Christ is so great that the apostle not only longs for his return, but even prefers to leave this present body if, by doing so, he may be with him—and there, with him, know no more of sin. Warfield exhorts us to let our hearts dwell on this great truth. God has revealed to us what he has in store for us, and what a comforting and sanctifying truth it is.

Explaining his point more fully Warfield stresses that we are taught by the Scriptures, then, that

---

[8] *PrS*, 332.

the bliss of the intermediate state is thus infinitely more to be desired than anything that can come to us on earth; it is only less desirable than the completed redemption which is yet to come. And of this complete redemption it is the earnest and pledge. It is the completion of the salvation of the higher element of our nature, and bears in itself the prophecy and promise of the completion of the salvation of the whole man. It is to be desired, then, as the storm-tossed mariner desires the haven which his vessel has long sought to win through the tossing waves and adverse winds—gate only though it be of the country which he calls home, and long though he may need to wait until all his goods are landed. It is the end of the journey, when the friends come out to meet us. It is within the Father's house, where the greeting rings, "Bring forth the best robe and put it on him."[9]

And so the apostle's chief joy is not in this present life but in the life to come, for Christ is there. To be with him will be such glory that the horror of dissolution of body and soul pales in comparison with it.

Fifth, and finally, Warfield pointedly instructs us to share in the desires of the apostle, and not the desire to be with Christ only, but the resolve of the apostle that we will indeed be with our Lord in death. Can we dare to consider that we may *not* be with Christ in death? Warfield points out that this seems to be the apostle's consideration exactly. Paul reaches the climax of his thought when he writes, "Yes, we are of good courage, and we would rather be away from the body and at home with the Lord" (2 Cor. 5:8). Then he continues with a note of somber reflection: "So whether we are at home or away, we make it our aim to please him. For we must all appear before the judgment seat of Christ, so that each one may receive what is due for what he has done in the body, whether good or evil" (vv. 9–10). Warfield observes here that the apostle has turned from the thought of what he will attain in Christ "to the danger of losing it all; from the bliss of dwelling with Christ to the dread of standing before his judgment-seat." Paul's purpose in this, Warfield notes, is to stress that "it is not enough to contemplate the glories of heaven; we must seek to make those glories ours," for the judgment of that day will be final and without possibility of reversal. Thus "it behooves us to be well-pleasing to him."[10]

Warfield preached this sermon at a memorial service for a Princeton colleague, Charles Augustus Aiken (1827–1892), who had died a few days before. Making reference to him and so many others like him who, well

---

[9] *PrS*, 334.
[10] *PrS*, 336–37.

pleasing to our Lord, had entered their rest with him, he concludes with this word of encouragement:

> While yet our farewell to them on this side of the separating gulf was sounding in their ears, the glad "Hail!" of their Lord was welcoming them there. May God grant to each of us to follow them. May he give us his Holy Spirit to sanctify us wholly and enable us when we close our eyes in our long sleep to open them at once, not in terrified pain in torment, but in the soft, sweet light of Paradise, safe in the arms of Jesus![11]

Summary

Clearly, Warfield's point in all this is not just to articulate certain points of doctrine, but by this to encourage us, his readers, to live in light of the glory that awaits us. Our life here is lived in Christ, for Christ, by Christ, and in view of Christ and the glory that shall be ours when we are with him. Everywhere in Warfield's works this certain hope is held out as an encouragement to the saints of God: their assurance of final success. We may be sure that if we belong to him, we shall one day see him. And when we see him as he is, we shall be like him (1 John 3:2). Here is a hope that is intended—and is well suited—to sustain us and to stir us to continued faithfulness until our Lord comes again for us, or until in death we are taken to him.

---

[11]*PrS*, 337.

PART 5

THE BIG PICTURE

CHAPTER 20

SUMMARY REFLECTIONS

All that we know about Warfield's own Christian life suggests that it was marked by continual reflection on Christ and gospel truth. For him the Christian life is simply the experience of the gospel, and his life was informed accordingly. Warfield was deeply convinced that Christianity is, at its very core, a redemptive religion. Beginning with the forgiveness of sins, the gospel offers the experience of peace and fellowship with God—redeemed sinners now made to be God's children rejoicing in the loving presence of their glorious Father. And it is these truths that are revealed to animate us at every step.

Warfield understands very clearly the Christian difference between "do" and "done." There is much the Christian must do. Responsibility is essential. Fulfilling Christian duty is essential to the very character of Christian salvation. But for Warfield duty and responsibility must ever be seen in light of what God in Christ has done for us and in us. Warfield lived—and he exhorts us to live—in light of a crucified Redeemer and in sight of his glorious return. These two bookends—Christ has come to save, and Christ is coming to save—shaped his perspective and must shape ours also. Warfield never minimizes Christian duty in any way, as some have mistakenly accused. But he does view Christian duty consistently within the context of divine provision, and his exhortations are therefore filled with every encouragement and assurance. And so, again, for Warfield it is in a deepening understanding and appreciation of these blessed truths that he looks to find encouragement to remain faithful in his own responsibilities in service to Christ.

Thus the Christian is responsible to be faithful, but Warfield's focus is on the God who promises to keep us faithful, on the Christ who remains faithful to us in keeping us for himself, and on the Holy Spirit who exercises sovereign control over us and who woos us with his great love. We also pray, not merely for "things" and temporal favors but in heartfelt worship and adoration. We strive for holiness, not merely out of mere moralistic concerns but in loving pursuit of Christ, our ideal, and with hearts filled with love and appreciation for his grace to us and his work for us. Our perspective is large: we look back to a crucified and risen Redeemer, we look ahead to his glorious return for us, and we see ourselves as belonging to him all the while.

For Warfield there is no greater incentive to Christian life and devotion than a frequent reminding of and a deepening acquaintance with the saving grace of God in Christ. He acknowledges that the writers and preachers of the New Testament, including Jesus, appeal to the sense of fear as well as to higher motives such as gratitude and love. Each has its place in Christian ministry. But he insists that appeal to the higher motives ought primarily to mark ministers of the gospel in their churches.

> Deal with people on a low plane and they may sink to that plane and become incapable of occupying any other. Cry to them, "Lift up your hearts" and believe me you will obtain your response. It is a familiar experience that, if you treat a man as a gentleman, he will tend to act like a gentleman; if you treat him like a thief, only the grace of God and strong moral fibre can hold him back from stealing. Treat Christian men like Christian men; expect them to live on Christian principles; and they will strive to walk worthily of their Christian profession.[1]

Throughout Warfield's writings and especially his sermons, he reflects the conviction that reminders of God's mercy in salvation promote Christians to progress in holiness. Throughout his works this line of thought is prominent, that the Christian life is fueled by a growing appreciation of divine grace. And so as we saw in chapter 4, for example, his expositions of the two natures of Christ and of the meaning of the cross form the ground of exuberant worship. These truths are intended to strengthen, uphold, and enliven the Christian. For Warfield there is no stronger nourishment and no other means of worshipful living than increased acquaintance with

---

[1]*FL*, 296.

the grace of God given to us in Christ and an increased appreciation of the privileged status we have attained in him. Warfield's own Christian life and his ministry bear this mark throughout.

Let us take as an example these comments from Warfield's exposition of Ephesians 4:30 on the "sealing" of the Spirit:

> If the Holy Spirit has done this for me; if He in all His holiness is dwelling in me, to seal me unto the day of redemption, shall I have no care not to grieve Him? Fear is paralyzing. Despair is destruction of effort. Hope is living and active in every limb, and when that hope becomes assurance, and that assurance is recognized as based on the act of a Person, lovingly dealing with us and winning us to holiness, can we conceive of a motive to holiness of equal power?[2]

So also, as we have seen throughout this book, to draw out our love for Christ, Warfield points us to the love of Christ and the infinite condescension he displayed in the incarnation. To stimulate our sense of trust he reminds us of our status in Christ as God's children and points us to God's all-embracing and tender fatherly care. To encourage us to persevere he reminds us of the faithfulness of Christ, the love of the Holy Spirit, and the promise of God to finish in us the great work he has already begun. And he points us always to the coming glory when we shall be with Christ and like him. These grand truths are for Warfield the very stuff of the Christian life.

In short, Warfield's own Christian life is marked by a fervent and adoring appreciation of gospel truth, especially the person of Christ and his work for us and in us. And to encourage us in our Christian walk he offers the same. Warfield teaches us that we will never outgrow the gospel. We will never reach such levels that we should "move on to better things." There is no better thing. And there is nothing so well suited to our growth and faithfulness than this.

---

[2]*FL*, 297.

GENERAL INDEX

SCRIPTURE INDEX